CIMA
STUDY TEXT

Final level Paper 14

Management Accounting:
Information Strategy

IN THIS JULY 2002 EDITION

- Targeted to the **syllabus** and **learning outcomes**

- **Quizzes** and **questions** to check your understanding

- Clear layout and style designed to save you time

- Plenty of **exam-style questions,** some with **NEW** detailed guidance from BPP

- **Chapter Roundups** to help revision

- **Mind Maps** to integrate the key points

- **Links** to help you with the **Final Level Case Study**

BPP Publishing
July 2002

First edition July 2000

Third edition July 2002

ISBN 0 7517 3768 2   (Previous edition 0 7517 3170 6)

British Library Cataloguing-in-Publication Data
A catalogue record for this book
is available from the British Library

Published by

BPP Publishing Limited
Aldine House, Aldine Place
London W12 8AW

www.bpp.com

We are grateful to the Chartered Institute of Management Accountants for permission to reproduce the Pilot Paper. The suggested solutions to the questions have been prepared by BPP Publishing Limited.

Contents

BPP
PUBLISHING

LEARNING TO LEARN ACCOUNTANCY

BPP's ground-breaking **Learning to learn accountancy** book is designed to be used at the outset of your CIMA studies and throughout the process of learning accountancy. It challenges you to consider how you study and gives you helpful hints about how to approach the various types of paper which you will encounter. It can help you **get your studies both subject and exam focused**, enabling you to acquire **knowledge, practice and revise efficiently and effectively.**

THE BPP STUDY TEXT

Aims of this Study Text

To provide you with the knowledge and understanding, skills and application techniques that you need if you are to be successful in your exams

This Study Text has been written around the **Management Accounting: Information Strategy** syllabus.

- It is **comprehensive**. It covers the syllabus content. No more, no less.

- It is written at the **right level**. Each chapter is written with CIMA's precise learning outcomes in mind.

- It is targeted to the **exam**. We have taken account of the pilot paper, questions put to the examiners at the recent CIMA conference and the assessment methodology.

To allow you to study in the way that best suits your learning style and the time you have available, by following your personal Study Plan (see pages (viii) – (x))

You may be studying at home on your own until the date of the exam, or you may be attending a full-time course. You may like to (and have time to) read every word, or you may prefer to (or only have time to) skim-read and devote the remainder of your time to question practice. Wherever you fall in the spectrum, you will find the BPP Study Text meets your needs in designing and following your personal Study Plan.

To tie in with the other components of the BPP Effective Study Package to ensure you have the best possible chance of passing the exam (see page (vi))

BPP PUBLISHING

Recommended period of use	Elements of the BPP Effective Study Package
From the outset and throughout	**Learning to learn accountancy** Read this invaluable book as you begin your studies and refer to it as you work through the various elements of the BPP Effective Study Package. It will help you to acquire knowledge, practice and revise, both efficiently and effectively.
Three to twelve months before the exam	**Study Text and i-Learn** Use the Study Text to acquire knowledge, understanding, skills and the ability to use application techniques. Use BPP's **i-Learn** product to reinforce your learning.
Throughout	**Virtual Campus** Study, practice, revise and take advantage of other useful resources with BPP's fully interactive e-learning site with comprehensive tutor support.
Throughout	**MCQ cards and i-Pass** Revise your knowledge and ability to use application techniques, as well as practising this key exam question format, with 150 multiple choice questions. **i-Pass**, our computer-based testing package, provides objective test questions in a variety of formats and is ideal for self-assessment.
One to six months before the exam	**Practice & Revision Kit** Try the numerous examination-format questions, for which there are realistic suggested solutions prepared by BPP's own authors. Then attempt the two mock exams.
From three months before the exam until the last minute	**Passcards** Work through these short, memorable notes which are focused on what is most likely to come up in the exam you will be sitting.
One to six months before the exam	**Success Tapes** These audio tapes cover the vital elements of your syllabus in less than 90 minutes per subject. Each tape also contains exam hints to help you fine tune your strategy.
Three to twelve months before the exam	**Breakthrough Videos** Use a Breakthrough Video to supplement your Study Text. They give you clear tuition on key exam subjects and allow you the luxury of being able to pause or repeat sections until you have fully grasped the topic.

HELP YOURSELF STUDY FOR YOUR CIMA EXAMS

Exams for professional bodies such as CIMA are very different from those you have taken at college or university. You are likely to be under greater **time pressure** before the exam - as you may be combining your study with work. There are many different ways of learning; the BPP Study Text offers you a number of different tools to help you. Here are some hints and tips: based on **research** and **experience**.

The right approach

1   **The right attitude**

Believe in yourself	Yes, there is a lot to learn. Yes, it is a challenge. But thousands have succeeded before and you can too.
Remember why you're doing it	Studying might seem a grind at times, but you are doing it for a reason: to advance your career.

2   **The right focus**

Read through the syllabus and learning outcomes section	These tell you what you are expected to know and are supplemented by Exam Focus Points in the text.
Study the Exam Paper section	Past papers are a reasonable guide of what you should expect in the exam. Take note of the form of assessment that will be used in the exam *you* will be facing.

3   **The right method**

The big picture	You need to grasp the detail - but keeping in mind how everything fits into the big picture will help you understand better. • The **Introduction** of each chapter puts the material in context. • The **Syllabus content**, **Learning outcomes** and **Exam focus points** show you what you need to **grasp**. • **Mind Maps** show the links and key issues in key topics.
In your own words	To absorb the information (and to practise your written communication skills), it helps **put it into your own words**. • **Take notes.** • Answer the **questions** in each chapter. As well as helping you absorb the information you will practise your written communication skills, which become increasingly important as you progress through your CIMA exams. • Draw **mind maps**. We have some examples. • Try 'teaching' to a colleague or friend.

BPP PUBLISHING

Give yourself cues to jog your memory	The BPP Study Text uses **bold** to **highlight key points** and **icons** to identify key features, such as **Exam focus points** and **Key terms**. • Try **colour coding** with a highlighter pen. • Write **key points** on cards or **post-it notes** for your room.

4   The right review

Review, review, review	It is a **fact** that regularly reviewing a topic in summary form can **fix it in your memory**. Because **review** is so important, the BPP Study Text helps you in many ways. • **Chapter roundups** summarise the key points in each chapter. Use them to recap each study session. • The **Quick quiz** is another review technique to ensure that you have grasped the essentials. • Go through the **Examples** in each chapter a second or third time.

Developing your personal Study Plan

One thing that the BPP Learning to learn accountancy book emphasises (see page (iv)) is the need to prepare (and use) a study plan. Planning and sticking to the plan are key elements of learning success.

There are four steps you should work through.

Step 1. **How do you learn?**

First you need to be aware of your style of learning. The BPP Learning to learn accountancy book commits a chapter to this **self-discovery**. What types of intelligence do you display when learning? You might be advised to brush up on certain study skills before launching into this Study Text.

> BPP's **Learning to learn accountancy** book helps you to identify what intelligences you show more strongly and then details how you can tailor your study process through your preferences. It also includes handy hints on how to develop intelligences you exhibit less strongly, but which might be needed as you study accountancy.

Are you a **theorist** or are you more **practical**? If you would rather get to grips with a theory before trying to apply it in practice, you should follow the study sequence on pages (ix) and (x). If the reverse is true (you like to know why you are learning theory before you do so), you might be advised to flick through Study Text chapters and look at questions, case studies and examples (Steps 7, 8 and 9 in the **suggested study sequence**) before reading through the detailed theory.

Step 2. **How much time do you have?**

Work out the time you have available per week, given the following.

- The standard you have set yourself
- The time you need to set aside later for work on the Practice & Revision Kit and Passcards
- The other exam(s) you are sitting
- Very importantly, practical matters such as work, travel, exercise, sleep and social life

Note your time available in box A.

Hours

A [   ]

Step 3. Allocate your time

- Take the time you have available per week for this Study Text shown in box A, multiply it by the number of weeks available and insert the result in box B.

B [   ]

- Divide the figure in Box B by the number of chapters in this text and insert the result in box C.

C [   ]

Remember that this is only a rough guide. Some of the chapters in this book are longer and more complicated than others, and you will find some subjects easier to understand than others.

Step 4. Implement

Set about studying each chapter in the time shown in box C, following the key study steps in the order suggested by your particular learning style.

This is your personal **Study Plan**. You should try and combine it with the study sequence outlined below. You may want to modify the sequence a little (as has been suggested above) to adapt it to your **personal style**.

Suggested study sequence

It is likely that the best way to approach this Study Text is to tackle the chapters in the order in which you find them. Taking into account your individual learning style, you could follow this sequence.

Key study steps	Activity
Step 1 **Topic list**	Each numbered topic is a numbered section in the chapter.
Step 2 **Introduction**	This gives you the **big picture** in terms of the **context** of the chapter, the **content** you will cover, and the **learning outcomes** the chapter assesses - in other words, it sets your **objectives for study.**
Step 3 **Explanations**	Proceed methodically through the chapter, reading each section thoroughly and making sure you understand.
Step 4 **Key terms and Exam focus points**	• **Key terms** can often earn you *easy marks* if you state them clearly and correctly in an appropriate exam answer (and they are highlighted in the index at the back of the text). • **Exam focus points** give you a good idea of how we think the examiner intends to examine certain topics.
Step 5 **Note taking**	Take brief notes, if you wish. Avoid the temptation to copy out too much. Remember that being able to put something into your own words is a sign of being able to understand it. If you find you cannot explain something you have read, read it again before you make the notes.
Step 6 **Examples**	Follow each through to its solution very carefully.

BPP PUBLISHING

Key study steps	Activity
Step 7 **Case examples**	Study each one, and try to add flesh to them from your own experience – they are designed to show how the topics you are studying come alive (and often come unstuck) in the real world.
Step 8 **Questions**	Make a very good attempt at each one.
Step 9 **Answers**	Check yours against ours, and make sure you understand any discrepancies.
Step 10 **Chapter roundup**	Work through it very carefully, to make sure you have grasped the major points it is highlighting.
Step 11 **Quick quiz**	When you are happy that you have covered the chapter, use the **Quick quiz** to check how much you have remembered of the topics covered and to practise questions in a variety of formats.
Step 12 **Question(s) in the Exam Question bank**	Either at this point, or later when you are thinking about revising, make a full attempt at the **Question(s)** suggested at the very end of the chapter. You can find these at the end of the Study Text, along with the **Answers** so you can see how you did. We highlight those that are introductory, and those which are of the standard you would expect to find in an exam.

Short of time: Skim study technique?

You may find you simply do not have the time available to follow all the key study steps for each chapter, however you adapt them for your particular learning style. If this is the case, follow the **skim study** technique below (the icons in the Study Text will help you to do this).

- Study the chapters in the order you find them in the Study Text.

- For each chapter, follow the key study steps 1/2, and then skim-read through step 3. Jump to step 10, and then go back to step 4. Follow through steps 6 and 7, and prepare outline answers to questions (steps 8/9). Try the Quick quiz (step 11), following up any items you can't answer, then do a plan for the Question (step 12), comparing it against our answers. You should probably still follow step 5 (note-taking), although you may decide simply to rely on the BPP Passcards for this.

Moving on...

However you study, when you are ready to embark on the practice and revision phase of the BPP Effective Study Package, you should still refer back to this Study Text, both as a source of **reference** (you should find the index particularly helpful for this) and as a way to **review** (the Chapter roundups and Quick quizzes help you here). Remember to keep this Study Text – you may find it useful in your work.

SYLLABUS AND LEARNING OUTCOMES

Syllabus overview

This syllabus is concerned with the strategic importance of information to organisations in the current and future business environment. It recognises that although many organisations employ IT professionals, Chartered Management Accountants have a key role to play in the provision of information that adds significant value to the ever-increasing volume of data that is available.

Aims

This syllabus aims to test the student's ability to:

- Identify how information supports business strategy
- Evaluate the use of IS/IT to improve the competitiveness of an organisation
- Prepare a coherent plan to manage information
- Identify the ways in which IS/IT is changing the nature and structure of the working environment

Assessment

There will be a written paper of 3 hours. Section A will contain a compulsory question up to a maximum of 50 marks, based upon a scenario. Section B will contain a choice of questions, normally two from four.

Learning outcomes and syllabus content

14(i) Strategic information management   *(study weighting 25%)*

Learning outcomes

On completion of their studies students should be able to:

- Evaluate the use of information as a key resource in different organisational contexts
- Evaluate information and information systems
- Evaluate the appropriate channels of communication available
- Identify and evaluate the various support systems available for the management of knowledge
- Explain and apply the rules for the disclosure of related parties to a business
- Evaluate the impact of electronic commerce on the way business is conducted and recommend an appropriate strategy

Syllabus content

	Covered in chapter
• Typical information requirements of organisations operating in different sectors such as manufacturing, service and the public sector as well as non-profit making organisations such as charities	1
• Chief reasons why information is important for organisations	1

	Covered in chapter
• Process of cost-benefit analysis and how to assess the value of information	1
• Characteristics of information at all levels of the organisation	1
• Use of qualitative information by organisations in planning, control and performance monitoring	2
• Typical methods of data collection in various business sectors (eg bar codes and scanners in retailing)	1
• Various IT systems that deliver information to different levels in the organisation (eg Transaction Processing, Decision Support and Executive Information Systems)	1
• Potential benefits and drawbacks of Internet use by organisations for activities such as data collection and dissemination of information (including the security issues to be borne in mind), as well as the concept of Intranets and their use by organisations in information management	2, 5
• Concept of electronic commerce and the potential impact it has on the business strategy	5
• Concept of knowledge management and why it is seen as a key element to an organisation's success	2
• Use of databases and planning models in assisting the strategic planning process, (eg external databases, economic models, forecasting and modelling packages/applications)	2

14(ii)   Strategic dimension - using IS/IT competitively   *(study weighting 35%)*

Learning outcomes

On completion of their studies students should be able to:

- Identify and evaluate appropriate IS/IT systems and recommend changes to meet the strategic information needs of an organisation

- Evaluate the use of IS/IT to gain competitive advantage and recommend appropriate strategies

- Evaluate the importance of process innovation and re-engineering

- Evaluate the strategic benefits of IT and advise managers on the development of an IS/IT/IM strategy

Syllabus content

	Covered in chapter
• Why an organisation needs an IS/IT strategy which is complementary to the organisation strategy	3
• How organisations can compete through better use of information as opposed to technology, eg using a database to identify potential customers or market segments as opposed to creating a barrier to entry through investment in IT	4
• The link between IS/IT and business strategies and how one supports the other, whilst at the same time potentially using IT as the key element of the competitive strategy	4

	Covered in chapter
• The way IT can impact upon an industry by utilising frameworks such as Porter's Five Forces and Value Chain, and how organisations can use IT to enhance their competitive position	4
• How CSFs (Critical Success Factors) link to performance indicators and the corporate strategy and how they can be used to drive the information needs in the organisations	2, 3
• The strategic business use of the Internet and WWW in terms of marketing and sales activities, and utilising the technology to provide enhanced value to customers and suppliers	5
• Use the applications portfolio to improve IS/IT strategy (McFarlan)	3
• Data warehousing and data mining as tools for managing data and the likely benefits that can be gained from their use, together with the implications of data warehousing	4
• The concept of business integration - links between strategy, people, technology and operations in determining the role of IS/IT	3
• The role of IT in innovation and Business Process Engineering	3
• The strategic case for IT investment particularly where the benefits and value of information are difficult to quantify with any degree of reliability	3

14(iii) Planning, and implementation of IS/IT strategies   *(study weighting 25%)*

Learning outcomes

On completion of their studies students should be able to:

• Analyse the contents of IS, IT and IM strategies and recommend improvements thereto

• Evaluate the organisation of the IS/IT function within a given organisation

• Recommend strategies for achieving the integration of technical and business staff

• Evaluate and recommend strategies for managing change in an IT context

Syllabus content

	Covered in chapter
• The purpose and contents of IS, IT and IM strategies	3, 6
• How to develop a plan and implement the various strategies in a positive way	3, 6, 7
• The potential ways of organising the IT function involving the use of steering committees, support centres for advice and help desk facilities, end user participation	7
• The argument for and against outsourcing	7
• The criteria for selecting outsourcing/Facilities Management partners and for managing ongoing relationships, service level agreements, discontinuation/change of supplier, hand-over considerations	7

BPP PUBLISHING

14(iv)   The social and organisational impact of IS/IT   *(study weighting 15%)*

Learning outcomes

On completion of their studies students should be able to:

- Identify and recommend new working patterns to improve a given situation

- Identify and evaluate the impact of developments in telecommunications

- Recommend ways of achieving co-ordination of activities via IS/IT in a decentralised organisation

- Explain and interpret the concept of Human Information Processors

- Evaluate the user of 'intelligent agents' software

- Identify and evaluate the cultural dimensions of IT acceptance

Syllabus content

	Covered in chapter
• The way IS/IT is changing the method of working and the increase in the knowledge content of many jobs	8
• The organisational impact of technology, its implications for structure and working relationships, and how individuals may be faced with a role change	8
• The Human Information Processor and the implications of providing a user friendly interface to gain maximum benefits whilst minimising the potential drawbacks, such as physical and emotional effects, providing the right volume of information, easy retrieval and storage facilities and merging sources of information reaching individuals so that they become a manageable number	9
• How intelligent agent software can be applied to monitor an individual's use of a system and learn what the user's day-to-day information needs are	9
• The growing awareness of remote working and the implication for the individual and the organisation	8
• The impact of IS/IT on the social aspect of the organisation and implications for organisational culture	8
• The management of change and potential staff reactions, particularly in respect of actual or perceived role changes	8

Syllabus Mind-Map

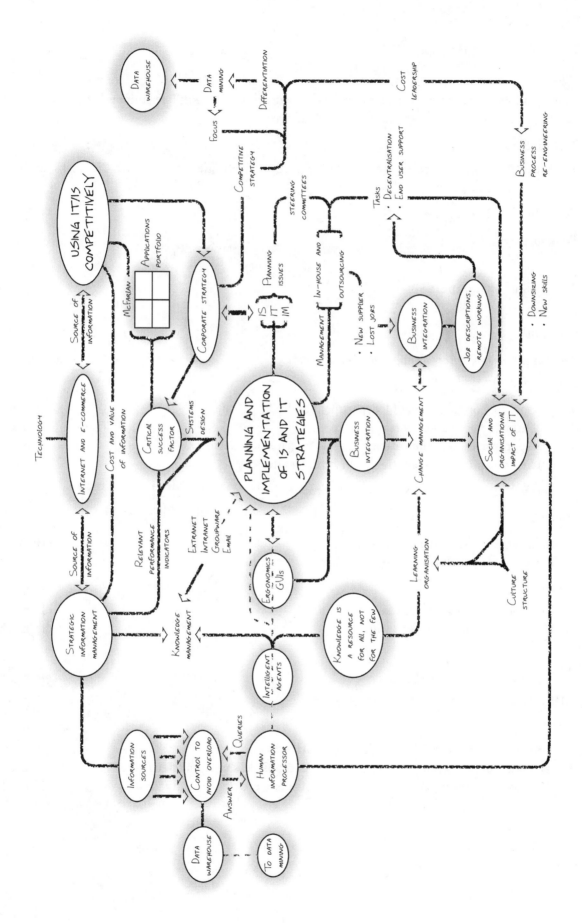

THE EXAM PAPER

Format of the paper

There will be a written paper of 3 hours, divided into two sections.

Section A

One compulsory question worth 50 marks, based on a scenario. The number of parts to the question will normally be in the range of three to five.

Section B

Two questions to be answered, **from a choice of four. Each question is worth 25 marks,** and is based on a short scenario.

Time allowed: 3 hours

Total marks: 100

Analysis of past papers

May 2002

Section A *(one compulsory question based on a scenario)*

Question 1

(a) Outsourcing or an internal IT department and related issues.	(18 marks)
(b) McFarlan's Application Portfolio.	(12 marks)
(c) (i) Appropriate communication channel (Internet and database).	(8 marks)
(ii) Design and implementation of an Internet site.	(12 marks)

Section B *(answer two questions from the four available)*

Question 2

(a) Internet and system deficiencies.	(10 marks)
(b) Problems implementing a system to share information.	(15 marks)

Question 3

(a) Intelligent Agent software characteristics.	(10 marks)
(b) Using intelligent agents software.	(15 marks)

Question 4

(a) Barriers to knowledge sharing.	(13 marks)
(b) Systems to facilitate knowledge sharing.	(12 marks)

Question 5

(a) Framework for prioritising investment in systems.	(10 marks)
(b) (i) Difference between process innovation and business process re-engineering.	(5 marks)
(ii) Importance of process innovation and business process re-engineering.	(10 marks)

November 2001

Section A (*one compulsory question based on a scenario*)

Question 1

(a) (i) Performance Indicators and Critical Success Factors.	(8 marks)
(ii) Information systems required for Performance Indicator monitoring.	(12 marks)
(b) Decision-making process when updating information systems.	(15 marks)
(c) An information system to co-ordinate information transfer.	(15 marks)

Section B (*answer two questions from the four available*)

Question 2

(a) Information system deficiencies and effect on decision-making.	(15 marks)
(b) Why implementing a new information system is difficult.	(10 marks)

Question 3

(a) The use of Intelligent Agents in data mining.	(10 marks)
(b) Strategic benefits of governmental data collection; Data limitations.	(15 marks)

Question 4

(a) Information system evaluation; intranet.	(15 marks)
(b) Extranet limitations.	(10 marks)

Question 5

(a) Developing and implementing an Internet banking strategy.	(13 marks)
(b) Outsourcing website operation.	(12 marks)

May 2001

Section A (*one compulsory question based on a scenario*)

Question 1

(a) A report advising whether to implement the new stock ordering system.	(20 marks)
(b) IT strategy development and systems investigation.	(15 marks)
(c) The information requirements of a manager and the Board.	(15 marks)

Section B (*Answer two questions from the four available*)

Question 2

(a) Benefits and limitations of cost-benefit analysis relating to information.	(10 marks)
(b) Information required to assess the success of a web-based ordering system.	(15 marks)

Question 3

(a) Porter's competitive forces and the Internet.	(15 marks)
(b) Adding value with a website.	(10 marks)

Question 4

(a) Mobile banking service - social and technological issues.	(15 marks)
(b) Service provider contract issues.	(10 marks)

Question 5

(a) The steps used by Human Information Processors (HIPs) to process information; contrast with computer data processing.	(15 marks)
(b) HIP problems.	(10 marks)

Pilot paper

Section A *(one compulsory question based on a scenario)*

Question 1

(a) Competitive advantage and Porters' Five Forces Model.   (20 marks)
(b) Staff turnover and retention.   (15 marks)
(c) Purpose of an information strategy.   (5 marks)
(d) IT system supporting business strategy.   (10 marks)

Section B *(answer two questions from the four available)*

Question 2

(a) The effect of a new IT system on fixed costs.   (18 marks)
(b) IT system and competitive advantage.   (7 marks)

Question 3

(a) Amending an information system to reduce information volume.   (17 marks)
(b) Characteristics of good information.   (8 marks)

Question 4

A report explaining weaknesses in information systems, and recommending solutions.   (25 marks)

Question 5

Brief descriptions of two organisations – local garden equipment supplier and an international consultancy.

(a) Should e-commerce be adopted.   (20 marks)
(b) Which organisation would benefit more from e-commerce.   (5 marks)

WHAT THE EXAMINER MEANS

The table below has been prepared by CIMA to help you interpret exam questions.

Learning objective	Verbs used	Definition
1 Knowledge What you are expected to know	• List • State • Define	• Make a list of • Express, fully or clearly, the details of/facts of • Give the exact meaning of
2 Comprehension What you are expected to understand	• Describe • Distinguish • Explain • Identify • Illustrate	• Communicate the key features of • Highlight the differences between • Make clear or intelligible/state the meaning of • Recognise, establish or select after consideration • Use an example to describe or explain something
3 Application Can you apply your knowledge?	• Apply • Calculate/ compute • Demonstrate • Prepare • Reconcile • Solve • Tabulate	• To put to practical use • To ascertain or reckon mathematically • To prove with certainty or to exhibit by practical means • To make or get ready for use • To make or prove consistent/compatible • Find an answer to • Arrange in a table
4 Analysis Can you analyse the detail of what you have learned?	• Analyse • Categorise • Compare and contrast • Construct • Discuss • Interpret • Produce	• Examine in detail the structure of • Place into a defined class or division • Show the similarities and/or differences between • To build up or compile • To examine in detail by argument • To translate into intelligible or familiar terms • To create or bring into existence
5 Evaluation Can you use your learning to evaluate, make decisions or recommendations?	• Advise • Evaluate • Recommend	• To counsel, inform or notify • To appraise or assess the value of • To advise on a course of action

Part A
Strategic information management

Chapter 1

INFORMATION REQUIREMENTS

Topic list	Syllabus reference	Ability required
1 Organisational information requirements	(i)	Evaluation
2 Information requirements in different sectors	(i)	Evaluation
3 Types of information system	(i)	Evaluation
4 Information sources and data capture	(i)	Evaluation
5 Choosing the communication channel	(i)	Evaluation

Introduction

Welcome to Paper 14 Information Strategy. As with all Final level papers, the examination for this paper will require you to **apply knowledge** to 'real' scenarios. So, when working through this Study Text, consider how the material could be applied or adapted for use in a range of business situations.

We start with the **information requirements** of the modern organisation.

Learning outcomes covered in this chapter

- **Evaluate** the use of information as a key resource in different organisational contexts

- **Evaluate** information and information systems

- **Evaluate** the appropriate channels of communication available

Syllabus content covered in this chapter

- Chief reasons why information is important for organisations

- Characteristics of information at all levels of the organisation

- Typical information requirements of organisations operating in different sectors such as manufacturing, service and the public sector as well as non-profit making organisations such as charities

- Typical methods of data collection in various business sectors (eg bar codes and scanners in retailing

- Various Information Technology (IT) systems that deliver information to different levels in the organisation (eg Transaction Processing, Decision Support and Executive Information Systems)

1 ORGANISATIONAL INFORMATION REQUIREMENTS 5/01

> **KEY TERMS**
>
> **Data** is the raw material for data processing. Data consists of numbers, letters and symbols and relates to facts, events, and transactions.
>
> **Information** is data that has been processed in such a way as to be meaningful to the person who receives it.

1.1 All organisations require information for a range of **purposes**. These can be categorised as follows.

- Information for **planning**
- Information for **controlling**
- Information for **recording transactions**
- Information for **performance measurement**
- Information for **decision making**

Planning

1.2 Planning requires a knowledge of the available resources, possible time-scales and the likely outcome under alternative scenarios. Information is required that helps **decision making**, and how to implement decisions taken.

Controlling

1.3 Once a plan is implemented, its actual performance must be controlled. Information is required to assess **whether it is proceeding as planned** or whether there is some unexpected deviation from plan. It may consequently be necessary to take some form of corrective action.

Recording transactions

1.4 Information about **each transaction or event** is required. Reasons include:

(a) Documentation of transactions can be used as **evidence** in a case of dispute.

(b) There may be a **legal requirement** to record transactions, for example for accounting and audit purposes.

(c) **Operational information** can be built up, allowing control action to be taken.

Performance measurement

1.5 Just as individual operations need to be controlled, so overall performance must be measured. **Comparisons against budget or plan** are able to be made. This may involve the collection of information on, for example, costs, revenues, volumes, time-scale and profitability.

Decision making

1.6 Strategic planning, management control and operational control may be seen as a hierarchy of planning and control decisions. (This is sometimes called the Anthony hierarchy, after the writer *Robert Anthony*.)

Strategic information

1.7 **Strategic information** is used to **plan** the **objectives** of the organisation, and to **assess** whether the objectives are being met in practice. Such information includes overall profitability, the profitability of different segments of the business, future market prospects, the availability and cost of raising new funds, total cash needs, total manning levels and capital equipment needs.

1.8 Strategic information is:

- Derived from both **internal and external** sources
- **Summarised** at a high level
- Relevant to the **long term**
- Concerned with the **whole organisation**
- Often prepared on an 'ad hoc' basis
- Both **quantitative and qualitative**
- **Uncertain,** as the future cannot be accurately predicted

BPP PUBLISHING

Tactical information

1.9   Tactical information is used to decide **how the resources of the business should be employed,** and to **monitor** how they are being and have been employed. Such information includes productivity measurements (output per hour) budgetary control or variance analysis reports, and cash flow forecasts, staffing levels and profit results within a particular department of the organisation, labour turnover statistics within a department and short-term purchasing requirements.

1.10   Tactical information is:

- Primarily generated internally (but may have a limited external component)
- **Summarised** at a relatively low level
- Relevant to the **short-** and **medium-**terms
- Concerned with **activities** or **departments**
- Prepared **routinely** and regularly
- Based on **quantitative** measures

Operational information

1.11   Operational information is used to ensure that **specific operational tasks** are planned and carried out as intended.

1.12   In a payroll office, for example, operational information would include the hours worked by each employee and the rate of pay per hour.

1.13   Operational information is:

- Derived from **internal** sources
- **Detailed**, being the processing of raw data
- Relevant to the **immediate term**
- **Task-specific**
- Prepared very **frequently**
- Largely **quantitative**

The qualities of good information   **Pilot paper, 5/01**

1.14   'Good' information is information that adds to the understanding of a situation. The qualities of good information are outlined in the following table.

Quality	Example
A ccurate	Figures should add up, the degree of rounding should be appropriate, there should be no typos, items should be allocated to the correct category, assumptions should be stated for uncertain information.
C omplete	Information should include everything that it needs to include, for example external data if relevant, or comparative information.
C ost-beneficial	It should not cost more to obtain the information than the benefit derived from having it. Providers or information should be given efficient means of collecting and analysing it. Presentation should be such that users do not waste time working out what it means.
U ser-targeted	The needs of the user should be borne in mind, for instance senior managers need summaries, junior ones need detail.
R elevant	Information that is not needed for a decision should be omitted, no matter how 'interesting' it may be.
A uthoritative	The source of the information should be a reliable one (**not**, for instance, 'Joe Bloggs Predictions Page' on the Internet unless Joe Bloggs is known to be a reliable source for that type of information).
T imely	The information should be available when it is needed.
E asy to use	Information should be clearly presented, not excessively long, and sent using the right medium and communication channel (e-mail, telephone, hard-copy report etc).

Exam focus point

You will **not be asked simply to produce a list** of the qualities of good information in the exam. Exam questions will expect you to be able to **recognise the information problems** that a company is having or to **analyse specific examples** of company documents and **suggest improvements** to overcome the problems you identify.

Improvements to information

1.15 The table on the following page contains suggestions as to how poor information can be **improved**.

Feature	Example of possible improvements
Accurate	Use computerised systems with automatic input checks rather than manual systems.
	Allow sufficient time for collation and analysis of data if pinpoint accuracy is crucial.
	Incorporate elements of probability within projections so that the required response to different future scenarios can be assessed.
Complete	Include past data as a reference point for future projections.
	Include any planned developments, such as new products.
	Information about future demand would be more useful than information about past demand.
	Include external data.
Cost-beneficial	Always bear in mind whether the benefit of having the information is greater than the cost of obtaining it.
User-targeted	Information should be summarised and presented together with relevant ratios or percentages.
Relevant	The purpose of the report should be defined. It may be trying to fulfil too many purposes at once. Perhaps several shorter reports would be more effective.
	Information should include exception reporting, where only those items that are worthy of note - and the control actions taken by more junior managers to deal with them - are reported.
Authoritative	Use reliable sources and experienced personnel.
	If some figures are derived from other figures the method of derivation should be explained.
Timely	Information collection and analysis by production managers needs to be speeded up considerably, probably by the introduction of better information systems.
Easy-to-use	Graphical presentation, allowing trends to be quickly assimilated and relevant action decided upon.
	Alternative methods of presentation should be considered, such as graphs or charts, to make it easier to review the information at a glance. Numerical information is sometimes best summarised in narrative form or vice versa.
	A 'house style' for reports should be devised and adhered to by all. This would cover such matters as number of decimal places to use, table headings and labels, paragraph numbering and so on.

2 INFORMATION REQUIREMENTS IN DIFFERENT SECTORS

2.1 The following table provides examples of the typical information requirements of organisations operating in different sectors.

Sector	Information type	Example(s)	General comment
Manufacturing	Strategic	Future demand estimates New product development plans Competitor analysis	The information requirements of commercial organisations are influenced by the need to make and monitor profit. Information that contributes to the following measures is important: • Changeover times • Number of common parts • Level of product diversity • Product and process quality
	Tactical	Variance analysis Departmental accounts Stock turnover	
	Operational	Production reject rate Materials and labour used Stock levels	
Service	Strategic	Forecast sales growth and market share Profitability, capital structure	Organisations have become more customer and results-oriented over the last decade. As a consequence, the difference between service and other organisations information requirements has decreased. Businesses have realised that most of their activities can be measured, and many can be measured in similar ways regardless of the business sector.
	Tactical	Resource utilisation such as average staff time charged out, number of customers per hairdresser, number of staff per account Customer satisfaction rating	
	Operational	Staff timesheets Customer waiting time Individual customer feedback	

Sector	Information type	Example(s)	General comment
Public	Strategic	Population demographics Expected government policy	Public sector (and non-profit making) organisations often don't have one overriding objective. Their information requirements depend on the objectives chosen. The information provided often requires interpretation (eg student exam results are not affected by the quality of teaching alone). Information may compare actual performance with: • Standards • Targets • Similar activities • Indices • Activities over time as trends
	Tactical	Hospital occupancy rates Average class sizes Percent of reported crimes solved	
	Operational	Staff timesheets Vehicles available Student daily attendance records	
Non-Profit / charities	Strategic	Activities of other charities Government (and in some cases overseas government) policy Public attitudes	Many of the comments regarding Public Sector organisations can be applied to not-for-profit organisations. Information to judge performance usually aims to assess economy, efficiency and effectiveness. A key measure of efficiency for charities is the percentage of revenue that is spent on the publicised cause, (eg rather than on advertising or administration).
	Tactical	Percent of revenue spent on admin Average donation 'Customer' satisfaction statistics	
	Operational	Households collected from / approached Banking documentation Donations	

3 TYPES OF INFORMATION SYSTEM

3.1 A modern organisation requires a **wide range of systems** to hold, process and analyse information. We will now examine the various information systems used to serve organisational information requirements.

3.2 Organisations require different **types of information system** to provide different **levels of information** in a range of **functional areas**. One way of portraying this concept is shown on the following diagram (taken from *Laudon* and *Laudon*, *Management Information Systems*).

Types of information systems

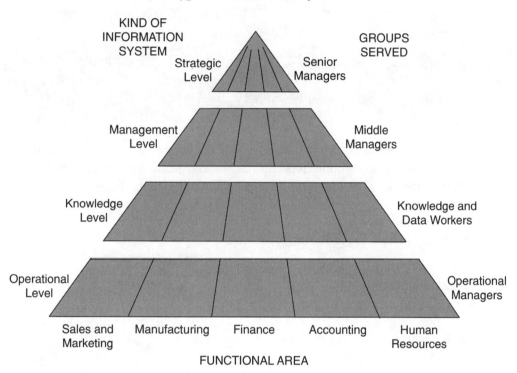

3.3

System level	System purpose
Strategic	To help senior managers with long-term planning. Their main function is to ensure changes in the external environment are matched by the organisation's capabilities.
Management	To help middle managers monitor and control. These systems check if things are working well or not. Some management-level systems support non-routine decision making such as 'what if?' analyses.
Knowledge	To help knowledge and data workers design products, distribute information and perform administrative tasks. These systems help the organisation integrate new and existing knowledge into the business and to reduce the reliance on paper documents.
Operational	To help operational managers track the organisation's day-to-day operational activities. These systems enable routine queries to be answered, and transactions to be processed and tracked.

3.4 There are six **types of information system**:

- Executive Information Systems (EIS)
- Management Information Systems (MIS)
- Decision-Support Systems (DSS)
- Knowledge Work Systems (KWS)
- Office Automation Systems (OAS)
- Transaction Processing Systems (TPS)

Executive Information Systems (EIS)

> **KEY TERM**
>
> An **Executive Information System (EIS)** pools data from internal and external sources and makes information available to senior managers in an easy-to-use form. EIS help senior managers make strategic, unstructured decisions.

3.5 An EIS should provide senior managers with easy access to key **internal and external** information. The system summarises and tracks strategically critical information, possibly drawn from internal MIS and DSS, but also including data from external sources eg competitors, legislation, external databases such as Reuters.

3.6 An EIS is likely to have the following **features**.

- Flexibility
- Quick response time
- Sophisticated data analysis and modelling tools

3.7 A model of a typical EIS is shown below.

An Executive Information System (EIS)

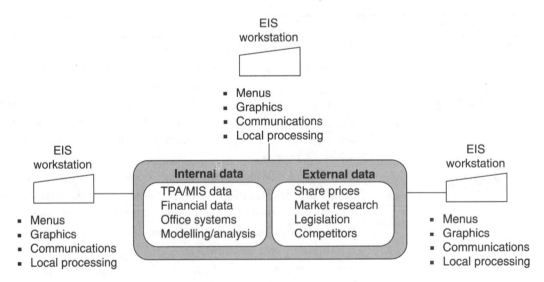

Management Information Systems (MIS)

> **KEY TERM**
>
> **Management Information Systems (MIS)** convert data from mainly internal sources into information (eg summary reports, exception reports). This information enables managers to make timely and effective decisions for planning, directing and controlling the activities for which they are responsible.

3.8 An MIS provides regular reports and (usually) on-line access to the organisation's current and historical performance.

3.9 MIS usually transform data from underlying transaction processing systems into summarised files that are used as the basis for management reports.

3.10 MIS have the following characteristics:

- Support **structured** decisions at operational and management control levels
- Designed to report on **existing** operations
- Have little analytical capability
- Relatively **inflexible**
- Have an **internal** focus

Decision Support Systems (DSS)

> **KEY TERM**
>
> **Decision Support Systems (DSS)** combine data and analytical models or data analysis tools to support semi-structured and unstructured decision making.

3.11 DSS are used by management to assist in making decisions on issues which are subject to high levels of uncertainty about the problem, the various **responses** which management could undertake or the likely **impact** of those actions.

3.12 Decision support systems are intended to provide a wide range of alternative information gathering and analytical tools with a major emphasis upon **flexibility** and **user-friendliness**.

3.13 DSS have more analytical power than other systems enabling them to analyse and condense large volumes of data into a form that helps managers make decisions. The objective is to allow the manager to consider a number of **alternatives** and evaluate them under a variety of potential conditions.

Knowledge Work Systems (KWS)

> **KEY TERMS**
>
> **Knowledge Work Systems (KWS)** are information systems that facilitate the creation and integration of new knowledge into an organisation.

> **Knowledge Workers** are people whose jobs consist of primarily creating new information and knowledge. They are often members of a profession such as doctors, engineers, lawyers and scientists.

3.14 KWS help knowledge workers create new knowledge and expertise. Examples include:

- Computer Aided Design (CAD)
- Computer Aided Manufacturing (CAM)
- Specialised financial software that analyses trading situations

Office Automation Systems (OAS)

> **KEY TERM**
>
> **Office Automation Systems (OAS)** are computer systems designed to increase the productivity of data and information workers.

3.15 OAS support the major activities performed in a typical office such as document management, facilitating communication and managing data. Examples include:

- Word processing, desktop publishing, and digital filing systems
- E-mail, voice mail, videoconferencing, groupware, intranets, schedulers
- Spreadsheets, desktop databases

Transaction Processing Systems (TPS)

> **KEY TERM**
>
> A **Transaction Processing System (TPS)** performs and records routine transactions.

3.16 TPS are used for **routine tasks** in which data items or transactions must be processed so that operations can continue. TPS support most business functions in most types of organisations. The following table shows a range of TPS applications.

Transaction processing systems				
	Sales/ marketing systems	**Manufacturing /production systems**	**Finance/ accounting systems**	**Human resources systems**	**Other types (eg university)**
Major functions of system	• Sales management • Market research • Promotion • Pricing • New products	• Scheduling • Purchasing Shipping/ receiving • Engineering • Operations	• Budgeting • General ledger • Billing • Management accounting	• Personnel records • Benefits • Salaries • Labour relations • Training	• Admissions • Student academic records • Course records • Graduates
Major application systems	• Sales order information system • Market research system • Pricing system	• Materials resource planning • Purchase order control • Engineering • Quality control	• General ledger • Accounts receivable /payable • Budgeting • Funds management	• Payroll • Employee records • Employee benefits • Career path systems	• Registration • Student record • Curriculum/ class control systems • Benefactor information system

Batch processing and On-line processing

3.17   A TPS will process transactions using either **batch** processing or **on-line** processing.

3.18   Batch processing involves transactions being **grouped** and **stored** before being processed at regular intervals, such as daily, weekly or monthly. Because data is not input as soon as it is received the system will not always be up-to-date.

3.19   The lack of up-to-date information means batch processing is usually not suitable for systems involving customer contact. Batch processing is suitable for internal, regular tasks such as payroll.

3.20   On-line processing involves transactions being input and processed immediately. An airline ticket sales and reservation system is an example.

3.21   The workings of both processing methods are shown in the following diagram.

BPP PUBLISHING

Batch processing and on-line processing

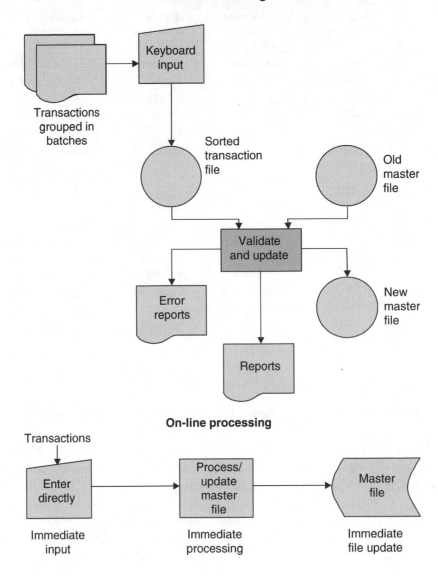

System dependencies and integration

3.22 The six types of system we have identified exchange data with each other. The ease with which data flows from one system to another depends on the extent of **integration** between systems.

3.23 The level of integration will depend on the nature of the organisation and the systems involved. The cost of integrating systems (eg programmer time) should be considered against benefits of integration (quicker availability of information, less time spent inputting information).

3.24 Interrelationships between systems are shown in the following diagram from *Loudon and Loudon*.

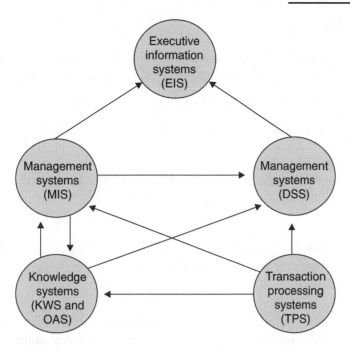

Information systems: levels, types and functions

3.25 Examples of the levels and types of information system we have discussed in this section are shown in the following diagram.

TYPES OF SYSTEMS

Strategic-Level Systems				
5-year sales trend forecasting	5-year operating plan	5-year budget forecasting	Profit planning	Human resource planning

Executive Information Systems (EIS)

Management-Level Systems				
Sales management	Inventory control	Annual budgeting	Capital investment analysis	Relocation analysis
Sales region analysis	Production scheduling	Cost analysis	Pricing/profit ability analysis	Contract cost analysis

Management Information Systems (MIS)

Decision Support Systems (DSS)

Knowledge-Level System		
Engineering workstations	Graphics workstations	Managerial workstations
Word processing	Document imaging	Electronic calendars

Knowledge Work Systems (KWS)

Office Automation Systems (OAS)

Operational-Level Systems				
	Machine control	Securities trading	Payroll	Compensation
Order tracking	Plant scheduling		Accounts payable	Training & development
Order processing	Material movement control	Cash management	Accounts receivable	Employee record keeping
Sales and Marketing	**Manufacturing**	**Finance**	**Accounting**	**Human Resources**

Transaction Processing Systems (TPS)

4 INFORMATION SOURCES AND DATA CAPTURE

4.1 Data and information come from sources both inside and outside an organisation. An organisation's information systems should be designed so as to obtain - or **capture** - all the relevant data and information required.

BPP PUBLISHING

Internal information

4.2 Capturing data and information from **inside** the organisation involves designing a system for collecting or measuring data and information which sets out procedures for:

- What data and information is collected
- How frequently
- By whom
- By what methods
- How data and information is processed, filed and communicated

The accounting records

4.3 The accounting ledgers provide an excellent source of information regarding what has happened in the past. This information may be used as a basis for predicting future events eg budgeting.

4.4 Accounting records can provide more than purely financial information. For example a stock control system includes purchase orders, goods received notes and goods returned notes that can be analysed to provide information regarding the speed of delivery or the quality of supplies.

Other internal sources

4.5 Much information that is not strictly part of the accounting records nevertheless is closely tied in to the accounting system.

(a) Information about **personnel** will be linked to the **payroll** system. Additional information may be obtained from this source if, say, a project is being costed and it is necessary to ascertain the availability and rate of pay of different levels of staff, or the need for and cost of recruiting staff from outside the organisation.

(b) Much information will be produced by a **production** department about machine capacity, fuel consumption, movement of people, materials, and work in progress, set up times, maintenance requirements and so on. A large part of the traditional work of cost accounting involves ascribing costs to the **physical information** produced by this source.

(c) Many **service** businesses, notably accountants and solicitors, need to keep detailed records of the **time spent** on various activities, both to justify fees to clients and to assess the efficiency and profitability of operations.

4.6 **Staff** themselves are one of the primary sources of internal information. Information may be obtained either informally in the course of day-to-day business or through meetings, interviews or questionnaires.

External information

4.7 **Formal** collection of data from outside sources includes the following.

(a) A company's **tax specialists** will be expected to gather information about changes in tax law and how this will affect the company.

(b) Obtaining information about any new legislation on health and safety at work, or employment regulations, must be the responsibility of a particular person - for example the company's **legal expert** or **company secretary** - who must then pass on the information to other managers affected by it.

(c) Research and development (R & D) work often relies on information about other R & D work being done by another company or by government institutions. An **R & D official** might be made responsible for finding out about R & D work in the company.

(d) **Marketing managers** need to know about the opinions and buying attitudes of potential customers. To obtain this information, they might carry out market research exercises.

4.8 **Informal** gathering of information from the environment occurs naturally, consciously or unconsciously, as people learn what is going on in the world around them - perhaps from newspapers, television reports, meetings with business associates or the trade press.

4.9 Organisations hold external information such as invoices, letters, advertisements and so on **received from customers and suppliers**. But there are many occasions when an active search outside the organisation is necessary.

KEY TERM

The phrase **environmental scanning** is often used to describe the process of gathering external information, which is available from a wide range of sources.

(a) The government.

(b) Advice or information bureaux.

(c) Consultants.

(d) Newspaper and magazine publishers.

(e) There may be specific reference works which are used in a particular line of work.

(f) Libraries and information services.

(g) Increasingly businesses can use each other's systems as sources of information, for instance via extranets or electronic data interchange (EDI).

(h) **Electronic sources** of information are becoming increasingly important.

  (i) For some time there have been 'viewdata' services such as **Prestel** offering a very large bank of information gathered from organisations such as the Office for National Statistics, newspapers and the British Library. **Topic** offers information on the stock market. Companies like **Reuters** operate primarily in the field of provision of information.

  (ii) The **Internet** is a vast source of information. Prestel, for example, is now delivered via the Internet, Prestel On-line.

Efficient data collection

4.10 To produce meaningful information it is first necessary to capture the underlying data. The method of data collection chosen will depend on the nature of the organisation, cost and efficiency. Some common data collection methods are outlined below.

Document reading methods

4.11 **Document reading methods** save time and money and also **reduce errors.** Some common document reading methods are described below.

MICR

4.12 Magnetic ink character recognition (**MICR**) involves the recognition by a machine of special formatted characters printed in magnetic ink. The characters are read using a specialised reading device. The main advantage of MICR is its speed and accuracy, but MICR documents are expensive to produce. The main commercial application of MICR is in the banking industry – on cheques and deposit slips.

Optical mark reading

4.13 **Optical mark reading (OMR)** involves the marking of a pre-printed form with a ballpoint pen or typed line or cross in an appropriate box. The card is then read by an OMR device which senses the mark in each box using an electric current and translates it into machine code. Applications in which OMR is used include National Lottery entry forms, and answer sheets for multiple choice questions.

Scanners and OCR

4.14 A scanner is a device that can read text or illustrations printed on paper and translate the information into a form the computer can use. A scanner works by digitising an image; the resulting matrix of bits is called a **bit map.**

4.15 To edit text read by an optical scanner, you need **optical character recognition (OCR)** software to translate the image into text. Most optical scanners sold today come with OCR packages. Businesses may use a scanner and OCR to obtain 'digital' versions of documents they have only paper copies of. For good results the copy must be of good quality.

Bar coding and EPOS

4.16 Bar codes are groups of marks which, by their spacing and thickness, indicate specific codes or values.

4.17 Large retail stores have Electronic Point of Sale (EPOS) devices, which include bar code readers. This enables the provision of immediate sales and stock level information.

EFTPOS

4.18 Many retailers have now introduced EFTPOS systems (Electronic Funds Transfer at the Point of Sale). An EFTPOS terminal is used with a customer's credit card or debit card to pay for goods or services. The customer's credit card account or bank account will be debited automatically. EFTPOS systems combine point of sale systems with electronic funds transfer.

Magnetic stripe cards

4.19 The standard magnetic stripe card contains machine-sensible data on a thin strip of magnetic recording tape stuck to the back of the card. The magnetic card reader converts this information into directly computer-sensible form. The widest application of magnetic stripe cards is as bank credit or service cards.

Smart cards

4.20 A smart card is a plastic card in which is embedded **a microprocessor chip**. A smart card would typically contain a **memory** and a **processing capability**. The information held on smart cards can therefore be updated (eg using a PC and a special device).

Touch screens

4.21 A type of display screen that allows users to make selections by touching areas of the screen with their finger. Sensors built into the screen surround detect which area has been touched. These devices are widely used in vending situations, such as the selling of train tickets.

Voice recognition

4.22 Computer software has been developed that can convert speech into computer-sensible form via a microphone. Users are required to speak clearly and reasonably slowly.

Question 1

Drawing on personal experience (if possible), give examples of the inefficient use of information.

Answer

Some examples are:

(a) Information which is collected but not needed.

(b) Information stored long after it is needed.

(c) Useful information which is inaccessible to potential users.

(d) Information disseminated more widely than is necessary.

(e) Inefficient methods used to collect, analyse, store and retrieve information.

(f) Collection of the same information by more than one group of people.

(g) Duplication of the same information.

5 CHOOSING THE COMMUNICATION CHANNEL — Pilot paper, 5/02

5.1 We now turn our attention to the range of communication methods available. How information is communicated will impact on how it is interpreted. A channel that will help the receiver correctly interpret the information should be used.

5.2 The choice of medium will depend upon numerous factors, including the following.

(a) **Time**

How long will be needed to prepare the message, and how long will it take to transmit it in the chosen form? This must be weighed against the **urgency** with which the message must be sent.

(b) **Complexity**

What medium will enable the message to be most readily understood? If detailed or highly technical information is to be exchanged or where a message has many interdependent parts, oral communication alone is not appropriate.

(c) **Distance**

How far is the message required to travel? Must it be transmitted to an office on a different floor of the building, or across town, or to the other end of the country?

(d) **Written record**

A written record may be needed as proof, confirming a transaction, or for legal purposes, or as an aid to memory. It can be duplicated and sent to many recipients. It can be stored and later retrieved for reference and analysis as required.

(e) **Interaction**

Sometimes instant feedback is needed for effective communication, for example when you are questioning a customer to find out their precise requirements ('small, medium or large?', 'green, red or blue?').

(f) **Degree of confidentiality**

Telephone calls may be overheard; faxed messages can be read by whoever is standing by the fax machine; internal memos may be read by colleagues or by internal mail staff; highly personal letters may be read by the recipient's secretary.

On the other hand a message may need to be spread widely and quickly to all staff: the notice-board, or a public announcement or the company newsletter may be more appropriate.

(g) The **recipient**

It may be necessary to be reserved and tactful, warm and friendly, or impersonal, depending upon the desired effect on the recipient. If you are trying to impress, a high quality document may be needed.

(h) **Cost**

Cost must be considered in relation to all of the above factors. The aim is to achieve the best possible result at the least possible expense.

5.3 The **features and limitations of common communication tools** are outlined in the following table.

Tool	Features / Advantages	Limitations
Conversation	Usually unstructured so can discuss a wide range of topics	Temptation to lose focus
	Requires little or no planning	May be easily forgotten
	Gives a real impression of feelings	
Presentation	Complex ideas can be communicated	Requires planning and skill
	Visual aids such as slides can help the communication process	Poorly researched or presented material can lead to an audience doubting all of the information provided
	The best presentations will leave a lasting impression	

Tool	Features / Advantages	Limitations
Meeting	Allows multiple opinions to be expressed Can discuss and resolve a wide range of issues	Can highlight differences and conflict if not managed efficiently – have been known to turn into time-wasting confrontations 'Louder' personalities may dominate proceedings Costly in terms of personnel time A focused agenda and an effective Chair should prevent these limitations hindering the meeting
Letter	Provides a permanent record of an external message Adds formality to external communications	If inaccurate or poorly presented provides a permanent record of incompetence May be slow to arrive depending on distance and the postal service
Report	Provides a permanent, often comprehensive written record Should use a clear, simple structure	Complex messages may be misunderstood in the absence of immediate feedback
Memorandum	Provides a permanent record of an internal message Adds formality to internal communications	If used too often or the message is too general people may ignore it Can come across as impersonal
Telephone	Good for communications that do not require (or you would prefer not to have) a permanent written record Can provide some of the 'personal touch' to people in geographically remote locations Conference calls allow multiple participants	Receiver may not be available; 'phone-tag' is a frustrating pass-time! (Voice-mail may help) Can be disruptive to receiver if in the middle of another task No written record gives greater opportunity for misunderstandings
Facsimile	Enables reports and messages to reach remote locations quickly	Easily seen by others Fax machine may not be checked for messages Complex images do not transmit well

BPP PUBLISHING

Tool	Features / Advantages	Limitations
Electronic mail	Provides a written record	Requires some computer literacy to use effectively
	Attachments (eg Reports or other documents) can be included	People may not check their e-mail regularly
	Quick – regardless of location	Lack of privacy – can be forwarded on without your knowledge
	Automated 'Read receipts' or a simple request to acknowledge receipt by return message mean you know if the message has been received	Is impersonal
	Can be sent to multiple recipients easily, can be forwarded on to others	Long messages (more than one 'screen') may best be dealt with via other means, or as attached documents

5.4 Study the following case example, it introduces topics that will be covered later in this Text.

Case example: SAP's R/3 system

The R/3 System: Thinking and Acting in Business Processes

As a company, you need dynamic strategies to meet the challenges of today's fast-paced business world. The ability to respond to customer needs and market opportunities as they arise is crucial. The answer? A powerful, open IT infrastructure that will optimally support your business activities and let you adjust flexibly to change and progress: **SAP's R/3 System**.

Flexible. R/3 enables you to respond quickly by making you more flexible so you can leverage changes to your advantage. Your everyday business will surge, letting you concentrate on strategically expanding to address new products and markets.

Comprehensive. SAP's R/3 System is ideal for companies of all sizes and industries. It gives them both a forward-looking information management system and the means to optimise their business processes. At R/3's core are powerful programs for accounting and controlling, production and materials management, quality management and plant maintenance, sales and distribution, human resources management, and project management. And the **Business Information Warehouse** conveniently edits external and internal data to support decision making at all corporate levels.

Open. The R/3 System is an unbeatable combination of functionality and technology. Although designed as an integrated system, R/3's modules can also be used individually. You can expand it in stages to meet the specific requirements of your business. R/3 runs on the hardware platforms of leading international vendors, and will mesh smoothly with your in-house applications. Open to allow interoperability with third-party solutions and services, it is quick and efficient to install.

Integrated. Sales and materials planning, production planning, warehouse management, financial accounting, and human resources management are all integrated into a workflow of business events and processes across departments and functional areas. Employees receive the right information and documents at the right time at their desktops.

Beyond the company. But R/3 does more than open up completely new IT solutions within your company. Its applications also link your business processes with those of customers and suppliers to create complete logistical chains covering the entire route from supply to delivery. R/3 lets you integrate banks and other business partners into inter-company communications.

Best business practices. R/3 software lets you integrate all your business operations in an overall system for planning, controlling and monitoring. They include **best business practices that reflect the experiences, suggestions and requirements of leading companies in a host of industries**. R/3 lets you profit directly from this wealth of business and organisational know-how.

New technologies. R/3 continues to evolve in close dialog with our customers. We incorporate cutting-edge technologies such as object orientation into our development work and translate them into practical customer benefits. We also harness innovative applications to extend the ways in which you can use R/3. Take the Internet, for example. More and more companies are using the Internet not just for marketing and communications, but also for procurement, customer service, and order processing. R/3 is directly **linked to the Internet and ready for electronic commerce**.

Controlling. A complete array of compatible planning and control instruments for company-wide controlling systems, with a uniform reporting system for co-ordinating the contents and procedures of your company's internal processes.

Enterprise Controlling. Continuously monitors your company's success factors and performance indicators on the basis of specially prepared management information.

Production Planning. Provides comprehensive processes for all types of manufacturing including repetitive, make-to-order, assemble-to-order and process manufacturing. Also includes integrated supply chain management with functions for extended MRP II plus optional interfaces to PDC, process control systems, CAD, and PDM.

Materials Management. Optimises all purchasing processes with workflow-driven processing functions, enables automated supplier evaluation, lowers procurement and warehousing costs with accurate inventory and warehouse management, and integrates invoice verification.

Plant Maintenance and Service Management. Provides planning, control, and processing of scheduled maintenance, inspection, damage-related maintenance, and service management to ensure availability of operational systems, including plants and equipment delivered to customers.

Quality Management. Monitors, captures, and manages all processes relevant to your quality assurance along the entire supply chain, co-ordinates inspection processing, initiates corrective measures, and integrates laboratory information systems.

Project System. Co-ordinates and controls all phases of a project, in direct co-operation with Purchasing and Controlling, from quotation to design and approval, to resource management and cost settlement.

Sales and Distribution. Actively supports sales and distribution activities with outstanding functions for pricing, prompt order processing, and on-time delivery, interactive multilevel variant configuration, and a direct interface to Profitability Analysis and Production.

Human Resources Management. Provides solutions for planning and managing your company's human resources, using integrated applications that cover all personnel management tasks and help simplify and speed the processes.

SAP Business Information Warehouse. This independent data warehouse solution summarises data from R/3 applications and external sources to provide executive information for supporting decision making and planning. Reports covering a wide range of information requirements, automated data staging, and standard R/3 business process models ensure rapid implementation and low operating costs.

Chapter roundup

- Organisations **require information for** recording transactions, measuring performance, making decisions, planning and controlling.

- **Strategic information** is used to **plan** the **objectives** of the organisation, and to **assess** whether the objectives are being met in practice.

- Tactical information is used to decide **how the resources of the business should be employed**, and to **monitor** how they are being and have been employed.

- Operational information is used to ensure that **specific operational tasks** are planned and carried out as intended.

- 'Good' information **aids understanding**. ACCURATE is a handy mnemonic for the qualities of good information.

- An information system should be designed to obtain information from **all relevant sources** - both internal and external.

- An organisation's information requirements will be influenced by the **sector** they operate in.

- There are six major types of Information Systems: Executive Information Systems (**EIS**), Management Information Systems (**MIS**), Decision Support Systems (**DSS**), Knowledge Work Systems (**KWS**), Office Automation Systems (**OAS**) and Transaction Processing Systems (**TPS**).

- The ease with which data flows from one system to another depends on the extent of **integration** between systems.

- A range of **data collection methods** are available - depending on the situation.

- The choice of **communication medium** will depend on:

  ° Time
  ° Complexity of the message
  ° Distance
  ° The need for a written record
  ° Confidentiality
  ° The recipient
  ° Cost

Quick quiz

1   List five uses of information.

1   ....PLANNING.............................

2   ....CONTROLLING.......................

3   ....DECISION MAKING................

4   ....PERFORMANCE MEASUREMENT...

5   ....RECORD TRANSACTIONS.........

2   List five characteristics of strategic information.

1   ....LONG TERM..........................

2   ....HIGH LEVEL / SUMMARISED...

3   ....INTERNAL & EXTERNAL.........

4   ....DECISION MAKING (STRAT)...

5   ....UNCERTAIN..........................

3   List five characteristics of tactical information.

1   ....MED-TERM............................

2   ....SUMMARISED AT LOWER LEG....

3   ....MOSTLY INTERNALLY GEN......

4   ....PLANNING RESOURCES...........

5   ....PREPARED ROUTINELY/REG....

    ✗ TIME BOUND

    ✗ DETAIL

    ✗ GENERATION

    ✗ USEFULNESS

    ✗ PREPARATION

4   List five characteristics of operational information.

1   ....IMMEDIATE / DAILY...............

2   ....DETAILED.............................

3   ....INTERNALLY GENERATED........

4   ....OPERATIONAL ACTIVITIES.....

5   ....PREPARED FREQUENTLY.........

5   Match the following abbreviations with the appropriate description.

Abbreviation				Description
(i)	OAS ~D~	A ~KWS~		Information systems that facilitate the creation and integration of new knowledge into an organisation.
(ii)	KWS ~A~	B ~MIS~		A system that converts data, mainly from internal sources into information (eg summary reports, exception reports).
(iii)	EIS ~F~	C ~DSS~		A system that combines data and analytical models or data analysis tools to support semi-structured and unstructured decision making.
(iv)	DSS ~C~	D ~OAS~		Computer systems designed to increase the productivity of data and information workers.
(v)	MIS ~B~	E ~TPS~		A system to perform and record routine transactions.
(vi)	TPS ~E~	F ~EIS~		A system that pools data from internal and external sources and makes information available to senior managers in an easy-to-use form.

6   'Full integration across all organisational information systems is vital.' Do you agree with this statement? Justify your answer (very briefly).

NO - DEPENDS ON - SIZE
BUT   - COST / BENEFIT
IMPORTANT   - COMPLEXITY
    - NEED / RELEVANCE

Answers to quick quiz

1   Planning, controlling, recording transactions, measuring performance and making decisions.

2   [Five of]

Derived from both internal and external sources

Summarised at a high level

Relevant to the long term

Concerned with the whole organisation

Often prepared on an 'ad hoc' basis

Both quantitative and qualitative

Uncertain, as the future cannot be predicted accurately

3   [Five of]

Primarily generated internally (but may have a limited external component)

Summarised at a lower level

Relevant to the short and medium term

Concerned with activities or departments

Prepared routinely and regularly

Based on quantitative measures

4   [Five of]

Derived from internal sources

Detailed, being the processing of raw data

Relevant to the immediate term

Task-specific

Prepared very frequently

Largely quantitative

5   (i)   D.

(ii) A.

(iii) F.

(iv) C.

(v)   B.

(vi) E.

6   Disagree. A high degree of integration is usually desirable, but in all cases the costs of integration should be considered against the value of the expected benefits integration would bring.

Question to try	Level	Marks	Time
17(b)	Examination	8	14 mins

Chapter 2

INFORMATION AND KNOWLEDGE MANAGEMENT

Topic list	Syllabus reference	Ability required
1 Information management	(i)	Evaluation
2 Information for planning and control	(i)	Evaluation
3 Knowledge management	(i)	Evaluation
4 Databases and planning models	(i)	Evaluation
5 Data warehousing and data mining	(i)	Evaluation

Introduction

The modern business environment can be volatile. Businesses are increasingly reliant on good quality information and knowledge to anticipate and ensure an appropriate response to change. As the importance of information and knowledge has increased, organisations have come to realise that like any other valuable resource, **information and knowledge should be managed effectively**.

Learning outcomes covered in this chapter

- **Evaluate** and **advise** managers on the development of knowledge management strategy

- **Identify** and **evaluate** the various support systems available for the management of knowledge

Syllabus content covered in this chapter

- Use of qualitative information by organisations in planning, control and performance monitoring

- Concept of knowledge management and why it is seen as a key element to an organisation's success

- The concept of intranets and their use by organisations in information management

- Use of databases and planning models in assisting the strategic planning process, (eg external databases, economic models, forecasting and modelling packages/applications)

- Data warehousing and data mining as tools for managing data and the likely benefits that can be gained from their use, together with the implications of data warehousing

BPP PUBLISHING

1 INFORMATION MANAGEMENT

1.1 Information must be managed just like any other organisational resource.

> ### KEY TERM
>
> **Information Management (IM) strategy** refers to the basic approach an organisation has to the management of its information systems, including:
>
> - Planning IS/IT developments
> - Organisational environment of IS
> - Control
> - Technology

1.2 Information management entails the following **tasks**.

(a) Identifying current and future **information needs**.

(b) Identifying information **sources**.

(c) **Collecting** the information.

(d) **Storing** the information.

(e) Facilitating existing methods of **using** information and identifying new ways of using it.

(f) Ensuring that information is **communicated** to those who need it, and is **not communicated** to those who are not entitled to see it.

1.3 Developments in technology provide new sources of information, new ways of collecting it, storing it and processing it, and new methods of communicating and sharing it.

1.4 Although computing and telecommunications technology provide fabulous tools for carrying out the information management tasks listed above, they are not always the best tools; nor are they always available.

Users of information

1.5 The information generated by an organisation may be used internally or externally.

1.6 **Internal** users of information include (by status) the following.

- The board (or equivalent)
- Directors with functional responsibilities
- Divisional general managers
- Divisional heads
- Departmental heads
- Section leaders, supervisors
- Employees

Question 1

Information is often required by people **outside** the organisation for making judgements and decisions relating to an organisation. Give four examples of decisions which may be taken by outsiders.

Answer

There are many possible suggestions, including those given below.

(a) The organisation's **bankers** take decisions affecting the amount of money they are prepared to lend.

(b) The **public** might have an interest in information relating to an organisation's products or services.

(c) The **media** (press, television etc) use information generated by organisations in news stories, and such information can adversely or favourably affect an organisation's relationship with its environment.

(d) The **government** (for example the Department of Trade and Industry) regularly requires organisational information.

(e) The **Inland Revenue** and **HM Customs and Excise** authorities require information for taxation and VAT assessments.

(f) An organisation's **suppliers** and **customers** take decisions whether or not to trade with the organisation.

---

2 INFORMATION FOR PLANNING AND CONTROL   5/01

2.1 As we explained in Chapter 1, **strategic planning**, **management control** and **operational control** may be seen as a hierarchy of planning and control decisions, sometimes called the Anthony hierarchy.

> **KEY TERM**
>
> **Strategic planning** is a process of deciding on objectives of the organisation, on changes in these objectives, on the resources used to attain these objectives and on the policies that are to govern the acquisition, use and disposition of these resources.

2.2 Strategic decision making:

- Is medium- to **long-term**
- Involves high levels of **uncertainty** and risk (the future is unpredictable)
- Involves situations that **may not recur**
- Deals with **complex** issues

> **KEY TERMS**
>
> **Tactical planning/control** (also called **management control**) means ensuring that resources are obtained and used effectively and efficiently in the accomplishment of the organisation's objectives.
>
> - **Efficiency** means that resources input to a process produce the optimum (maximum) amount of outputs.
>
> - **Effectiveness** means that the resources are used to achieve the desired ends.

2.3 Tactical control decisions are taken within the framework of strategic plans and objectives which have previously been made, or set.

> ### KEY TERM
>
> **Operational control** ensures that specific tasks are carried out effectively and efficiently. It focuses on individual tasks, and is carried out within the strictly defined guidelines issued by strategic planning and tactical control decisions.

2.4 It may help to clarify the above to consider it in terms of how well **structured** the problem situation is. Examples of unstructured and structured decisions at the different levels of management are shown in the following table.

Decision level	Structured	Semi-structured	Unstructured
Operational	Stock control procedures	Selection of new supplier	Hiring supervisor
Tactical	Selection of products to discount	Allocation of budget	Expanding into a new design
Strategic	Major investment decisions	Entry to new market; new product line	Reorganisation of whole company

Question 2

Consider management decisions as they affect work in a purchase ledger department. Classify each of the following three decisions according to the three types of decision identified above.

(a) The payment cycle will be extended by five days to improve cash flow.

(b) On receipt of an invoice, the purchase order form and goods received note relating to the order must be checked to the invoice. Specified details must be checked, and the invoice stamped to show that the checks have been carried out fully and satisfactorily.

(c) Suppliers who supply over £50,000 worth of goods per annum will be asked to join the company's EDI network.

Answer

The first is a tactical control decision, the second is an operational control decision and the third is a strategic planning decision.

The nature of decision making

2.5 Decisions are made in different ways in different situations.

(a) In some organisations decisions are arrived at **collectively** through negotiation or voting. A referendum is a means of taking such a decision.

(b) In many cases, the right to make decisions is delegated to certain **individuals**. In most limited companies, the owners will appoint directors to act on their behalf, and to manage the organisation's activities.

(c) Within an organisation, different types of decision are taken at different **levels**. Senior management will be involved in decisions that affect the business as a whole; decisions that affect only one aspect of the business will be delegated to lower levels of management.

(d) Certain kinds of decision are **routine**, in that the same remedy will be applied to a situation which recurs regularly, or which is relatively simple.

The decision making process   **11/01**

2.6   The stages in making a decision are as follows.

> *Step 1.*   Problem **recognition**.
> *Step 2.*   Problem **definition** and structuring.
> *Step 3.*   Identifying **alternative courses of action**.
> *Step 4.*   Making and **communicating** the decision.
> *Step 5.*   **Implementation** of the decision.
> *Step 6.*   **Monitoring** the effects of the decision.

Information and decision-making

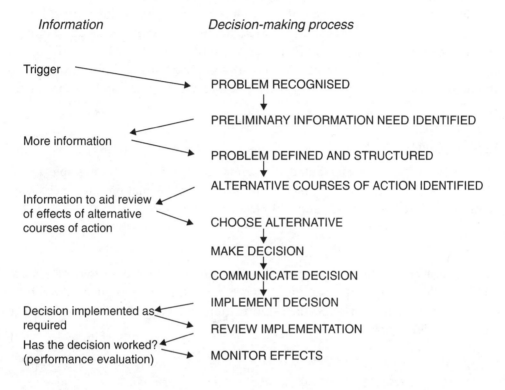

Problem recognition

2.7   Decisions are not made without **information**. The decision-maker needs to be informed of a problem in the first place. This is sometimes referred to as the **decision trigger**.

Problem definition and structuring

2.8   Normally **further information** is then required. This further information is **analysed** so that the problem can be **defined** precisely.

2.9   Consider, for example, a company with falling sales. The fall in sales would be the **trigger**. **Further information** would be needed to identify where the deficiencies were occurring. The company might discover that sales of product X in area Y are falling, and the problem can be **defined** as:

> 'Decline of sales of product X in area Y due to new competitor: how can the decline be reversed?'

2.10   One of the purposes of **defining** the problem is to identify the **relationships** between the **various factors** in it, especially if the problem is complex.

BPP PUBLISHING

Identifying alternative courses of action

2.11 Where alternative courses of action are identified, **information** is needed about the likely effect of each, so they can be assessed.

2.12 As a simple example, if our company wishes to review the price of product X in area Y, information will be needed as to the effect of particular price levels on demand for the product. Such information can include external information such as market research (demand at a particular price) and the cost of the product, which can be provided internally.

Making and communicating the decision

2.13 The decision is **made** after review of the information relating to alternatives. However, the decision is useless if it is not **communicated**. So, in our example, if the **marketing director** decides to lower the price of product X and institute an intensive **advertising** campaign, nothing will happen unless the advertising department is informed, and also the **manufacturing** department, who will have to prepare new packaging showing the lower price.

Implementation of the decision

2.14 The decision is then **implemented**. For large-scale decisions (for example to relocate a factory 100 miles away from its current site), implementation may need substantial **planning**, detailed information and very clear communication.

Monitoring the effects of the decision

2.15 Once a decision has been implemented, information is needed so that its effects can be **reviewed**. For example, if a manufacturing organisation has installed new equipment in anticipation of savings in costs, then information will need to be obtained as to whether these are achieved in practice.

Exam Focus Point
You could use this six-stage process as a means of analysing an exam question scenario and as a structure for your answer. What is the problem; what are the alternatives; how will your solution be implemented, etc?

Risk and uncertainty in decision making

2.16 Decision making involves **making decisions now about what will happen in the future**. Obviously, decisions can turn out badly, or actual results can prove to be very different from the estimates on which the original decision was made because the necessary **information is not available** when the decision is made.

KEY TERMS

Risk involves situations or events which may or may not occur, but whose probability of occurrence can be calculated statistically and the frequency of their occurrence predicted from past records.

Uncertainty involves situations or events whose outcome cannot be predicted with statistical confidence.

2.17 The management accountant, who must present relevant cost and revenue data to assist a manager who is about to make a decision, should consider two things.

(a) If the figures are **only slightly in doubt** or the amounts themselves are not material, a **best estimate** with a note that the figures are not certain may be good enough.

(b) If the amount or the **degree of uncertainty was large,** to present just one set of forecast figures would be unwise. For example, if a forecast of sales demand is 'anywhere between 1,000 and 10,000 units', it would be naive and unhelpful to prepare a **single point estimate** of sales - just one forecast figure - of, say, 5,000 units.

If the uncertainty in a situation does warrant special attention in the figures, the next problem is **how the uncertainty** in the figures should be presented.

2.18 There are various methods of bringing uncertainty and risk analysis into the evaluation of decisions. They include the following.

(a) **Conservative estimates:** estimating outcomes in a conservative manner in order to provide a built-in safety factor.

(b) Looking at the **worst possible** and **best possible** outcomes, as well as the most likely outcome, and reaching a decision which takes these into account.

(c) **Sensitivity analysis:** any technique that tests decision options for their vulnerability to changes in a 'variable' such as expected sales volume.

(d) Assessing **probabilities** and calculating, for each decision alternative, either the **expected value** of costs or benefits with, possibly, the standard deviation of the possible outcomes, or a probability distribution of the possible outcomes. **Decision trees** might be used to illustrate in a 'pictorial' or 'graphical' form the alternatives facing the decision-maker.

Perfect information

2.19 Obtaining more information first about what is likely to happen can sometimes reduce the uncertainty about the future outcome from taking a decision. We can categorise information depending upon **how reliable** it is likely to be for predicting what will happen in the future and hence for helping managers to make better decisions.

> **KEY TERMS**
>
> **Perfect information** is information that is guaranteed to predict the future with 100% accuracy.
>
> **Imperfect information** is information which cannot be guaranteed to be completely accurate. Almost all information is therefore imperfect - but may still be very useful.

3   KNOWLEDGE MANAGEMENT   5/02

3.1   Studies have indicated that 20 to 30 percent of company resources are wasted because organisations are not aware of what **knowledge they already possess**.

KEY TERMS

Knowledge is information within people's minds.

Knowledge management describes the process of collecting, storing and using the knowledge held within an organisation.

Knowledge Work Systems (KWS) are information systems that facilitate the creation and integration of new knowledge into an organisation.

Knowledge workers are people whose jobs consist primarily of creating new information and knowledge. They are often members of a profession such as doctors, engineers, authors, lawyers and scientists.

Data workers process and distribute information eg secretary, accounts clerk.

3.2   Knowledge is now commonly viewed as a sustainable source of **competitive advantage**. Producing unique products or services or producing products or services at a lower cost than competitors is based on superior knowledge.

3.3   Knowledge is valuable as it may be used to create new ideas, insights and interpretations and for decision making. However knowledge, like information, is of no value unless it is applied.

3.4   As the importance of knowledge increases, the success of an organisation becomes increasingly dependant on its ability to gather, produce, hold and disseminate knowledge.

3.5   **Knowledge management** programmes are attempts at:

(a)   Designing and installing techniques and processes to create, protect and use **explicit knowledge** (that is knowledge that the company knows that it has). Explicit knowledge includes facts, transactions and events that can be clearly stated and stored in management information systems.

(b)   Designing and creating environments and activities to discover and release **tacit knowledge** (explained below).

3.6   **Tacit knowledge** is expertise held by people within the organisation that has not been formally documented. It is a difficult thing to manage because it is **invisible** and **intangible**. We do not know what knowledge exists within a person's brain, and whether he or she chooses to share knowledge is a matter of choice.

3.7   The **motivation to share** hard-won experience is sometimes low; the individual is 'giving away' their value and may be very reluctant to lose a position of influence and respect by making it available to everyone.

3.8   Organisations should encourage people to share their knowledge. This can be done through a culture of openness and rewards for sharing knowledge and information.

Where does knowledge reside?

3.9   There are various actions that can be taken to try to determine the prevalence of knowledge in an organisation.

3.10   One is the **identification and development of informal networks** and communities of practice within organisations. These self-organising groups share common work interests, usually cutting across a company's functions and processes. People exchange what they know freely and develop a shared language that allows knowledge to flow more efficiently.

3.11   It is then possible to **'map' a knowledge network** and make it available to others in the organisation. Knowledge maps are guides that assist employees to ascertain who knows what.

3.12   Another means of establishing the prevalence of knowledge is to look at knowledge-related business **outcomes**. One example is **product development and service innovation**. While the knowledge embedded within these innovations is invisible, the products themselves are tangible.

3.13   Every day companies make substantial **investments in improving their employees' knowledge** and enabling them to use it more effectively. Analysis of these investments is a third way of making KM activities visible. For example how much technical and non-technical training are individuals consuming? How much is invested in competitive and environmental scanning, and in other forms of strategic research?

Knowledge creation

3.14   Japanese companies have a strong focus on **tacit knowledge**. They motivate knowledge creation through visions of products and strategies coupled with organisational cultures that promote sharing, transparency and proactive use of knowledge and innovation.

3.15   Human resource policies such as rotation of employees through different jobs and functions support the expansion of knowledge.

Organisational learning

3.16   The process by which an organisation develops its store of knowledge is sometimes called organisational learning.

3.17   A learning organisation is centred on the **people** that make up the organisation and the **knowledge** they hold. The organisation and employees feed off and into the central pool of knowledge. The organisation uses the knowledge pool as a tool to teach itself and its employees.

Knowledge management or information management?

3.18   There are dozens of **different approaches** to KM, including document management, information management, business intelligence, competence management, information systems management, intellectual asset management, innovation, business process design, and so on.

BPP PUBLISHING

3.19 Many KM projects have a significant element of information management. After all, people need information about where knowledge resides, and to share knowledge they need to transform it into more or less transient forms of information.

3.20 But beyond that, KM does have two distinctive tasks: to facilitate the **creation** of knowledge and to manage the way people **share** and **apply** it. Companies that prosper with KM will be those that realise that it is as much about managing people as about information and technology.

Case example

How to facilitate knowledge sharing

The business trend for the new millennium might well be summed up as, 'Tradition is out, innovation is in.' World-class companies now realise that the best ideas do not necessarily come from the executive boardroom but from all levels of the company; from line workers all the way through to top management.

Companies that have cultures that **encourage best practice sharing** can unlock the rich stores of knowledge within each employee: sharing promotes overall knowledge, and facilitates further creativity. World-class companies are innovatively implementing best practice sharing to shake them of out of the rut of 'the way it's always been done.' Programs such as General Electric's Work-Out sessions or Wal-Mart's Saturday meetings help employees challenge conventions and suggest creative new ideas that drive process improvement, increased efficiency, and overall, **a stronger bottom line**.

The fundamental goal of **knowledge management** is to capture and disseminate knowledge across an increasingly global enterprise, enabling individuals to avoid repeating mistakes and to operate more intelligently - striving to create an entire **learning organisation** that works as efficiently as its most seasoned experts.

Best Practices recently updated report, '*Knowledge Management of Internal Best Practices*', profiles innovative methods used by world-class companies to communicate best practices internally. The study provides recommendations for how to create a best-practice-sharing culture through all levels of the organisation, how to use both external and internal sources to find best practices and how to capture that knowledge and communicate it to all employees.

Best Practices contacted over fifty leading companies at the vanguard of knowledge management to compile its report. Some of the vital issues these thought leaders addressed include **measurement and management of intellectual assets**, best practice identification and recognition systems, best practice prioritisation systems, communication of best practices, and **knowledge sharing through technology**. For example, in the area of best practice communications, the report examines how General Electric spreads best practices with **regular job rotations**.

Adapted from Chapel Hill, N.C. (Business Wire) Feb 2000 via News Edge Corporation

---

Systems that aid knowledge management

3.21 Information systems play an important role in knowledge management, helping with **information flows** and helping to formally **capture** the knowledge held within the organisation.

3.22 Any system that encourages people to work together and share information and knowledge will aid knowledge management. Examples are shown in the following table.

What the systems facilitate	Examples
Knowledge distribution	**Office automation systems**
	• Word processing
	• Electronic schedulers
	• Desktop databases
	• Web publishing
	• Voice mail
	• E-mail
Knowledge sharing	**Group collaboration systems**
	• Groupware
	• Intranets
	• Extranets
Knowledge creation	**Knowledge work systems**
	• Computer Aided Design (CAD) (explained in Chapter 4)
	• Virtual Reality
	• Investment workstations
Knowledge capture and codification	**Artificial intelligence systems**
	• Expert systems
	• Neural Nets
	• Fuzzy logic
	• Intelligent agents (covered in Chapter 9)

Distributing knowledge

Office automation systems (OAS)

3.23 As discussed in Chapter 1, an OAS is any application of information technology that increases productivity within an office.

3.24 Knowledge work is dependant on the efficient production and distribution of documents and other forms of communication such as voice messaging systems.

3.25 Document imaging systems convert documents and images to digital form, reducing the amount of paper required. Electronic information should be easier to retrieve as electronic searches should be quicker than hunting through a mountain of paper.

Knowledge sharing   11/01, 5/02

Groupware

> ### KEY TERM
>
> **Groupware** is a term used to describe software that provides functions for the use of collaborative work groups.

3.26 Typically, groups utilising groupware are small project-oriented teams that have important tasks and tight deadlines Perhaps the best-known groupware product at present is Lotus Notes. However, there are many related products and technologies.

3.27 Features might include the following.

(a) A **scheduler** allowing users to keep track of their schedule and plan meetings with others.

(b) An **address book**.

(c) '**To do**' lists.

(d) A **journal**, used to record interactions with important contacts, record items (such as e-mail messages) and files that are significant to the user, and record activities of all types and track them all without having to remember where each one was saved.

(e) A **jotter** for jotting down notes as quick reminders of questions, ideas, and so on.

(f) File sharing and distribution utilities.

3.28 There are clearly advantages in having information such as this available from the desktop at the touch of a button, rather than relying on scraps of paper, address books, and corporate telephone directories. However, it is when groupware is used to **share information** with colleagues that it comes into its own. Here are some of the features that may be found.

(a) **Messaging**, comprising an **e-mail** in-box which is used to send and receive messages from the office, home, or the road and **routing** facilities, enabling users to send a message to a single person, send it sequentially to a number of people (who may add to it or comment on it before passing it on), or sending it to everyone at once.

(b) Access to an **information database**, and customisable 'views' of the information held on it, which can be used to standardise the way information is viewed in a workgroup.

(c) **Group scheduling**, to keep track of colleagues' itineraries. Microsoft Exchange Server, for instance, offers a 'Meeting Wizard' which can consult the diaries of everyone needed to attend a meeting and automatically work out when they will be available, which venues are free, and what resources are required.

(d) **Public folders**. These collect, organise, and share files with others on the team or across the organisation.

(e) One person (for instance a secretary or a stand-in during holidays or sickness) can be given '**delegate access**' to another's groupware folders and send mail on their behalf, or read, modify, or create items in public and private folders on their behalf.

(f) **Conferencing**. Participation in public, online discussions with others.

(g) **Assigning tasks**. A task request can be sent to a colleague who can accept, decline, or reassign the task. After the task is accepted, the groupware will keeps the task status up-to-date on a task list.

(h) **Voting** type facilities that can, say, request and tally responses to a multiple-choice question sent in a mail message (eg 'Here is a list of options for this year's Christmas party').

(i) **Hyperlinks** in mail messages. The recipient can click the hyperlink to go directly to a Web page or file server.

(j) **Workflow management** (see below) with various degrees of sophistication.

3.29 **Workflow** is a term used to describe the defined series of tasks within an organisation to produce a final outcome. Sophisticated workgroup computing applications allow the user to define different **workflows** for different types of jobs. For example, in a publishing setting, a document might be automatically routed from writer to editor to proofreader to production.

3.30 At **each stage** in the workflow, **one individual** or group is **responsible** for a specific task. Once the task is complete, the workflow software ensures that the individuals responsible for the **next** task are notified and receive the data they need to do their stage of the process.

3.31 Workflow systems can be described according to the type of process they are designed to deal with. There are three common types.

(a) **Image-based workflow systems** are designed to automate the flow of paper through an organisation, by transferring the paper to digital "images". These were the first workflow systems that gained wide acceptance. These systems are closely associated with 'imaging' (or 'document image processing' (DIP)) technology, and help with the routing and processing of digitised images.

(b) **Form-based workflow systems** (formflow) are designed to route forms intelligently throughout an organisation. These forms, unlike images, are text-based and consist of editable fields. Forms are automatically routed according to the information entered on them. In addition, these form-based systems can notify or remind people when action is due.

(c) **Co-ordination-based workflow systems** are designed to help the completion of work by providing a framework for **co-ordination** of action. Such systems are intended to improve organisational productivity by addressing the issues necessary to **satisfy customers**, rather than automating procedures that are not closely related to customer satisfaction.

Intranets

> **KEY TERM**
>
> An **intranet** is an internal network used to share information. Intranets utilise Internet technology and protocols. The firewall surrounding an internet fends off unauthorised access.

3.32 The idea behind an 'intranet' is that companies set up their own **mini version of the Internet.** (We look at the Internet in detail in Chapter 5). Intranets use a combination of the organisation's own networked computers and Internet technology. Each employee has a browser, used to access a server computer that holds corporate information on a wide variety of topics, and in some cases also offers access to the Internet.

3.33 Potential applications include company newspapers, induction material, online procedure and policy manuals, employee web pages where individuals post details of their activities and progress, and **internal databases** of the corporate information store.

3.34 Most of the **cost** of an intranet is the **staff time** required to set up the system.

3.35 The **benefits** of intranets are diverse.

(a) Savings accrue from the **elimination of storage, printing** and **distribution** of documents that can be made available to employees on-line.

(b) Documents on-line are often **more widely used** than those that are kept filed away, especially if the document is bulky (eg manuals) and needs to be searched. This means that there are **improvements in productivity** and **efficiency**.

(c) It is much **easier to update** information in electronic form.

(d) Wider access to corporate information should open the way to **more flexible working patterns,** eg material available on-line may be accessed from remote locations..

Case example

Groupware and intranets

The original idea of a 'personal' computer was to allow people to work together and share information across a network through a mainframe computer. However, users became so frustrated at their inability to get what they wanted from mainframe systems that they welcomed the IBM PC, used in stand-alone mode, with open arms.

This meant in turn that groupware (software designed to let users work together and share information through computers) had to be invented. (Examples are Lotus Notes (now **Lotus Domino**), **Novell GroupWise**, and **Microsoft Exchange**.) Groupware technology has been widely used to enable people to communicate, to share information, to work together and, most importantly, to carry out business processes and execute transactions, often using unstructured data.

The current fashion for intranets has given new impetus to these ideas, and all of the major products have now adopted Internet-type standards. Such products may have an advantage over intranets built from scratch because they recognise and address the problems of bringing about the **cultural changes** needed to get better business processes and **generate competitive advantage**.

Extranets

KEY TERM

An **extranet** is an intranet that is accessible to authorised outsiders.

3.36 Whereas an intranet resides behind a firewall and is accessible only to people who are members of the same company or organisation, an extranet provides various levels of accessibility to outsiders.

3.37 Only those outsiders with a valid username and password can access an extranet, with varying levels of access rights enabling control over what people can view. Extranets are becoming a very popular means for **business partners to exchange information**.

3.38 Extranets therefore allow better use of the knowledge held by an organisation - by facilitating access to that knowledge.

Creating knowledge

Knowledge work systems (KWS)

3.39 Knowledge Work Systems (KWS) are information systems that facilitate the creation and integration of new knowledge into an organisation. They provide knowledge workers with tools such as:

- Analytical tools
- Powerful graphics facilities
- Communication tools
- Access to external databases
- A user-friendly interface

3.40 The workstations of knowledge workers are often designed for the specific tasks they perform. For example, a design engineer would require sufficient graphics power to manipulate 3-D Computer Aided Design (**CAD**) images; a financial analyst would require a powerful desktop computer to access and manipulate a large amount of financial data (an **investment workstation**).

3.41 The components of a KWS are shown in the following diagram.

Knowledge work system

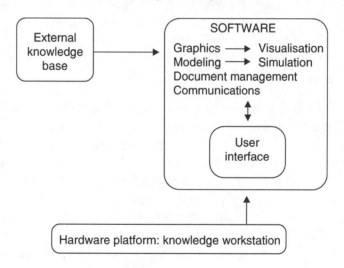

3.42 **Virtual reality systems** are another example of KWS. These systems create computer-generated simulations that emulate real-world activities. Interactive software and hardware (eg special headgear) provide simulations so realistic that users experience sensations that would normally only occur in the real world.

Case examples

Virtual reality

Burger King have used virtual reality stores to test new store designs.

Volvo have used virtual reality test drives in vehicle development.

BPP
PUBLISHING

Capturing and codifying knowledge

Artificial intelligence (AI)

KEY TERM

Artificial intelligence (AI) is the development of computer-based systems designed to behave as humans. Artificial intelligence systems are based on human expertise, knowledge and reasoning patterns.

3.43 The field of AI includes:

- Robotics
- 'Natural language' programming tools
- Perceptive systems
- Expert systems

3.44 The main commercial applications of AI have involved **expert systems**.

KEY TERM

An **expert system** is a computer program that captures human expertise in a limited domain of knowledge.

3.45 Expert system software uses a knowledge base that consists of facts, concepts and the relationships between them on a particular domain of knowledge and uses pattern-matching techniques to 'solve' problems.

3.46 Rules of thumb or ('heuristics') are important. A simple example might be 'milk in first' when making a cup of tea: this is a rule of thumb for tea making that saves people having to rethink how to make a cup of tea every time they do so. A simple business example programmed into a credit check may be: 'Don't allow credit to a person who has no credit history and has changed address twice or more within the last three years'.

3.47 For example, many financial institutions now use expert systems to process straightforward **loan applications**. The user enters certain key facts into the system such as the loan applicant's name and most recent addresses, their income and monthly outgoings, and details of other loans. The system will then:

(a) **Check the facts** given against its database to see whether the applicant has a good previous credit record.

(b) **Perform calculations** to see whether the applicant can afford to repay the loan.

(c) **Make a judgement** as to what extent the loan applicant fits the lender's profile of a good risk (based on the lender's previous experience).

(d) Suggest a decision.

3.48 A decision is then suggested, based on the results of this processing. This is why it is now often possible to get a loan or arrange insurance **over the telephone**, whereas in the past it would have been necessary to go and speak to a bank manager or send details to an actuary and then wait for him or her to come to a decision.

3.49 Other applications of expert systems include:

(a) **Legal** advice.

(b) **Tax** advice.

(c) **Forecasting** of economic or financial developments, or of market and customer behaviour.

(d) **Surveillance,** for example of the number of customers entering a supermarket, to decide what shelves need restocking and when more checkouts need to be opened, or of machines in a factory, to determine when they need maintenance.

(e) **Diagnostic systems,** to identify causes of problems, for example in production control in a factory, or in healthcare.

(f) **Education and training** (diagnosing a student's or worker's weaknesses and providing or recommending extra instruction as appropriate).

Exam Focus Point

An exam question could ask you to explain how a particular system (such as an intranet or an expert system) could help with the activities of a company described in a scenario. Give some thought to this for different sorts of organisation, for example a local authority, a transport company, a manufacturer of fast-moving consumer goods, a firm of accountants and so on.

3.50 An organisation can use an expert system when a number of conditions are met.

(a) The problem is **well defined**.
(b) The expert can define **rules** by which the problem can be solved.
(c) The **investment** in an expert system is cost-justified.

3.51 The knowledge base of an expert system must be kept up-to-date.

3.52 Expert systems are not suited to high-level unstructured problems as these require information from a wide range of sources rather than simply deciding between a few known alternatives.

3.53 A diagram of an expert system follows.

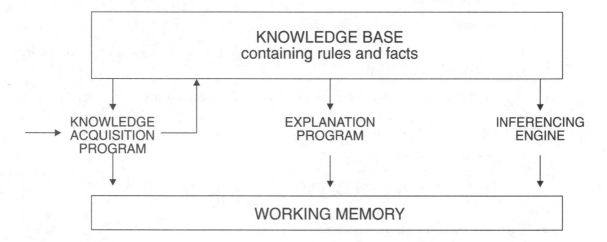

(a) The **knowledge base** contains facts (for example 'Postcode AX9 9ZZ had 104 reported burglaries in 2002') and rules ('next year the burglary rate is likely to be 5% higher than last year'). These facts and rules enable the system to make a 'judgement' such as; 'In 2002 homes in postcode AX9 9ZZ have a 6% chance of being burgled'.

(b) The **knowledge acquisition program** is a program which enables the expert system to acquire new knowledge and rules.

(c) The **working memory** is where the expert system stores the various facts and rules used during the current enquiry, and the current information given to it by the user.

(d) The **inferencing engine** is the software that executes the reasoning. It needs to discern which rules apply, and allocate priorities.

Question 3

Why do you think organisations wish to automate reasoning or decision-making tasks which humans are naturally better able to perform than computers?

Answer

The primary reason has to do with the relative cost of information. A human expert builds up a specialised body of knowledge over time. This knowledge has a commercial value. With human resource 'time is money'. Expert systems aim to use this expertise without requiring the human expert to spend time making the decision. The system also protects the organisation against loss of this expertise should the human expert leave the organisation.

Capturing knowledge in a computer system means that this wisdom can be accessed by more people. Thus, the delivery of complicated services to customers, decisions whether or not to extend credit and so forth, can be made by less experienced members of staff if the expert's knowledge is available to them.

If a manufacturing company has a complicated mixture of plant and machinery, then the repair engineer may accumulate a lot of knowledge over a period of time about the way it behaves: if a problem occurs, the engineer will be able to make a reasoned guess as to where the likely cause is to be found. If this accumulated expert information is made available to less experienced staff, it means that some of their learning curve is avoided.

An expert system is advantageous because it saves time, and therefore costs less. It is particularly useful as it possesses both knowledge and a reasoning ability.

3.54 **Advantages** of expert systems include the following.

(a) AI and expertise is **permanent,** whereas human experts may leave the business.

(b) AI is **easily copied**.

(c) AI is **consistent,** whereas human experts and decision makers may not be.

(d) AI can be **documented**. The reasoning behind an expert recommendation produced by a computer will be recorded.

(e) Depending on the task the computer may be much **faster** than the human being.

3.55 **Disadvantages** of expert systems include the following:

(a) Systems are **expensive**.

(b) The technology is still relatively new. Systems will probably need extensive testing and debugging.

(d) People are naturally **more creative**.

(e) Systems have a very **narrow focus**.

Neural networks

3.56 Neural networks are another application of AI, seen by some as the 'next step' in computing. Neural computing is modelled on the biological processes of the human brain.

3.57 Neural networks can **learn from experience**. They can analyse vast quantities of complex data and **identify patterns** from which predictions can be made. They have the ability to cope with incomplete or 'fuzzy' data, and can deal with previously unspecified or **new situations**.

3.58 Neural techniques have been applied to similar areas as expert systems eg credit risks. Neural techniques are more advanced in that they don't rely on a set of hard rules, but develop a 'hidden' layer of experience and come to a decision based on this hidden layer.

3.59 A neural network is shown below.

Neural network

Input layer	Hidden layer	Output layer
Income		
Debt		Good credit risks
Age		Bad credit risks
Payment record		

Fuzzy logic

3.60 Artificial intelligence applications are increasingly making use of 'fuzzy logic'. Traditionally computer programs have required precision such as 'yes' or 'no'.

3.61 Fuzzy logic involves using more complex rules than the traditional IF-THEN statements. For example, a traditional statement may say '*IF room temperature is less than 60 degrees THEN raise the heat*'.

3.62 A system using fuzzy logic would have a range of membership functions which are less precise than rules. A membership function may say '*If the temperature is warm or hot and the humidity is high lower the temperature and humidity.*'

3.63 The parameters for *warm, hot, high, low* etc would be defined elsewhere in the system (and may overlap). The program would combine the function readings and using weightings decide on the required course of action.

4   DATABASES AND PLANNING MODELS   5/02

4.1   The way in which data is held on a system affects the ease by which the data is able to be accessed and manipulated. Many modern software packages are built around a database. A database provides a comprehensive set of data for a number of different users.

> ### KEY TERMS
>
> A **database** is a collection of data organised to service many applications. The database provides convenient access to data for a wide variety of users and user needs.
>
> A **database management system** (**DBMS**) is the software that centralises data and manages access to the database. It is a system which allows numerous applications to extract the data they need without the need for separate files.
>
> The **logical structure** of a database refers to how various application programs access the data. The **physical structure** relates to how data is organised within the database.
>
> The independence of data items from the programs which access them is referred to as **data independence**.
>
> Duplication of data items is referred to as **data redundancy**.
>
> In a database environment, the ease with which applications access the central pool of data is referred to as **integration**.
>
> **Integrity** relates to data accuracy and consistency. Data independence and integration should reduce data redundancy resulting in improved data integrity.

The characteristics of a database system

4.2   A database system has the following characteristics.

(a)   **Shared**. Different users are able to access the same data for their own processing applications. This removes the need for duplicating data on different files.

(b)   **Controls** to preserve the **integrity** of the database. Users should not be able to alter the data on file so as to **spoil** the database records for other users. However, users must be able to make **valid** alterations to the data.

(c)   **Flexibility.** The database system should provide for the **needs of different users**, who each have their own processing requirements and data access methods. The database should be capable of **evolving** to meet **future** needs.

4.3   The **advantages** of a database system are as follows.

(a)   **Avoidance of unnecessary duplication of data**

It recognises that data can be used for many purposes but only needs to be input and stored once.

(b)   **Multi-purpose data**

From (a), it follows that although data is input once, it can be used for several purposes.

(c)   **Data for the organisation as a whole, not just for individual departments**

The database concept encourages management to regard data as a resource that must be **properly managed** just as any other resource. Database systems encourage management to analyse data, relationships between data items, and how data is used in different applications.

(d) **Consistency**

Because data is only held once, it is easier to ensure that it is up-to-date and consistent across departments.

(e) **New uses for data**

Data is held independently of the programs that access the data. This allows greater flexibility in the ways that data can be used. New programs can be easily introduced to make use of existing data in a different way.

(f) **New applications**

Developing new application programs with a database system is easier as a central pool of data is already available to be drawn upon.

(g) **Flexibility**

Relational systems are extremely flexible, allowing information from several different sources to be combined and providing answers to ad-hoc queries.

4.4 The **disadvantages** of a database systems relate mainly to security and control.

(a) There are potential problems of **data security** and **data privacy**. Administrative procedures for data security should supplement software controls.

(b) Since there is only one set of data, it is essential that the data should be **accurate** and free from corruption. A back-up routine is essential.

(c) Initial **development costs** may be high.

(d) For hierarchical and network structures, the access paths through the data must be **specified in advance**.

(e) Both hierarchical and network systems require intensive **programming** and are **inflexible**.

Using databases for planning

4.5 Planning will always involve an element of risk – as it deals with the **future**. Databases can at least ensure that information we have about the present and the past is available to aid planning. Organised data retrieval techniques make the data available in an effective way. In a world in which decisions must be ever more rapid, it is crucial to be able to access diverse, complex, multiple data bits and to analyse them to rapidly and correctly extract the knowledge they contain.

4.6 Databases can be used in conjunction with a variety of tools and techniques, eg Decision Support Systems, Executive Information Systems, data warehousing, and data mining. (DSS and EIS were explained in Chapter 1, data warehousing and data mining will be explained later in this Chapter.)

BPP PUBLISHING

4.7 An **object model,** as described below, has characteristics of both a database and a **planning model**. The article explains how models can assist the strategic planning process.

Case example

Using models for strategic planning

Financial and business planning is probably the most important activity that an organisation will undertake. However, traditional tools like spreadsheets were never designed for planning and have inherited the task. This article will demonstrate the **strategic value of objects** over traditional spreadsheets.

So what are 'objects'?

Objects are based on **models organised around real-world concepts**. Essentially **they consist of data and a program held together in a single entity**.

Although 'objects' are a technology that were developed more than ten years ago it is only now that they have reached a stage where they can be **considered of strategic importance** for organisations. This is because, unlike traditional tools, they can **capture knowledge** and guarantee integrity. This means that managers are equipped to become strategic planners rather than spreadsheet programmers.

It is easy to see why spreadsheets are so popular—they can be efficient, cost-effective and flexible. However, the explosive growth in their use has far outpaced the understanding of the associated risks or the application of best practice. In an investigation into blue-chip companies using large spreadsheets, KPMG Management Consulting reported that up to 95% of models were found to contain major errors (ie those that could affect decisions).

In 1995 Commercial and General Systems undertook some research, talking to management consultancies, accountants, venture capitalists and banks about the main **problems in financial and business planning**. Those identified were:

Consolidation: Time is incurred in agreeing a common standard for each model, as there are many different accounting formats and standards that need to be applied. Figures to be consolidated tend to come from a variety of sources and those from colleagues are often looked upon with distrust. This means that with revisions or new sets of figures being consolidated there is constant checking and re-checking for errors which means increased time and costs.

Sharing: The business plan should reflect the plan of the business but very often it is difficult for different departments to contribute successfully. Planning 'knowledge' is not shared, with users ending up speaking different languages. This can lead to bad assumptions being incorporated into financial models which are inevitably carried through to the final plan.

Re-invention: PC stands for 'personal computer' and that is exactly what it is - personal. Using spreadsheets, users tend to work on their own models, which are developed in isolation of each other. This leads to duplication of effort and substantial time is wasted in reinventing similar models.

Re-scheduling: Business planning involves conducting 'what if' scenario analysis and spreadsheets prove to be inflexible in this—try moving all of the costs for a new project out, say, three months on your spreadsheet models and watch the formulas 'fall over'. This inflexibility means that managers are not really planning.

Hidden mistakes: With spreadsheets, mistakes are made unknowingly and these are often amplified when refinements are made to the plan. The revenue and cost drivers are not always fully understood and are buried deep inside the spreadsheet. Models are therefore inherently incorrect, leading to bad decision-making.

Managers become programmers: The skills now required to be competent with spreadsheets are fairly significant and many business models are being compromised by lack of programming skills. Managers become frustrated and end up doing the wrong job. They are technically programming instead of financial and business planning.

Limited audit trail: Audit-trails in spreadsheets are very limited at best, and you can't review what you did very easily, let alone tracking someone else's changes! Managers **cannot therefore learn from mistakes** and capture or evolve organisational best practice.

How can object type models be of strategic value?

Planning objects: the next generation

Individual planning objects can be considered 'products' in their own right. As objects can vary widely in their features and capabilities, one-day objects may be traded between organisations and individuals. Objects like 'Rent objects' and 'Electricity objects' might simply 'feed' and manipulate a cost or revenue centre, whereas a hypothetical 'British Telecom' object, might carry BT's most recent profit and loss and balance sheet data. When 'corporate' data is 'packaged' into a planning object, the data 'inside' the object can be flexed and explored with an ease and efficiency not achievable in a spreadsheet.

Polymorphism (explained later in this article) allows objects to be mixed, matched and freely arranged in a single, internally consistent plan without regard to individual object types. This means **that consolidating and sharing plans is made easier** whilst reducing re-invention. New objects dynamically adapt to the planning model and, unlike a spreadsheet plan, an object-based plan guarantees 100% plan calculation integrity whilst simultaneously enabling the user to reorganise the timing of individual events in the plan. Making last-minute changes using the traditional spreadsheet plans can take hours, but using the object-based approach this takes a matter of seconds.

From a visual perspective planning with objects is much more intuitive than using the spreadsheet. As the plan is 'pushed, pulled and flexed', **the objects maintain 'live' connections to the chart of accounts**. The timing of 'planned' events can be changed and the **financial consequences reported upon**.

Planning with 'objects' **actively encourages managers to use models created from other managers**, rather than continually 're-inventing new spreadsheet models', managers can freely explore and manipulate 'other people's financial models' simply by importing them into the model. The chart of accounts automatically performs consolidations to the same accounting structure and, due to encapsulation, a deep understanding of complicated underlying formulas and logic frequently found in 'other people's spreadsheets' is not required. For further academic and professional research material about planning objects and the limitations of spreadsheets refer to the Internet site at www.planningobjects.com.

Strategic value

The appeal of an object-orientated approach is that the **information in each object can be re-used** repeatedly in a variety of applications. As can be seen, the common tasks that are performed in financial and business planning are much more effectively done by the use of objects. The value of this re-usability **facilitates the capture of knowledge and organisational learning**. With guaranteed integrity, managers are secure about the figures they use, whether self-generated or from colleagues. Taking all these factors into account it is easy to see how objects can be of strategic value.

It is important to recognise that objects will not replace spreadsheets, just as spreadsheets didn't replace paper. They do, however, represent a new set of tools for managers that complement existing ones. Using objects can confer competitive advantage for organisations and offer the benefits of **knowledge capture and guaranteed integrity**.

Objects can be considered to consist of three components:

Encapsulation: The object's interface hides all the details about its composition, structure and internal workings. For example, the 'interface' of a computer keyboard is the keys and the internal details of how a keystroke translates into a character on the screen are 'encapsulated' behind the interface. This offers the benefits of allowing the user to remove one object and seamlessly replace it with another— say, a 'Barclays loan' object with a 'Bank of Scotland loan' object.

Polymorphism: This concept allows two similar objects to be viewed through a common interface, thereby eliminating the need to differentiate between the two objects. Consider the structure of most writing implements. Each may have a different kind of ink, lead or colour but they all share the common interface of how you hold and write with that implement. Thus different supplier objects can be created to work seamlessly together, eg you could use a sales object from 'Dixons' and a payroll object from 'Arthur Andersen' within the same plan.

Inheritance: Here each object can be defined and similarities of different classes of objects are described by a common base class. For example, a base class could be 'Shape' and this derives 'Square' and 'Triangle'. Thus the derived class is said to inherit properties and characteristics from the base class. This is important since it allows the enterprise to share knowledge and facilitate learning by

BPP PUBLISHING

building on top of other people's work. You could take the 'Dixons' sales object as a base to create a 'Dixons' sales object which supports commissions.

Adapted from an article by Les Porter, John Oakland and Ken Gadd, CIMA articles database
September 1999

5 DATA WAREHOUSING AND DATAMINING

5.1 Two techniques designed to utilise the ever-increasing amounts of data held by organisations are **data warehousing** and **datamining**.

Data warehousing

> **KEY TERM**
>
> A **data warehouse** consists of a database, containing data from various operational systems, and reporting and query tools.

5.2 A data warehouse contains data from a range of internal (eg sales order processing system, nominal ledger) and external sources. One reason for including individual transaction data in a data warehouse is that if necessary the user can drill-down to access transaction level detail. Data is increasingly obtained from newer channels such as customer care systems, outside agencies or websites.

5.3 Data is copied to the data warehouse as often as required – usually either daily, weekly or monthly. The process of making any required changes to the format of data and copying it to the warehouse is usually automated.

5.4 The result should be a coherent set of information available to be used across the organisation for management analysis and decision making. The reporting and query tools available within the warehouse should facilitate management reporting and analysis.

5.5 The reporting and query tools should be flexible enough to allow multidimensional data analysis, also known as on-line analytical processing (**OLAP**). Each aspect of information (eg product, region, price, budgeted sales, actual sales, time period etc) represents a different dimension. OLAP enables data to be viewed from each dimension, allowing each aspect to be viewed and in relation to the other aspects.

Features of data warehouses

5.6 A data warehouse is subject-oriented, integrated, time-variant, and non-volatile.

(a) **Subject-oriented**

A data warehouse is focussed on data groups not application boundaries. Whereas the operational world is designed around applications and functions such as sales and purchases, a data warehouse world is organised around major **subjects** such as customers, supplier, product and activity.

(b) **Integrated**

Data within the data warehouse must be consistent in format and codes used – this is referred to as **integrated** in the context of data warehouses.

For example, one operational application feeding the warehouse may represent **gender** as an 'M' and an 'F' while another represents **gender** as '1' and '0'.

While it does not matter how **gender** is represented in the data warehouse (let us say that 'M' and 'F' is chosen), it **must** arrive in the data warehouse in a **consistent integrated** state. The data import routine should 'cleanse' any inconsistencies.

(c) **Time-variant**

Data is organised by time and stored in 'time-slices'.

Data warehouse data may cover **a long time horizon,** perhaps from five to ten years. Data warehouse data tends to deal with **trends** rather than single points in time. As a result, each data element in the data warehouse environment must carry with it the time for which it applies.

(d) **Non-volatile**

Data **cannot be changed** within the warehouse. Only load and retrieval operations are made.

5.7 Organisations may build a single central data warehouse to serve the entire organisation or may create a series of smaller **data marts**. A data mart holds a selection of the organisation's data for a specific purpose.

5.8 A data mart can be constructed more quickly and cheaply than a data warehouse. However, if too many individual data marts are built, organisations may find it is more efficient to have a single data warehouse serving all areas.

Advantages of data warehouses

5.9 Advantages of setting up a data warehouse system include the following.

(a) Decision makers can access data without affecting the use of operational systems.

(b) Having a wide range of data available to be queried easily encourages the taking of a wide perspective on organisational activities.

(c) Data warehouses have proved successful in some businesses for:

(i) Quantifying the effect of marketing initiatives.
(ii) Improving knowledge of customers.
(iii) Identifying and understanding an enterprise's most profitable revenues streams.

5.10 Some organisations have found they have invested considerable resources implementing a data warehouse for little return. To benefit from the information a data warehouse can provide, organisations need to be flexible and prepared to act on what they find. If a warehouse system is implemented simply to follow current practice it will be of little value.

5.11 The components of a data warehouse are shown in the following diagram.

Components of a data warehouse

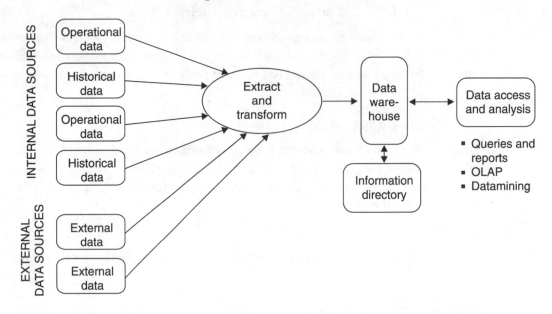

Case example: Seven steps to bring your systems into the 21st century

Step One. Implement a data warehouse

A data warehouse is a computer loaded with a database product such as Oracle or Microsoft SQL server. **This database is configured to hold the key information** you want to look at and is interfaced with the 'transaction processing' systems.

For larger volumes of data a toolset has been developed called **OLAP (on-line analytical processing)** which allows **summary information** to be created and stored across the different business performance metrics. As a consequence of this, on-line and instant enquiries can potentially be made on the balances of any combination of customer/product/regional performance by date/period range.

The performance of the transaction-processing systems will not be affected by heavy use of the data warehouse for a complex set of enquiries, as you will not be working with the live information.

Once this warehouse has been set up, information can be combined from the different operations systems into a consistent format and can be accessed by a wide variety of reporting/analysis/web tools.

Step Two. Reporting tools

Time and time again finance directors say that their key IT issue is lack of reporting capabilities in the systems they are using. Reporting problems tend to fall into three categories.

First, the **inability to access the source data**. This is either because it is in a format that cannot be accessed by PC technology or it is held in so many places that its structure is incomprehensible to a member of the finance team.

Second, the **tools to make the enquiries** or produce the reports are often **difficult to use** and do not produce the reports in a 'user friendly' format with 'drill down' capabilities.

Third, there is the issue of **consistency of information** across systems. In order to get an overall picture of your organisation's performance you will usually need to access data from different operation applications. All too often the data is not the same across these systems.

The argument for replacing what you have is well rehearsed. New systems promise the latest technology for reporting and enquiries. **Enterprise Resource Planning (ERP)** packages promise to integrate your different applications smoothly and give you a single point of access to all data. **Customer Relationship Management (CRM)** software has been added to this recipe to give this approach a better chance of happening.

There are a myriad of reporting tools costing from a few pounds to hundreds of thousands of pounds. One that is regularly overlooked is the **spreadsheet**. Excel is the product most commonly used by accountants. With the advent of Microsoft Office 2000 there is a bewildering array of features to present information on your desktop or paper. **Pivot tables** are starting to be used more widely for multi-dimensional analysis and can be combined with the increasingly powerful **graphical capabilities** of Excel. Spreadsheets are much underrated and it is surprising how many organisations go out and buy expensive new knowledge-management tools when they already have a product on their computer that will deliver all the reporting/enquiry performance they require.

So, see how far your spreadsheet will take you and see if you can avoid the cost of another new IT tool.

Step Three. Intranet-enabled-reporting/enquiries

Larger companies have by now started to implement a **corporate intranet**. This typically holds information on employee phone and contact details, standard forms for holiday requests, terms and conditions of employment and so on.

It is possible now to integrate financial reporting into an intranet. The leading web page development tools allow the display of information from a data warehouse. Excel has facilities to post spreadsheets and pivot table information straight to a web page and for users to drill down to the detail from a summary level. There are a number of **benefits** to this.

First, the information is presented in a **user-friendly** format and can be made 'idiot proof' for non-IT literate staff.

Second, the benefit of using a web browser is that it allows for **remote access** to the information quickly and easily. This means that people working at different parts of the organisation or away from the office can access this data rapidly.

Third, the web browser technology is becoming an **industry standard** and as such is well supported and increasingly reliable.

So start to use a web browser to access your reports and **publish these to your intranet** server rather than printing them out.

Step Four. Client/supplier access to information

So you have implemented the above and have your core business data from your different systems in **a single data warehouse**. You will be using PC tools like Excel to access this and will have developed part of your intranet so that staff can access key information quickly and easily wherever they are.

Why not consider making **some of this information available to your business partners**? For example, if you have customer sales order information in your data warehouse, why not make it available to your customers and even suppliers? If you have internal information on the products and services that you sell, why not do likewise?

This is where the Internet can really start to bite and give your organisation real commercial benefit.

Step Five. Streamlined transaction processing

The next step is to look at the possibility of **streamlining your business processes**. How many times are you capturing your transactions in your organisation?

Why not allow customers to generate their own orders via the web? If the data warehouse holds information on the clients, the products and services you sell, it could be relatively straightforward to create an order front-end with a web browser to this information.

You could populate the data warehouse with these incoming orders and use this to upload your core transaction processing systems. Most packages now have data import modules and this process may be more straightforward than you think and a lot cheaper and easier than replacing your core business systems. Why not extend this to allowing your employees and even customers to 'self service' the information in your systems and keep it up-to-date themselves.

Clearly there are lots of caveats to this option. **Security** is always a concern, as is the resilience of the IT infrastructure necessary to support on-line order processing by clients. However, a number of forward-thinking businesses have achieved this without replacing all their systems.

Step Six. Train staff in what you already have

Do your staff really understand the features of your accounting and business systems? Are they familiar with what the web can offer your organisation? Put together a **comprehensive training programme**.

BPP PUBLISHING

Step Seven. Get board buy-in

A note of caution to conclude on: **you MUST get board and senior management buy-in to what you are planning**.

Source: Adapted from an article by *John Tate, Management Accounting*, April 2000

Datamining 11/01

> **KEY TERM**
>
> **Datamining** software looks for hidden patterns and relationships in large pools of data.

5.12 True datamining software discovers **previously unknown relationships**. The hidden patterns and relationships the software identifies can be used to guide decision making and to **predict future behaviour**.

Case example: Datamining

(1) The American retailer Wal-Mart discovered an unexpected relationship between the sale of **nappies** and **beer!** Wal-Mart found that both tended to sell at the same time, just after working hours, and concluded that men with small children stopped off to buy nappies on their way home, and bought beer at the same time. Logically therefore, if the two items were put in the same shopping aisle, sales of both should increase. Wal-Mart tried this and it worked.

(2) Some credit card companies have used datamining to predict which customers are likely to switch to a competitor in the next few months. Based on the datamining results, the bank can take action to retain these customers.

5.13 Datamining uses statistical analysis tools as well as neural networks, fuzzy logic and other **intelligent techniques**.

5.14 The types of relationships or patterns that datamining may uncover may be classified as follows.

Relationship\Discovery	Comment
Classification or cluster	These terms refer to the identification of patterns within the database between a range of data items. For example, datamining may find that unmarried males aged between 20 and 30, who have an income above £50,000 are more likely to purchase a high performance sports car than people from other demographic groups. This group could then be targeted when marketing material is produced/distributed.
Association	One event can be linked or correlated to another event – such as in Wal-Mart example (1) above.
Forecasting	Trends are identified within the data that can be extrapolated into the future.

Case example: Datamining software

Datamining software

The following is extracted from marketing material for a Datamining product called the NeoVista Decision Series.

Understand The Patterns In Your Business and Discover The Value In Your Data

Within your corporate database resides extremely valuable information - information that reflects how your business processes operate and how your customers behave. Every transaction your organisation makes is captured for accounting purposes, and with it, a wealth of potential knowledge.

When properly analysed, organised and presented, this information can be of enormous value. Conventional 'drill down' database query techniques may reveal some of these details, but much of the valuable **knowledge content will remain hidden**.

The NeoVista Decision Series is a suite of knowledge discovery software specifically designed to address this challenge. Analysing data without any preconceived notion of the patterns it contains, the Decision Series **seeks out relationships and trends**, and presents them in easy-to-understand form, enabling better business decisions.

The Decision Series is being used today by leading corporations to discover the hidden value in their data, providing them with major competitive advantages and organisational benefits.

- A Large Multi-National Retailer uses the Decision Series **to refine inventory stocking levels**, by store and by item, to dramatically reduce out-of-stock or overstocking situations and thereby improve revenues and reduce forced markdowns.

- A Health Maintenance Group uses the Decision Series to **predict which of its members are most at risk** from specific major illnesses. This presents opportunities for timely medical intervention and preventative treatment to promote the patient's well-being and reduce the healthcare provider's costs.

- An International Retail Sales Organisation uses the Decision Series to **optimise store and department layouts**, resulting in more accurate targeting of products to maximise sales within the scope of available resources.

NeoVista's unique software can be applied to a wide range of business problems, allowing you to:

- Determine the relationships that lie at the heart of your business.

- Make reliable **estimates of future behaviour** based on sophisticated analyses of past events.

- Make **business decisions with a higher degree of understanding** and confidence.

Datamining is renowned for exposing important facts and anomalies within data warehouses. The NeoVista Decision Series' knowledge discovery methodology has the proven ability to expose the patterns that are not merely interesting, but which are critical to your business. These patterns provide you with an advantage through insight and knowledge that your competition may never discover.

Chapter roundup

- **Information** is a **valuable resource** that requires efficient management.

- **Technology** has changed how information is collected, stored and processed, as well as changing the information needs of organisations.

- Strategic planning, management control and operational control may be seen as a **hierarchy** of planning and control decisions (the Anthony hierarchy).

- **Knowledge management** describes the process of collecting, storing and using the knowledge held within an organisation.

- Knowledge is now commonly viewed as a sustainable source of competitive advantage. Producing unique products or services or producing products or services at a lower cost than competitors is based on superior knowledge.

- Information systems play an important role in knowledge management, helping with **information flows** and helping formally **capture** the knowledge held within the organisation.

- There are a wide range of systems available that encourage knowledge management including:

  ° Office automation systems
  ° Group collaboration systems
  ° Workflow and workgroup applications
  ° Intranets and extranets

- A database is a collection of data organised to service many applications. The database provides convenient access to data for a wide variety of users and user needs.

- **Advantages of a database system** include the avoidance of data duplication, management is encouraged to manage data as a valuable resource, data consistency across the organisation, and the flexibility for answering ad-hoc queries.

- **Disadvantages of a database system** include initial development costs and the potential problems of data security.

- A **data warehouse** consists of a database, containing data from various operational systems, and reporting and query tools.

- Organisations may build a single central data warehouse to serve the entire organisation or may create a series of smaller **data marts**.

- **Datamining** software looks for **hidden** patterns and relationships in large pools of data. Datamining uses **statistical analysis tools** as well as **neural networks**, **fuzzy logic** and other **intelligent techniques**.

Quick quiz

1   Define 'risk' and 'uncertainty' in the context of decision-making.

2   Define 'efficiency' and 'effectiveness'.

3   Match the following types of system with how they help knowledge management.

System			Use
(i)	Knowledge work systems	A	Knowledge distribution.
(ii)	Artificial intelligence systems	B	Knowledge sharing.
(iii)	Office automation systems	C	Knowledge creation.
(iv)	Group collaboration systems	D	Knowledge capture and codification.

4   List five features of groupware.

   1   ....

   2   ....

   3   ....

   4   ....

   5   ....

5   'Artificial intelligence and expert systems are the same thing.'

   True   ☐

   False   ☐

6   Distinguish between a data warehouse and a data mart.

7   List four business applications of datamining.

   1   ....

   2   ....

   3   ....

   4   ....

BPP PUBLISHING

Answers to quick quiz

1   Risk involves situations or events which may or may not occur, but whose probability of occurrence can be calculated statistically, and the frequency of their occurrence predicted from past records. Uncertainty involves situations or events whose outcome cannot be predicted with statistically.

2   Efficiency refers to the resources input to a process and the amount of outputs. Effectiveness relates to whether resources are being used for the 'best' purpose.

3   (i)   C
    (ii) D
    (iii) A
    (iv) B

4   A scheduler.
    An address book.
    'To do' lists.
    A 'journal' to record significant interactions and activities.
    A 'jotter'.
    File sharing and distribution utilities.

5   False. Artificial intelligence (AI) systems are based on human expertise, knowledge and reasoning patterns. An expert system is one example of AI. Expert systems are computer programs that capture human expertise in a limited domain of knowledge.

6   A data warehouse consists of a database, containing data from various operational systems, and reporting and query tools. Organisations may build a single central data warehouse to serve the entire organisation or may create a series of smaller data marts. A data mart holds a selection of the organisation's data for a specific purpose.

7   Some examples include:
    Predicting what each website visitor is most interested in seeing.
    Predicting which customers are likely to switch to competitors.
    Identifying common characteristics of customers.
    Determining which products are often purchased together.
    Identifying which transactions are most likely to be fraudulent.

Question to try	Level	Marks	Time
5	Examination	25	45 mins

INFORMATION SYSTEMS AT DIFFERENT LEVELS

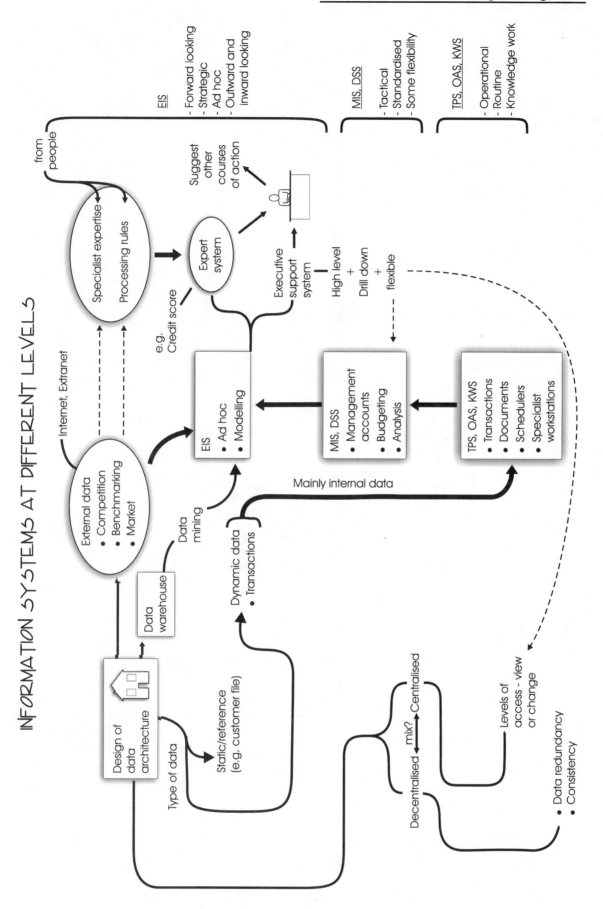

Part B
Using IS/IT competitively

Chapter 3

INFORMATION SYSTEMS AND STRATEGY

Topic list	Syllabus reference	Ability required
1 Strategic planning	(ii)	Evaluation
2 Developing a strategy for IS and IT	(ii)	Evaluation
3 Information system architectures	(ii)	Evaluation
4 Building a business case for investment in IS and IT	(ii)	Evaluation
5 Business process re-engineering	(ii)	Evaluation
6 Process innovation	(ii)	Evaluation

Introduction

In this chapter we look at the concept of **strategic planning** and the role of Information Technology in the strategic planning process. Some ideas will be familiar from your other studies of strategy (although you may not have thought about them in the context of information systems before); others, such as **Business Process Re-engineering** you may not have studied in detail before.

Learning outcomes covered in this chapter

- **Identify** and **evaluate** appropriate IS/IT systems and **recommend** changes to meet the strategic information needs of an organisation

- **Analyse** the contents of IS, IT and IM strategies and **recommend** improvements thereto *(Also see Chapter 6)*

- **Evaluate** the importance of process innovation and reengineering

Syllabus content covered in this chapter

- Process of cost-benefit analysis and how to assess the value of information

- The strategic case for IT investment particularly where the benefits and value of information are difficult to quantity with any degree of reliability

- The purpose and contents of IS, IT and IM strategies *(Also see Chapter 6)*

- Why an organisation needs an IS/IT strategy which is complementary to the organisation strategy

- Use the applications portfolio to improve IS/IT strategy (McFarlan)

- How Critical Success Factors (CSFs) link to performance indicators and corporate strategy and how they can be used to drive the information needs in organisations

- The concept of business integration - links between strategy, people, technology and operations in determining the role of IS/IT *(Also see Chapter 4)*

- The role of IT in innovation and Business Process Engineering

1 STRATEGIC PLANNING

1.1 Before looking at the role of information and information systems in strategic planning, we will briefly explain the general process of strategic planning. We provided one definition of strategic planning when looking at information for planning and control in Chapter 1 – CIMA's official definition is shown below.

> **KEY TERMS**
>
> **Strategy** can be defined as 'A course of action, including the specification of resources required, to achieve a specific objective.'
>
> **Strategic planning** is the formulation, evaluation and selection of strategies for the purpose of preparing a long-term plan of action to attain objectives.
>
> (CIMA, *Official Terminology*)

1.2 Strategic planning involves taking a view of the organisation and the future, and deciding how best to organise the structure and resources of the organisation. Three general **levels of strategy** can be identified: corporate, business and functional/operational.

Corporate strategy

1.3 **Corporate strategy** is concerned with what types of business the organisation is in. It denotes the most general level of strategy in an organisation.

Business strategy

1.4 **Business strategy** is concerned with how an organisation approaches a particular product or market. For example, a decision may be required as to whether a company should focus on a single market segment, or offer a wide range of products covering all market segments.

1.5 Some large, diversified firms have separate **strategic business units** dealing with particular areas.

1.6 **Characteristics of decisions relating to corporate and/or business strategy**

Characteristic	Comment
Scope of activities	Products and markets – decisions might involve diversifying into a new line of business or into a new market. It might mean global expansion or contraction.
Environment	The organisation counters threats and exploits opportunities in the environment (customers, clients, competitors).
Capability	The organisation matches its activities to its resources: ie it does what it is able to do.
Resources	Strategy involves choices about allocating or obtaining resources now and in future.
Operations	Strategic decisions always affect operations.
Values	The value systems of people in power influence them to understand the world in a certain way.

Characteristic	Comment
Direction	Strategic decisions have a medium or long-term impact.
Complex	Strategic decisions involve uncertainty about the future, integrating the operations of the organisation and change.

Functional/operational strategies; information systems strategy

1.7 Information systems strategy is an example of a **functional/operational strategy** (although in some cases it may have strategic implications). Functional/operational strategies deal with specialised areas of activity.

Functional area	Comment
Information systems	A firm's information systems are becoming increasingly important, as an item of expenditure, as administrative support and as a tool for competitive strength.
Marketing	Devising products and services, pricing, promoting and distributing them, in order to satisfy customer needs at a profit.
Production	Factory location, manufacturing techniques, outsourcing etc.
Finance	Ensuring that the firm has enough financial resources to fund its other strategies.
Human resources	Secure personnel of the right skills in the right quantity at the right time.
R&D	New products and techniques.

1.8 The relationship between corporate, business and operational strategies is shown in the following diagram.

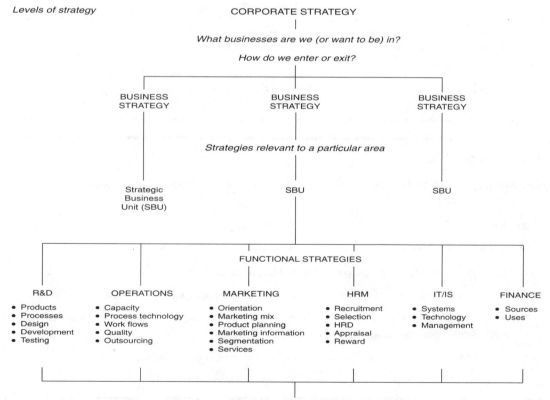

BPP
PUBLISHING

Formulating strategic business objectives: The rational model

1.9 Strategic planning divides into a number of different stages: strategic **analysis**, strategic **choice** and **implementation**.

(a) **Strategic analysis** involves the steps outlined in the following table (relevant models referred to are covered throughout this Text).

	Stage	Comment	Key tools, models, techniques
Step 1.	Mission and/or vision	Mission denotes values, the business's rationale for existing; vision refers to where the organisation intends to be in a few years	• Mission statement
Step 2.	Goals	Interpret the mission to different stakeholders	• Stakeholder analysis
Step 3.	Objectives	Quantified embodiments of mission	• Measures such as profitability, time scale, deadlines
Step 4.	Environmental analysis	Identify opportunities and threats	• PEST analysis • Porter's 5 forces • Scenario building
Step 5.	Position audit or situation analysis	Identify strengths and weaknesses Firm's **current** resources, products, customers, systems, structure, results, efficiency, effectiveness	• Resource audit • Distinctive competence • Value chain • Product life cycle • Boston (BCG) matrix • Marketing audit
Step 6.	Corporate appraisal	Combines Steps 4 and 5	• SWOT analysis charts
Step 7.	Gap analysis	Compares outcomes of Step 6 with Step 3	• Gap analysis

Question 1

List five ways in which corporate and business strategy are relevant to the types of information system required in an organisation?

Answer

Five ways are shown below. You may have come up with others.

(a) Information is needed to shape corporate and business strategy.

(b) Information systems provide information that monitors progress towards strategic objectives.

(c) Business objectives are becoming increasingly customer focused. Good customer service requires good quality information available on demand.

(d) A strategy of growth will require a corresponding increase in the information system.

(e) A change of strategy may mean a new information system is required.

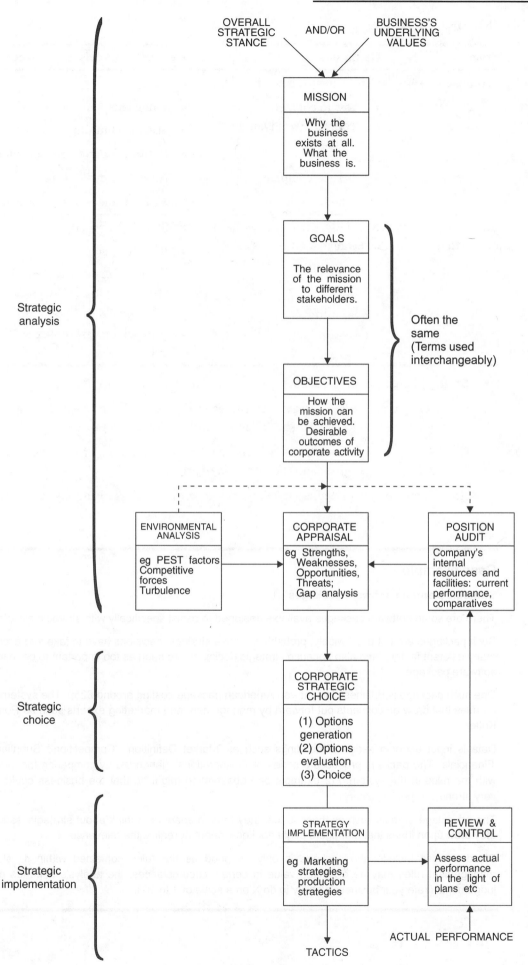

(b) Strategic choice

Stage	Comment	Key tools, models, techniques
Strategic options generation	Come up with new ideas: • How to compete (competitive advantage) • Where to compete • Method of growth	 • Value chain analysis • Scenario building • Porter's generic strategic choices • Ansoff's growth vector • Acquisition vs organic growth
Strategic options evaluation	Normally, each strategy has to be evaluated on the basis of • Acceptability • Suitability • Feasibility • Environmental fit	• Stakeholder analysis • Risk analysis • Decision-making tools such as decision trees, matrices, ranking and scoring methods • Financial measures (eg ROCE, DCF)

Strategy selection involves choosing between the alternative strategies.

(i) The competitive strategies are the generic strategies for competitive advantage an organisation will pursue. They determine **how** you compete.

(ii) Product-market strategies (which markets you should enter or leave) determine **where** you compete and the direction of growth.

(iii) Institutional strategies (ie relationships with other organisations) determine the method of **growth**.

Case example

Strategic planning software packages

There are some software packages available designed to assist specifically with strategic planning.

Such packages are not used widely, probably because strategic decisions have to take into account so many different factors, and also because strategic decisions are seen as too important to be made by a software package.

One such package is Business Insight - an American package costing around £250. The system is built on rules that draw on concepts put forward by management and marketing experts such as Porter and Kotler.

Data is input under a series of headings such as 'Market Definition', 'Competition', 'Suppliers' and 'Financials'. The package produces a series of 'Observations', generated by comparing the input data with the rules in the system. For example one observation might be that the business could 'expect very strong competitive rivalry'.

The advantage of tools such as these is that they force managers to think about strategic issues, and they draw upon ideas that managers might not know about or realise the relevance of.

Disadvantages include; the package is only as good as the rules contained within it, 'standard' management rules may be of limited value in certain circumstances, the analysis depends on user judgements ('rate your business's ability to do X on a scale of 1 to 10').

(c) **Strategy implementation** is the conversion of the strategy into detailed plans or objectives for operating units. This involves:

- **Resource** planning (ie finance, personnel): assessing the key tasks
- **Operations** planning
- **Organisation** structure and control systems

Case example

Goold and Quinn (in *Strategic Control*) cite Ciba-Geigy, a Swiss-based global firm with chemicals and pharmaceuticals businesses, as an example of formal strategic control and planning processes.

(a) Strategic planning starts with the identification of strategic business sectors, in other words, areas of activity where there are identifiable markets and where profit, management and resources are largely independent of the other sectors.

(b) Strategic plans containing:

(i) Long term objectives
(ii) Key strategies
(iii) Funds requirements

are drawn up, based on a 'comprehensive analysis of market attractiveness', competitors etc.

(c) At corporate level, these plans are reviewed. Head office examines all the different plans and, with a 7-10 year planning horizon, the total risk, profitability, cash flow and resource requirements are assessed. Business sectors are allocated specific targets and funds.

Why have an IS/IT strategy?

1.10 A strategy for information systems and information technology is **justified** on the grounds that IS/IT:

- Involves **high costs**
- Is **critical to the success** of many organisations
- Is now used as part of the commercial strategy in the battle for **competitive advantage**
- Impacts on **customer service**
- Affects **all levels of management**
- Affects the way **management information** is created and presented
- **Requires effective management** to obtain the maximum benefit
- Involves many **stakeholders** inside and outside the organisation

IS/IT is a high cost activity

1.11 Many organisations invest large amounts of money in IS, but not always wisely.

1.12 The unmanaged proliferation of IT is likely to lead to expensive mistakes. Two key benefits of IT, the ability to **share** information and the **avoidance of duplication**, are likely to be lost.

1.13 All IT expenditure should therefore require approval to ensure that it enhances rather than detracts from the overall information strategy.

IS/IT is critical to the success of many organisations

1.14 When developing an IS/IT strategy a firm should assess **how important IT is** in the provision of products and services. The role that IT fills in an organisation will vary depending on the type of organisations. IS/IT could be:

- A **support** activity
- A **key** operational activity
- **Potentially** very important
- A **strategic** activity (without IT the firm could not function at all)
- A source of **competitive advantage**

Information and competitive advantage

1.15 It is now recognised that information can be used as a source of competitive advantage. Many organisations have recognised the importance of information and developed an **information strategy**, covering both IS and IT.

1.16 Information systems should be tied in some way to **business objectives**.

(a) The **corporate strategy** is used to plan functional **business plans** which provide guidelines for information-based activities.

(b) On a year-by-year basis, the **annual plan** would try to tie in business plans with information systems projects for particular applications, perhaps through the functioning of a steering committee.

IT can impact significantly on the business context

1.17 IT is an **enabling** technology, and can produce dramatic changes in individual businesses and whole industries. For example, the deregulation of the airline industry encouraged the growth of computerised seat-reservation systems. IT can be both a **cause** of major changes in doing business and a **response** to them.

IT affects all levels of management

1.18 IT has become a routine feature of office life, **a facility for everyone to use**. IT is no longer used solely by specialist staff.

IT and its effect on management information

1.19 The use of IT has permitted the design of a range of information systems. Executive Information Systems (EIS), Management Information Systems (MIS), Decision Support Systems (DSS), Knowledge Work Systems (KWS) and Office Automation Systems (OAS) can be used to improve the quality of management information.

1.20 IT has also had an effect on **production processes**. For example, Computer Integrated Manufacturing (CIM) changed the methods and cost profiles of many manufacturing processes. The techniques used to **measure and record costs** have also adapted to the use of IT.

IT and stakeholders

1.21 Parties interested in an organisation's use of IT are as follows.

(a) **Other business users** - for example to facilitate Electronic Data Interchange (EDI).

(b) **Governments** – eg telecommunications regulation, regulation of electronic commerce.

(c) **IT manufacturers** looking for new markets and product development. User-groups may be able to influence software producers.

(d) **Consumers** - for example as reassurance that product quality is high, consumers may also be interested if information is provided via the Internet.

(e) **Employees** - as IT affects work practices.

Question 2

Babbage and Newman plc is a company with an established base of IT applications. The finance department has a fully computerised accounting system. The marketing department has developed a primitive customer modelling package. The production department 'does not need IT'.

The Finance Director is in charge of IT at Babbage and Newman. He proposes in the annual corporate budget a 10% increase in IT expenditure based on last year, for the relevant departments. This will enable system upgrades.

Comment briefly on the information strategy at Babbage and Newman.

Answer

There is no strategy at all. The Finance Director regards IT as a cost. Moreover the IT 'strategy' is directed to enhancing its existing base (eg in the accounts department) rather than areas where it might prove competitively valuable (eg in marketing).

Information systems and corporate/business strategy

1.22 It is widely accepted that an organisation's information system should **support** corporate and business strategy. In some circumstances an information system may have a greater influence and actually help **determine** corporate / business strategy. For example:

(a) IS/IT may provide a possible source of competitive advantage. This could involve new technology not yet available to others or simply using existing technology in a different way.

(b) The information system may help in formulating business strategy by **providing information** from internal and external sources.

(c) Developments in IT may provide **new channels** for distributing and collecting information, and /or for conducting transactions eg the Internet.

1.23 Some common ways in which IS/IT have had a major impact on organisations are explained below.

(a) **The type of products or services that are made and sold.** For example, consumer markets have seen the emergence of home computers, compact discs and satellite dishes for receiving satellite TV; industrial markets have seen the emergence of custom-built microchips, robots and local area networks for office information systems. Technological changes can be relatively minor, such as the introduction of tennis and squash rackets with graphite frames, fluoride toothpaste and turbo-powered car engines.

(b) **The way in which products are made.** There is a continuing trend towards the use of automation and computer aided design and manufacture. The manufacturing environment is undergoing rapid changes with the growth of advanced manufacturing technology. These are changes in both apparatus and technique.

(c) **The way in which services are provided**. High-street banks encourage customers to use 'hole-in-the-wall' cash dispensers, or telephone or Internet banking. Most larger shops now use computerised **Point of Sale terminals** at cash desks. Many organisations use **e-commerce**: selling products and services over the Internet.

(d) **The way in which markets are identified**. Database systems make it much easier to analyse the market place.

(e) **The way in which employees are mobilised**. Technology encourages workforce empowerment. Using technology frequently requires changes in working methods. This is a change in organisation.

(f) **The way in which firms are managed**. An empowered workforce often leads to the 'delayering' of organisational hierarchies (in other words, the reduction of management layers).

(g) The means and extent of **communications** with customers.

1.24 Benefits of technological change might therefore be as follows.

- To **cut production costs** and so (probably) to **reduce sales prices** to the customer
- To develop **better quality** products and services
- To develop products and services that **did not exist before**
- To **provide** products or services to customers **more quickly or effectively**
- To **free staff** from repetitive work and to tap their creativity

1.25 An important role of the information technology and finance functions is to help ensure the agreed strategy is proceeding according to plan. The table below outlines the rationale behind this view.

	Traditional view	Strategic implications
Cost	The finance and information technology functions can be relatively expensive	Shared services and outsourcing could be used to capture cost savings
IT	IT has traditionally been transaction based	IT/IS should be integrated with business strategy
Value	The finance and IT functions do not add value	Redesign the functions
Strategy	Accountants and IT managers are seen as scorekeepers and administrators rather than as a business partner during the strategic planning process	Change from cost-orientated to market-orientated ie development of more effective strategic planning systems

The importance of managing technology

1.26 The success of an organisation's use of technology depends largely on how technology is selected, implemented and **managed**. For example, **information systems** may **fail to deliver the benefits expected** for any of the following reasons.

(a) They are used to tackle the **wrong problem** (ie the use of IT has not been thought through in the context of the wider organisational context).

(b) Senior management are not interested.

(c) Users are ignored in design and development.

(d)   No attention is given to behavioural factors in design and operation.

1.27   If an organisation develops and follows a realistic information strategy and information systems plan for information systems and technology then there is less chance that these problems will arise.

1.28   Organisations should develop an **information systems plan** that supports their overall business plan. The plan should contain the following:

(a)   Overall organisation goals.

(b)   How information systems and information technology contributes to attaining these goals

(c)   Key management decisions regarding hardware, software, data and telecommunications

(d)   Specific dates and milestones relating to IS/IT projects

(e)   Financial information such as a budget and cost-benefit analysis

---

Case study link

The alignment of IT/IS strategy with the overall organisation strategy may be of relevance to the Final Level Case Study paper.

---

2   DEVELOPING A STRATEGY FOR INFORMATION SYSTEMS AND INFORMATION TECHNOLOGY
Pilot Paper

KEY TERMS

The **Information Systems (IS) strategy** refers to the long-term plan concerned with exploiting IS and IT either to support business strategies or create new strategic options.

Strategic information systems are systems at any level of an organisation that change goals, processes, products, services or environmental relationships with the aim of gaining competitive advantage.

Strategic-level systems are systems used by senior managers for long-term decision making.

2.1   An IS/IT strategy must deal with three issues.

- The organisation's overall **business needs**
- The organisation's **current use** of IS/IT
- The potential **opportunities** and **threats** that IS/IT can bring

2.2   Each of these three issues involves different personnel, and requires a slightly different approach. A diagrammatic representation of IS strategy development follows.

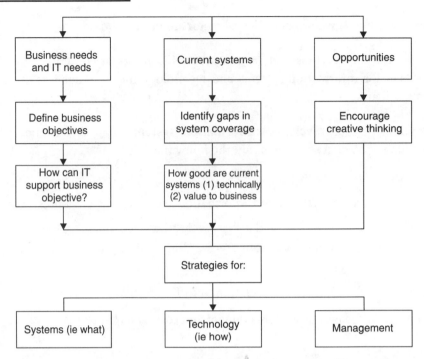

2.3 An **evaluation of current systems** will be necessary so that the organisation knows where it is starting from.

(a) For example, an organisation with good financial reporting systems may have no marketing information systems. **Gaps** in the IS coverage are identified here.

(b) The **efficiency** of current systems coverage is also evaluated. Are users happy? Is the system reliable?

2.4 **Users** and **system providers** can indicate the existing system's business value and technical quality.

(a) **Systems specialists and providers** indicate the system's technical quality in terms of:

- Reliability
- Ease of maintenance
- Cost efficiency

(b) **Users** can rate a system on its:

- Business impact (eg how would we manage without it?)
- Ease of use and user-friendliness
- Frequency of use (indicates its importance and value)

(c) **Users** may suggest valuable evolutionary add-ons to systems.

2.5 The identification of organisational information needs and the information systems framework to satisfy them is at the heart of a strategy for information systems and information technology.

2.6 The IS and IT strategies should complement the overall strategy for the organisation. It follows therefore that the IS/IT strategy should be considered whenever the organisation prepares its long-term marketing or production strategies.

2.7 We will now look at a range of tools and techniques that may be used to establish organisational information requirements and help establish an effective strategy for information systems and information technology.

Generic strategies for information systems

2.8   The writer Parsons identified six possible generic Information System (IS) strategies. These are outlined in the following table.

Generic strategy for IS	Comment
Centrally planned	The logic of this approach is that those planning IS developments should have an understanding of the overall strategic direction. Business and IS strategy are viewed as being closely linked.
Leading edge	There is a belief that innovative technology use can create competitive advantage, and therefore that risky investment in unproven technologies may generate large returns. The organisation must have the motivation and ability to commit large amounts of money and other resources. Users must be enthusiastic and willing to support new initiatives.
Free market	This strategy is based ion the belief that the market makes the best decisions. The IS function is a competitive business unit, which must be prepared to achieve a return on its resources. The department may have to compete with outside providers.
Monopoly	The direct opposite to the free market strategy. This strategy is based upon the because that information is an organisational asset that should be controlled by a single service resource.
Scarce resource	This strategy is based on the premise that information systems use limited resources, and therefore all IS development requires a clear justification. Budgetary controls are in place and should be adhered to. New projects should be subject to Cost Benefit Analysis (CBA).
Necessary evil	IS/IT is seen as a necessary evil of modern business. IS/IT is allocated enough resource only to meet basic needs. This strategy is usually adopted in organisations that believe that information is not important in their business.

Enterprise analysis

> **KEY TERM**
>
> **Enterprise analysis** involves examining the entire organisation in terms of structure, processes, functions and data elements to identify the key elements and attributes of organisational data and information.

2.9   Enterprise analysis is sometimes referred to as **business systems planning**. This approach involves the following steps.

Step 1.   Ask a large sample of managers about:

- How they use information
- Where they get information
- What their objectives are

- What their data requirements are
- How they make decisions
- The influence of the environment

Step 2. Aggregate the findings from *Step 1* into subunits, functions, processes and data matrices. Compile a process/data class matrix to show:

- What data classes are required to support particular organisational processes
- Which processes are the creators and users of data

Step 3. Use the matrix to identify areas that information systems should focus on, eg on processes that create data.

2.10

Enterprise analysis approach – strength	Comment
Comprehensive	The enterprise analysis approach gives a comprehensive view of the organisation and its use of data and systems.

2.11

Enterprise analysis approach – weaknesses	Comment
Unwieldy	The enterprise analysis approach results in a mountain of data that is expensive to collect and difficult to analyse.
Focussed on existing information	Survey questions tend to focus on how systems and information are currently used, rather than on how information that is needed could be provided. The analysis has tended to result in existing systems being automated rather than looking at the wider picture.

Critical success factors   11/01

2.12 The use of **critical success factors (CSFs)** can help to determine the information requirements of an organisation. CSFs are operational goals. If operational goals are achieved the organisation should be successful.

KEY TERM

Critical success factors are a small number of key operational goals vital to the success of an organisation. CSFs may be used to establish organisational information requirements.

2.13 The CSF approach is sometimes referred to as the **strategic analysis** approach. The philosophy behind this approach is that managers should focus on a small number of objectives, and information systems should be focussed on providing information to enable managers to monitor these objectives.

2.14 **Two separate types** of critical success factor can be identified. A **monitoring** CSF is used to keep abreast of existing activities and operations. A **building** CSF helps to measure the progress of new initiatives and is more likely to be relevant at senior executive level.

- **Monitoring** CSFs are important for **maintaining** business
- **Building** CSFs are important for **expanding** business

2.15 One approach to **determining the factors** which are critical to success in performing a function or making a decision is as follows.

- List the organisation's **objectives** and **goals**
- Determine which factors are **critical** for accomplishing the objectives
- Determine a small number of **key performance indicators** for each factor

2.16 The determination of **key performance indicators** for each of these CSFs is not necessarily straightforward. Some measures might use **factual**, verifiable data, while others might make use of 'softer' concepts, such as opinions, perceptions and hunches.

2.17 For example, the reliability of stock records can be measured by means of physical stock counts, either at discrete intervals or on a rolling basis. Forecasting of demand variations will be much harder to measure.

2.18 Where measures use quantitative data, performance can be measured in a number of ways.

- In **physical quantities,** for example units produced or units sold
- In **money terms,** for example profit, revenues, costs or variances
- In **ratios** and **percentages**

2.19 In general terms Rockart identifies four **sources** of CSFs.

(a) The **industry** that the business is in.

(b) The **company** itself and its situation within the industry.

(c) The **environment**, for example consumer trends, the economy, and political factors of the country in which the company operates.

(d) Temporal organisational factors, which are areas of corporate activity which are causing **concern**, for example, high stock levels.

2.20 More specifically, possible internal and external data sources for CSFs include the following.

(a) The **existing system**. The existing system can be used to generate reports showing failures to meet CSFs.

(b) Customer service department. This department will maintain details of **complaints, refunds** and **queries.**

(c) **Customers.** A survey of customers, provided that it is properly designed and introduced, would reveal (or confirm) those areas where **satisfaction** is high or low.

(d) **Competitors.** Competitors' operations, pricing structures and publicity should be closely monitored.

(e) **Accounting system.** The **profitability** of various aspects of the operation would be a key factor in any review of CSFs.

(f) **Consultants.** A specialist consultancy might be able to perform a detailed review of the organisation to identify CSFs.

2.21 The CSF approach to IS/IT planning is illustrated in the following diagram.

BPP PUBLISHING

The critical success factor approach to IS/IT planning

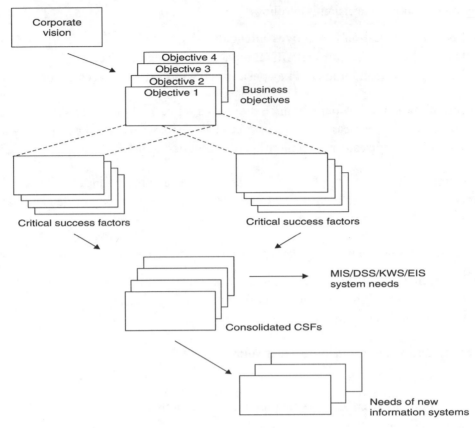

Source: IT Strategy for Business, Joe Peppard
Chapter 4, Garret Hickey

2.22 EXAMPLE

An organisation has an **objective** to fulfil customer orders promptly from stock on hand, but without holding uneconomic stock levels. This objective could be quantified in the form of a **goal**, eg 'to dispatch 90% of orders within 24 hours using goods held in stock, and to maintain an average monthly stock value below £X'.

CSFs might then be identified as the following.

- **Supplier performance** in terms of quality and lead times
- Reliability of **stock records**
- **Forecasting** of demand variations

CSF approach: strengths and weaknesses

2.23

CSF approach – strengths	Comment
Takes into account environmental changes	The CSF approach requires managers to examine the environment and consider how it influences their information requirements.
Focuses on information	The approach doesn't just aim to establish organisational objectives. It also looks at the information and information systems required to establish and monitor progress towards these objectives.
Facilitates top management participation in system development	The clear link between information requirements and individual and organisational objectives encourages top management involvement in system (DSS, EIS) design.

2.24

CSF approach - weaknesses	Comment
Aggregation of individual CSFs	Wide-ranging individual CSFs need to be aggregated into a clear organisational plan. This process relies heavily on judgement. Managers who feel their input has been neglected may be alienated.
Bias towards top management	When gathering information to establish CSFs it is usually top management who are interviewed. These managers may lack knowledge of operational activities.
CSFs change often	The business environment, managers and information systems technology are subject to constant change. CSFs and systems must be updated to account for change.

Question 3

Here is the first paragraph of an exam question scenario.

'HJK Ltd is a light engineering company which produces a range of components, machine tools and electronic devices for the motor and aircraft industry. It employs about 1,000 people in 12 main divisions.'

Identify some CSFs for HJK Ltd

Answer

CSFs might include technological excellence to keep pace with the industries served and co-ordination of divisional activities. You may have thought of others.

Information audit

2.25 An **information audit** aims to establish the information needs of users **and** how these needs could be met. The audit has three stages.

	Stage	Comment
1	**Information needs assessment**	This stage involves gathering information, usually through interviews and questionnaires.
		Information users are asked what information they require, why they require it, when they require it and the preferred format.
		People should be encouraged to think laterally about what information would help them do their job, rather than simply listing the information they currently receive.
		To encourage wide-ranging thought, users should be asked to state the information they would like in an 'ideal world'. Unrealistic and uneconomic needs can be rejected (tactfully) at a later stage.
2	**Information analysis**	This stage focuses on the information provided by the existing information system. Both the quantity and the quality of the information are analysed. For example, the timing of information may reduce the quality of otherwise excellent information as it is provided too late to influence decision making. Slightly less accurate information, provided earlier, may be more desirable.

	Stage	Comment
3	Gap analysis	This stage compares the information needs identified in stage 1 with the information identified as being provided in stage 2. Gaps between what is required and what is currently provided are identified.
		'Information gaps' are analysed to evaluate the costs and benefits of closing the gap.

2.26 An information system **resource analysis** involves a review of **all** information systems and information technology used within an organisation. The review includes all aspects of hardware, software, communications devices, network topologies, systems development methodologies, maintenance procedures, contingency plans and IS/IT personnel. The review looks at all of these aspects in the context of the organisation's overall strategy and the IS/IT strategy.

2.27 Resource analysis is sometimes called **Current Situation Analysis (CSA)**. The analysis establishes the current status of IS/IT within the organisation.

2.28 The CSA has similar problems to that of a cost-benefit analysis in that it relies on the **subjective judgements** of information users. A group of people using the same system for the same purpose may come up with different ratings for system efficiency and user-friendliness.

2.29 Two techniques that could be useful when conducting a CSA are **Earl's grid** and the **strategic grid** (applications portfolio).

Earl's grid

2.30 *Earl* suggests a grid to analyse an organisation's current use of information systems. Current systems are plotted on the following grid.

Business Value	*High*	Renew	Maintain, enhance
	Low	Divest	Reassess
		Low	*High*
			Technical Quality

(a) A system of poor quality and little value should be **disposed of** (divest).

(b) A system of high business value and low technical quality should be **renewed** (invested in). An important system of low quality carries a high business risk.

(c) A system of high quality but low business value should be **reassessed**. Is the system meeting an information need? Why is it under-utilised?

(d) High quality systems with a high business value should be **maintained** to preserve the high quality, and if possible **enhanced** in the quest for competitive advantage.

2.31 Establishing where to place systems on the grid is the difficult part. Consultation with system users and those for formulating and implementing information system strategy would be undertaken to form an opinion of each system. Again, judgements are subjective.

Strategic grid **5/02**

2.32 Peppard developed a strategic grid that analyses the **strategic importance of individual applications** within an organisation. The grid is an adaptation of an earlier grid developed by **McFarlan**, which in turn was based on the general Boston Consulting Group (BCG) matrix.

Strategic importance of individual applications in the predicted **future** competitive environment	High	High potential (or 'turnaround')	Strategic
	Low	Support	Key operational (or 'factory')
		Low	High

Strategic importance of individual applications in the **current** competitive environment

2.33 **Support applications** are not critical to business success. An example would be an accounting system.

2.34 **Key operational applications** support established core business activities. A production planning system is a good example.

2.35 **Strategic applications** are vital to the organisation's future success. Finance/service companies are becoming increasingly dependent on information systems and technology.

2.36 **High potential applications** are applications likely to have a significant impact in the future environment. A supermarket on-line ordering application is an example.

Innovation and creative thinking

2.37 The identification of opportunities and threats that could impact on IS/IT strategy relies on **creative thinking**. Threats are often opportunities that have not been identified by the organisation, but have been by competitors.

2.38 There are three ways in which creative thinking and opportunity 'spotting' can be encouraged.

(a) **Techniques** to foster innovation, such as think tanks, brainstorming sessions and so forth, are useful if they encourage ideas. Some of the most successful systems developments have resulted from ideas that **users** have had about how a system should evolve, or have come from **customers**.

(b) **Processes for innovation** require organisational investment. Fostering innovation activities include:

(i) Recruiting **outsiders.**
(ii) Experimenting with innovative projects outside the main business.
(iii) Looking to **users and suppliers** for ideas.

(c) **Technology**. Providing user-friendly systems enables users to develop creative applications. For example, providing an easy-to-use expert system shell might enable users to develop their own. The organisational environment has to allow innovation to happen.

2.39 **External analysis** is also necessary in all the stages in IS strategy, for example in monitoring developments in technology, or where possible, examining systems used by competitors.

Determining the best fit 5/01

2.40 Systems or applications very rarely operate in isolation. They will need to **integrate** directly or indirectly with other systems used in the firm. Systems should also **fit** with organisation strategy, culture and current systems.

2.41 If a system is proposed that is considered important to the future prosperity of the organisation, yet it does not fit well with existing systems, culture and staff skills, then a decision has to be made regarding business and information **strategy**.

2.42 For example, a traditional high street bookseller losing market share to Amazon.com may consider implementing an e-commerce enabled website. However, such a system is **unlikely to fit** well with existing systems (and culture) which are geared to over the counter sales. The organisation could decide to:

(a) Implement book selling over the web, and overhaul existing systems and staffing to fit the new environment.

(b) Enter into a strategic partnership with an organisation to run a separate book selling operation via the web.

(c) Ignore the web. Try to entice customers back into stores through improved décor and coffee shop ambience.

Question 4

Think about the role of Information Systems (IS) and Information Technology (IT) in achieving business objectives and securing an advantage over competitors. Try to think of an example of each of the following.

(a) The use of IT to 'lock out' competitors.
(b) The use of IS/IT to reduce the likelihood of customers changing suppliers.
(c) The use of IS/IT to secure a performance advantage.
(d) How IT may generate a new product or service.

Answer

(a) An example is an organisation that invests so heavily in technology that potential competitors lack both the expertise and the funds to compete successfully. Microsoft has not completely locked competitors out of the office software market but its domination is increasing.

(b) Once a bank customer has gone to the effort of installing a home banking system, he or she is unlikely to make a decision to change banks.

(c) Accurate stock systems that facilitate Just-In-Time (JIT) stock management, and organisations participating in Electronic Data Interchange (EDI) are two examples of how IT can increase efficiency and facilitate better service - providing an advantage over competitors. (They may also make an organisation more dependent on existing suppliers therefore discouraging the changing of suppliers.)

(d) Internet Service Providers (ISPs) did not exist before the advent of the Internet.

Case example

Extracts from the International Management Accounting Practice Statement

Strategic Planning for Information Resource Management (IRM)

An organisation's strategic plan describes how it will advance into the future. The IRM strategic plan should focus on how information and technology will support the goals and objectives outlined in the corporate strategy. IRM strategies must be creative and flexible to address current needs and potentially expanded future needs. There is a need for the organisation's IRM plan to mirror corporate strategy, eg if the enterprise's strategy emphasises customer service then the IRM plan must also.

IRM is an approach to strategic information systems planning that emphasises the importance of **information as a corporate resource**. It focuses on designing, implementing and maintaining a balanced, enterprise-wide system of information, processes and technology. In the IRM environment, technology is viewed as a means to assist the business to do things better, faster and cheaper - not as an end in itself.

Objectives of IRM

The fundamental objective of IRM is to ensure that an organisation's **information systems support its strategic direction** and business plans and enhance the quality, applicability, accessibility and value of the information resources of the enterprise. Its success in an organisation is dependent on the acceptance of four fundamental principles:

- Data is a valuable resource that requires proper management

- Most data is highly shareable

- The ability to share and use data more effectively is a **critical success factor** for most businesses

- Information systems should incorporate a broad view of the enterprise

An effective IRM program provides for continuously **scanning the environment** for opportunities that could drive the direction of an organisation's business. Information technology planners must have a strategic view on how information systems can increase the opportunities available to an organisation and also how to extend traditional business boundaries to include information resource links with customers and suppliers.

Organisations must emphasise strategic planning for IRM in order to gain a **competitive advantage** as they move into an era of increased automation and global competition. Information systems can help streamline business functions, improve managerial decision making, create new products and businesses and enhance relationships with suppliers and customers.

Developing the IRM strategic plan

The ultimate goal of an effective IRM strategic plan is the design, delivery and maintenance of a seamless, integrated information resource environment that responds successfully to the need for cross-functional flows of information while providing the flexibility and adaptability to respond to incessant business and technological change. The requirement is for a set of data transport capabilities and data management interfaces that are usable by each business function, but unique to and owned exclusively by none of them. Without a plan there are no objectives, no measures and, ultimately, no results.

There are three key steps involved in planning for the introduction of IRM practices into an organisation:

- Determine strategic information resource requirements
- Baseline the existing environment
- Design the IRM

Exhibit 1 **The Planning Process**

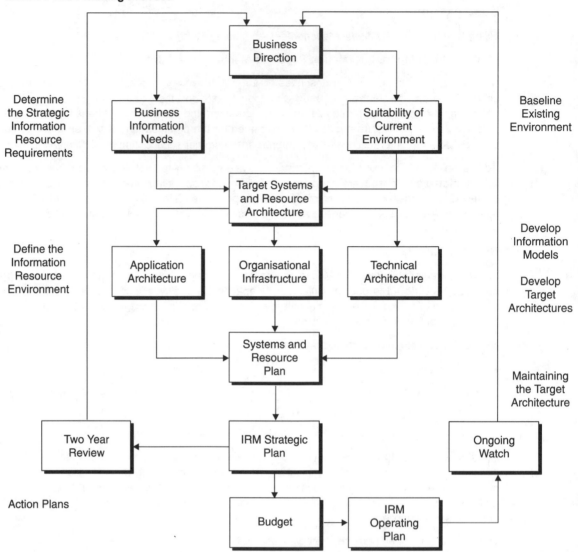

As shown in Exhibit 1, the planning process starts with a definition of the business direction, this is the foundation for all subsequent steps. The strategic business planning process ensures that an organisation understands its **critical success factors**, what it must do well to succeed and how it will measure success. Conversely, the strategic planning process provides an opportunity to identify areas of vulnerability, areas that may need to be monitored more closely and potentially subjected to stringent controls. Typical examples of what an organisation must do well to succeed in the next decade are customer service, new product development and cost control.

The business strategy drives the process of determining what information the business requires to **support its objectives** and how well the existing environment (systems, processes, information, organisational structure, etc.) supports, or has the potential to support, the achievement of the business objectives.

Technological issues are addressed in the third step, where a blueprint of the organisation's future computing infrastructure is designed. The blueprint takes the form of a set of 'target architectures,' ie systems and resource architecture, application architecture and the technical architecture, each of which describes a particular component of the infrastructure to be constructed. This is a plan, describing what hardware, software and databases are necessary to satisfy the strategic information requirements previously identified.

This set of target architectures supports the development of the IRM strategic plan, which, in turn, ensures the appropriate enabling technology and information infrastructure. It articulates how the organisation will make the most effective use of information, computers, database technology, decision support tools and telecommunications in combination with other resources to achieve its mission. The IRM Plan reflects the organisation's business focus, mirroring its emphasis on customer service, becoming the least-cost provider, expansion, decentralisation goals and objectives and clearly states how the IRM organisation will support the business mission.

The following principles guide the development of an effective IRM strategy:

- It must be linked to the business strategy
- Cross-functional business processes are central to the planning dimension
- The technology infrastructure must represent a 'model of the business'

In the past, the focus of information systems planning may have been limited to determining how to apply technology to automate a task. Using the IRM approach more relevant questions might be: 'How do I apply technology to **competitive advantage**? How do I get the right information to the decision makers? Where are the best opportunities to add value through information resources?'

---

3 INFORMATION SYSTEM ARCHITECTURES

3.1 The term **system architecture** refers to the way in which the various components of an information system are linked together, and the way they relate to each other. In the following paragraphs we discuss the theory behind centralised and distributed systems. However, in reality many systems include elements of both.

Centralised architecture

> **KEY TERM**
>
> A **centralised architecture** involves all computer processing being carried out on a single central processor. The central computer is usually a mainframe or minicomputer designed to be accessed by more than one user.

3.2 A centralised system using a central mainframe linked to 'dumb terminals' (which do not include a CPU and therefore rely on the central computer for processing power) is shown below.

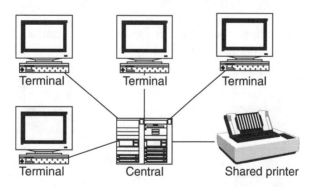

3.3 Many centralised systems also have shared peripherals, such as printers, linked to the central computer.

3.4 Centralised architectures could be based in a single location or spread over multiple locations. For example, both a local area network (LAN) and a wide area network (WAN) could utilise a centralised architecture.

3.5 A LAN is a network that spans a relatively small area. Most LANs are confined to a single building or group of buildings. A wide area network (WAN) is a computer network that spans a relatively large geographical area. A centralised WAN would have only one computer with processing power. (LANs may be linked to form a WAN – although such a configuration would not be considered a centralised architecture.)

3.6 **Advantages** of centralised architectures.

(a) There is one set of files. Everyone uses the same data and information.

(b) It gives better security/control over data and files. It is easier to enforce standards.

(c) Head office (where the computer is usually based) is able to control computing processes and developments.

(d) An organisation might be able to afford a very large central computer, with extensive processing capabilities that smaller 'local' computers could not carry out.

(e) There may be economies of scale available in purchasing computer equipment and supplies.

3.7 **Disadvantages** of centralised architectures.

(a) Local offices might experience processing delays or interruptions.

(b) Reliance on head office. Local offices rely on head office to provide information they need.

(c) If the central computer breaks down, or the software develops a fault, the entire system goes out of operation.

Decentralised or distributed architectures

KEY TERM

Distributed architectures spread the processing power throughout the organisation at several different locations. With modern distributed systems, the majority of processing power is held on numerous personal computers (PCs) spread throughout the organisation.

3.8 An example of a distributed architecture, with a combination of stand-alone PCs and networks spread throughout an organisation, is shown in the following diagram.

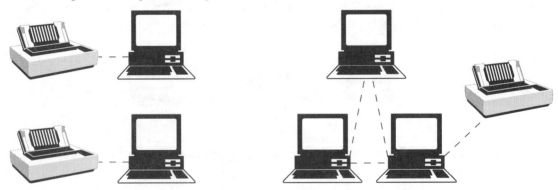

3.9 Key **features** of distributed architectures.

(a) Many computers have their own processing capability (CPU).

(b) Some sharing of information is possible via communication links.

(c) The systems are usually more user-friendly than mainframe based systems.

(d) End-users are given responsibility for, and control over, programs and data.

Advantages and disadvantages of distributed architectures

3.10 **Advantages**.

(a) There is greater flexibility in system design. The system can cater for both the specific needs of each local user of an individual computer and also for the needs of the organisation as a whole, by providing communications between different local computers in the system.

(b) Since data files can be held locally, data transmission is restricted because each computer maintains its own data files which provide most of the data it will need. This reduces the costs and security risks in data transmission.

(c) Speed of processing.

(d) There is a possibility of a distributed database. Data is held in a number of locations, but any user can access all of it for a global view.

(e) The effect of breakdowns is minimised, because a fault in one computer will not affect other computers in the system.

(f) Allows for better localised control over the physical and procedural aspects of the system.

(g) May facilitate greater user involvement and increase familiarity with the use of computer technology.

3.11 **Disadvantages**.

(a) There may be some duplication of data on different computers, increasing the risk of data inaccuracies.

(b) A distributed network can be more difficult to administer and to maintain, as several sites require access to staff with IT skills.

Client-server architecture

3.12 With a client-server architecture each computer or process on the network is either a 'client' or a 'server'. Servers are powerful computers or processes dedicated to managing disk drives (file servers), printers (print servers), or network traffic (network servers). Clients are PCs or workstations on which users run applications. Clients rely on servers for resources, such as files, devices, and sometimes processing power.

KEY TERMS

A **client** is a machine which requests a service, for example a PC running a spreadsheet application which the user wishes to print out.

A **server** is a machine which is dedicated to providing a particular function or service requested by a client. Servers include file servers (see below), print servers, e-mail servers and fax servers.

3.13 A typical client-server system includes three **hardware** elements.

- A central server (sometimes called the corporate server)
- Local servers (sometimes called departmental servers)
- Client workstations

3.14 A server computer (such as a file server) may be a powerful PC or a minicomputer. As its name implies, it **serves** the rest of the network offering a generally-accessible hard disk and sometimes offering other resources, such as a **shared printer**.

3.15 A typical client-server architecture is shown below.

Client-server architecture

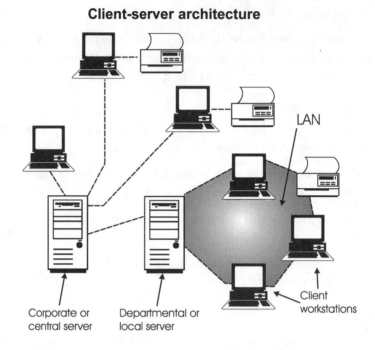

Corporate or central server

Departmental or local server

LAN

Client workstations

3.16 Client-server systems aim to locate software where it is most efficient - based on the number and location of users requiring access and the processing power required. There are three main types of software applications.

(a) **Corporate applications** are run on the central (or corporate) server. These applications are accessed by people spread throughout the organisation, and often require significant processor power (eg a centralised Management Information System).

(b) **Local applications** are used by users within a particular section or department, and therefore are run on the relevant local or departmental server (eg a credit-scoring expert system may be held on the server servicing the loans department of a bank).

(c) **Client applications** may be unique to an individual user, eg a specialised Executive Support System (ESS). Other software that may be run on client hardware could include 'office' type software, such as spreadsheet and word processing programs. Even though many people may use these applications, individual copies of programs are often held on client hardware - to utilise the processor power held on client machines.

The advantages of a client-server architecture

3.17	Advantage	Comment
	Greater resilience	Processing is spread over several computers. If one server breaks down, other locations can carry on processing.
	Scalability	They are highly scalable. Instead of having to buy computing power in large quantities you can buy just the amount of power you need to do the job.
	Shared programs and data	Program and data files held on a file server can be shared by all the PCs in the network. With stand-alone PCs, each computer would have its own data files, and there might be unnecessary duplication of data. A system where everyone uses the same data will help to improve data processing and decision making.
	Shared work-loads	The processing capability of each computer in a network can be utilised. For example, if there were separate stand-alone PCs, A might do job 1, B might do job 2 and C might do job 3. In a network, any PC, (A, B or C) could do any job (1, 2 or 3). This is more efficient.
	Shared peripherals	Peripheral equipment can be shared. For example, five PCs might share a single printer.
	Communication	LANs can be linked up to the office communications network, thus adding to the processing capabilities in an office. Electronic mail, calendar and diary facilities can also be used.
	Compatibility	Client/server systems are likely to include interfaces between different types of software used on the system, making it easier to move information between applications.
	Flexibility	For example, if a detailed analysis of existing data is required, a copy of this data could be placed on a separate server, allowing data to be manipulated without disrupting the main system.

The disadvantages of a client-server architecture

3.18 The client/server approach has some drawbacks.

(a) A single mainframe may be more efficient performing some tasks, in certain circumstances. For example, where the process involves routine processing of a very large number (eg millions) of transactions.

(b) It is easier to control and maintain a centralised system. In particular it is easier to keep data secure.

(c) It may be cheaper to 'tweak' an existing mainframe system rather than throwing it away and starting from scratch: for example it may be possible to give it a graphical user interface and to make data exchangeable between Windows and non-Windows based applications.

(d) Each location may need its own network administrator to keep things running smoothly - there may be unnecessary duplication of skills and staff.

(e) Duplication of information may be a problem if individual users do not follow a disciplined approach.

Peer-to-peer architecture

3.19 'Peer-to-peer' refers to a type of network in which each workstation has equivalent capabilities and responsibilities. This differs from client-server architectures, in which some computers are dedicated to serving the others. Peer-to-peer networks are generally simpler, but they usually do not offer the same performance under heavy workloads.

4 BUILDING A BUSINESS CASE FOR INVESTMENT IN IS AND IT 5/01

KEY TERM

A **business case** is a justification for a project or particular course of action (an investment) to be undertaken.

General framework

4.1 A business case aims to convince decision-makers within an organisation that an investment is justified. The case should provide a clear understanding of the implications of proceeding with the proposed investment.

4.2 Many organisations have a general framework under which all competing business cases are submitted. Using a standard framework enables comparisons to be made between different types of investments to be made more easily.

4.3 The general framework for business case development has four stages. We look at each of these stages in the following table – in the context of an investment in an improved information system.

	Stage	Comment
1	**Where are we now?**	A business case starts by establishing **what the current position is**. The person (or people) responsible for authorising the investment will use this information to develop an understanding as to why the new information system is being proposed.
		Documenting the current system may involve systems analysis techniques such as interviews, observations and system modelling.
		As the aim is to justify the investment in the context of the organisation's overall operations and strategy, an environmental analysis should also be undertaken (eg SWOT, PEST).
		The information compiled during this stage should provide a clear picture of where the organisation is at present.

	Stage	Comment
2	**Where do we want to be?**	This stage involves devising a statement of where the organisation would like to be (**the desired position**), and a justification (maybe a cost-benefit analysis) showing why the position described is desirable.
		The statement may be broken down into more detailed objectives for the investment. These objectives are in effect what the investment hopes to achieve (the benefits) – decision makers can compare these against the cost when assessing the investment.
3	**How are we going to get there?**	This stage focuses on the actual work that needs to be undertaken to move from the current position to the desired position. In an information system installation this would include Work Breakdown Structure and Network Analysis.
		A clear plan of exactly **what is involved in the project** should be developed.
4	**Overall justification**	This stage focuses on the information most relevant to making a decision on **whether to proceed** with, or reject, the investment.
		All (financial, commercial, strategic etc) costs and benefits should be summarised. For example, a supermarket chain may find that implementing on-line shopping with free delivery is not cost-effective when viewed in isolation, but is necessary to maintain market share.

Business case justification

4.4 **Cost-benefit analysis** is a key part of a business case justification. You should be familiar with the methods of evaluating the **financial viability** of a project from your earlier studies. Three common techniques are outlined in the following table.

Method	Comment
Payback period	Calculates the length of time a project will take to recoup the initial investment; in other words how long a project will take to pay for itself. The method is based on **cash flows**.
Accounting rate of return (ARR)	This method, also called **return on investment**, calculates the profits that will be earned by a project and expresses this as a percentage of the capital invested. The higher the rate of return, the higher a project is ranked. This method is based on **accounting** results rather than cash flows.
Internal rate of return (IRR)	**Internal rate of return (IRR)** involves comparing the rate of return expected from the project calculated on a discounted cash flow (NPV) basis with the rate used as the cost of capital. Projects with an IRR higher than the cost of capital are worth undertaking.

4.5 Cost-benefit analysis of information systems is complicated by the fact that many of the system cost elements are poorly defined and that benefits can often be highly qualitative and **subjective** in nature.

4.6 An added complication is that the benefits or returns are not certain – there is a **risk** that the benefit will not eventuate. Probabilities can be assigned to different levels of return and an **expected value** of the return established.

The costs of a proposed system

4.7 The costs of a new system will include costs in a number of different categories.

Cost	Example
Hardware costs	• Computers and peripherals
Installation costs	• New buildings (if necessary) • The computer room (wiring, air-conditioning if necessary) • Desks, security systems etc
Development costs	These include costs of measuring and analysing the existing system and costs of looking at the new system. They include **software**/consultancy work and systems analysis and programming. Changeover costs, particularly file conversion, may be very considerable.
Personnel costs	• Staff training • Staff recruitment/relocation • Staff salaries and pensions • Redundancy payments • Overheads
Operating costs	• Consumable materials (tapes, disks, stationery etc) • Maintenance • Accommodation costs • Heating/power/insurance/telephone • Standby arrangements, in case the system breaks down
Intangible costs	Some costs are **harder to quantify**. • 'Learning curve' – staff will work slower until they become familiar with the new system • Staff morale may suffer from the enforced changes • Investment opportunities forsaken – the opportunity cost • Incompatibility with other systems may mean an unforeseen change is required elsewhere in the organisation

Capital and revenue costs

4.8 The distinction between capital costs and revenue costs is important. Capital items will be capitalised and then depreciated, and revenue items will be expensed as incurred as a regular annual cost.

Question 5

Draw up a table with three headings: capital cost items, one-off revenue cost items and regular annual costs. Identify at least three items to be included under each heading.

Answer

Capital cost items	'One-off' revenue cost items	Regular annual costs
Hardware purchase costs	Consultancy fees	Operating staff salaries/wages
Software purchase costs	Systems analysts' and programmers' salaries	Data transmission costs
Purchase of accommodation (if needed)	Costs of testing the system (staff costs, consumables)	Consumable materials
Installation costs (new desks, cables, physical storage etc)	Costs of converting the files for the new system	Power
		Maintenance costs
	Staff recruitment fees	Cost of standby arrangements
		Ongoing staff training

The benefits of a proposed system

4.9 The benefits from a proposed new system must also be evaluated. These consist of direct and indirect or intangible benefits.

4.10 **Direct benefits**

(a) Savings because the old system is no longer operating. These include savings in staff salaries and other operating costs such as consumable materials.

(b) Efficiency savings resulting in less overtime and possibly increased turnover.

(c) Extra savings or revenue benefits because of the improvements or enhancements that the new system should bring:

(i) Possibly more sales revenue and so additional contribution.

(ii) Operational efficiencies such as better stock control (with a new stock control system) and so fewer stock losses from obsolescence and deterioration, or reduced bad debts from a new debtors system.

(d) Possibly, some one-off revenue benefits from the sale of equipment which the new system does not require. However, computer equipment depreciates very quickly. It is also possible that the new system will use **less office space**, possibly providing an opportunity to sell or rent the spare space.

4.11 Many of the benefits are **intangible**, or impossible to give a money value to.

(a) Greater **customer satisfaction** and **loyalty**, arising from better customer service.

(b) Improved **staff morale** from working with a more efficient system.

(c) Automating routine decisions and tasks should provide **more time for planning**.

(d) More informed **decision making**.

(e) Further savings in staff time, resulting perhaps in **reduced future staff growth**.

(f) Benefits accruing from gaining **competitive advantage**.

4.12 The fact that so many of the benefits a new information system provides are intangible means that it is difficult to construct a meaningful cost benefit analysis. There are three possible approaches to dealing with this problem.

Approach	Comment
Calculate a value for the benefits	We could estimate the worth of each of the intangible benefits and allocate an appropriate cash value.
	The problem with this approach is that realistically it is nothing more than **guesswork**.
Ignore the 'too intangible' benefits	Allocate a value to those intangible benefits we are able to estimate a realistic value for. Ignore the other intangible benefits.
	This approach will significantly **undervalue** the system.
Adopt a qualitative approach	Find a reasonable non-financial way of stating intangible benefits. For example customer satisfaction ratings could be established through questionnaires – as could staff time savings and staff morale. Market share could be used to assess competitive advantage.
	The problems with this approach are:
	• Much of the information would only be available **after** the system had been implemented
	• Determining **appropriate measures**
	• **Isolating the effect** of the information system from other factors

Sensitivity analysis

4.13 One way of taking into account the uncertainty of possible benefits is to use **sensitivity analysis**. This involves:

(a) **Identifying** the main factors or variables that the benefits the system could bring are dependent upon (eg staff acceptance, budgetary control, effective programming, integration with other systems etc)

(b) **Assessing** the effect on the benefits if the variable was amended by x% up or down.

4.14 Sensitivity analysis involves asking 'what if?' questions. By changing the value of different variables in the model, a number of different **scenarios** for the future will be produced.

4.15 This will highlight those variables which are most likely to have a significant effect on realising the benefits expected from the system. Once the most critical variables have been established, management then can:

(a) Apply the most stringent **controls** to the most critical variables.

(b) **Alter the plans** so that the most critical variables are no longer as critical. For example, if management is worried that existing staff do not possess the skills and motivation to operate the new system, new employees with the required skills may be recruited.

(c) Choose a **lower-risk** plan. For example, instead of outsourcing all IS/IT operations an organisation may decide to maintain a small IS/IT team to liase with the facilities management company and oversee operations and developments.

Business case report

4.16 The business case should be presented to the decision makers in report format. The report should **summarise** the findings of the activities carried out under the stages of the general framework. If detailed analyses are included they should be appended to the report as appendices.

4.17 The report should contain:

- An introduction stating the terms of reference
- An outline of the current position highlighting problem areas
- The relevant objectives from the organisation's information system strategy
- Different options explored and a summary of the cost-benefit analyses
- A conclusion, and a recommended course of action

Case example

Railtrack pays for poor information

Rail regulator Tom Winsor, in his strongest condemnation yet of Railtrack, gave the company until 21 May, effectively telling it: 'Get your act together.'

If Railtrack fails, Mr Winsor said he will issue an enforcement notice, a legal procedure which could result in the imposition of heavy and unspecified fines.

Railtrack, which is responsible for the national infrastructure, still has more than 200 speed limits in place as a result of the Hatfield disaster last October in which four died and 34 were injured. That was caused by a broken rail and resulted in chaos as other cracked rails were discovered.

Mr Winsor today put the blame squarely on Railtrack's shoulders. The company, he said, lacks 'crucial information about its own network'. It had also '**failed to organise and disseminate the information it does have in an accessible, consistent and efficient way**'.

Mr Winsor said that **if**, after Hatfield, **Railtrack had had the information it should have, speed restrictions could have been prevented**. He said: 'Customer confidence in the railways will revive when Railtrack gets the service back onto a reliable basis. That is the core of my action today.'

A Railtrack spokesman said the company was confident that it would have work completed before the deadline. 'We will seek to achieve Mr Winsor's timescale. Most of the work will be done by Easter. There may be one or two areas after that where work will remain, possibly on the longer-distance lines.'

He added: 'We strongly agree with the **development of a national asset register** (which would list the condition and location of equipment owned by the company). That is an important step in running a safer and more efficient network and we readily agree to that and we are working hard on it.'

The company, which used to make profits of £1.3 million a day, will announce its **first-ever loss** in two weeks' time.

Adapted from *The Evening Standard* March 20, 2001

---

5 BUSINESS PROCESS RE-ENGINEERING (BPR)   5/02

5.1 In recent years the emphasis has been very much on the **use of information technology for competitive advantage**. An earlier trend (still relevant to many situations) involved focussing attention **inwards** to consider how **business processes** could be redesigned or re-engineered to improve efficiency.

5.2 The changes that may be made to processes may be classified as automation, rationalisation or e-engineering.

KEY TERMS

Business automation is the use of computerised working methods to speed up the performance of existing tasks.

Business rationalisation is the streamlining of operating procedures to eliminate obvious inefficiencies. Rationalisation usually involves automation.

5.3 Automation and rationalisation are relatively the most common forms of organisational change. They usually offer modest returns and little risk. **Automation** usually involves assisting employees to carry out their duties more efficiently – for example introducing a computerised accounting package. **Rationalisation** involves not only the automation of a process but also efficient process design. For example, an automated banking system requires the standardisation of account number structure and standard rules for calculating daily account balances – in this situation automation encouraged a certain amount of rationalisation.

5.4 Business process re-engineering involves fundamental changes in the way an organisation functions. For example, processes which were developed in a paper-intensive processing environment may not be suitable for an environment which is underpinned by IT.

5.5 The main writing on the subject is Hammer and Champy's *Reengineering the Corporation* (1993), from which the following definition is taken.

KEY TERM

Business Process Re-engineering is the fundamental rethinking and radical redesign of business processes to achieve dramatic improvements in critical contemporary measures of performance, such as cost, quality, service and speed.

5.6 The key words here are **'fundamental'**, **'radical'**, **'dramatic'** and **'process'**.

(a) **Fundamental** and **radical** indicate that BPR assumes nothing: it starts by asking basic questions such as 'why do we do what we do', without making any assumptions or looking back to what has always been done in the past.

(b) **'Dramatic'** means that BPR should achieve 'quantum leaps in performance', not just marginal, incremental improvements.

(c) **'Process'** is explained in the following paragraphs.

KEY TERM

A **process** is a collection of activities that takes one or more kinds of input and creates an output.

5.7 For **example**, order fulfilment is a process that takes an order as its input and results in the delivery of the ordered goods. Part of this process is the manufacture of the goods, but under BPR the aim of manufacturing is **not merely to make** the goods. Manufacturing should aim to **deliver the goods that were ordered,** and any aspect of the manufacturing process that hinders this aim should be re-engineered. The first question to ask might be

'Do they need to be manufactured at all; should they be purchased from another organisation?'

5.8 A re-engineered process has certain **characteristics**.

- Often several jobs are **combined** into one
- Workers often **make decisions**
- The **steps** in the process are performed in **a logical order**
- **Work** is performed where it **makes most sense**
- Checks and controls may be reduced, and **quality 'built-in'**
- One manager provides a **single point of contact**
- The advantages of **centralised and decentralised** operations are combined

5.9 EXAMPLE: BPR

This scenario is based on a problem at Ford.

A company employs 25 staff to perform the standard accounting task of matching goods received notes with orders and then with invoices. About 80% of their time is spent trying to find out why 20% of the set of three documents do not agree.

One way of improving the situation would have been to computerise the existing process to facilitate matching. This would have helped, but BPR went further: why accept any incorrect orders at all?

> 'What if all the orders are entered onto a computerised database? When goods arrive at the goods inwards department they either agree to goods that have been ordered or they don't. It's as simple as that. Goods that agree to an order are accepted and paid for. Goods that are not agreed are *sent back* to the supplier. There are no files of unmatched items and time is not wasted trying to sort out these files.'
>
> (Alan Lewin, 'Business process re-engineering', *CIMA Student,* February 1996)

5.10 Lewin notes the gains for the company: less staff time wasted, quicker payment for suppliers, lower stocks, and lower investment in working capital.

Principles of BPR

5.11 Hammer presents **seven principles** for BPR.

(a) Processes should be designed to achieve a desired **outcome** rather than focusing on existing **tasks.**

(b) Personnel who use the **output** from a process should **perform** the process. For example, a company could set up a database of approved suppliers; this would allow personnel who actually require supplies to order them themselves, perhaps using on-line technology, thereby eliminating the need for a separate purchasing function.

(c) Information processing should be **included** in the work which **produces** the information. This eliminates the differentiation between information gathering and information processing.

(d) **Geographically-dispersed** resources should be treated as if they are **centralised.** This allows the benefits of centralisation to be obtained, for example, economies of scale through central negotiation of supply contracts, without losing the benefits of decentralisation, such as flexibility and responsiveness.

(e) Parallel activities should be **linked** rather than **integrated.** This would involve, for example, co-ordination between teams working on different aspects of a single process.

(f) 'Doers' should be allowed to be **self-managing.** The traditional distinction between workers and managers can be abolished: decision aids such as expert systems can be provided where they are required.

(g) Information should be captured **once** at **source.** Electronic distribution of information makes this possible.

Is there a BPR methodology?

5.12 *Davenport* and *Short* prescribe a **five-step approach** to BPR.

Step 1. Develop the **business vision and process objectives.** BPR is driven by a business vision which implies specific business objectives such as cost reduction, time reduction, output quality improvement, Total Quality Management and empowerment.

Step 2. **Identify the processes** to be redesigned. Most firms use the 'high impact' approach, which focuses on the most important processes or those that conflict most with the business vision. Lesser number of firms use the Exhaustive approach that attempts to identify all the processes within an organisation and then prioritise them in order of redesign urgency.

Step 3. Understand and **measure the existing processes** – to ensure previous mistakes are not repeated and to provide a baseline for future improvements.

Step 4. **Identify IT levers.** Awareness of IT capabilities could approve useful when designing processes.

Step 5. Design and **build a prototype** of the new process. The actual design should not be viewed as the end of the BPR process - it should be viewed as a prototype, with successive alterations. The use of a prototype enables the involvement of customers.

IT and BPR

5.13 Simply computerising existing ways of doing things does not mean a process has been re-engineered. Technology may be able to add value by re-designing business processes.

5.14 IT is not the solution in itself, it is an **enabler.** BPR uses IT to allow an organisation to do things that it is not doing already. For example, teleconferencing reduces the cost of travelling to meetings - a re-engineering approach takes the view that teleconferencing allows more frequent meetings.

5.15 As *Hammer* and *Champy* put it, 'It is this disruptive power of technology, its ability to break the rules that limit how we conduct our work, that makes it critical to companies looking for competitive advantage.'

5.16 Examples of how technology has changed the way work is conducted include:

(a) **Shared databases** allow information to be accessed simultaneously from many locations.

(b) **Expert systems** may allow non-specialists to do work that previously required an expert.

(c) **Telecommunications networks** mean that businesses can simultaneously reap the rewards of centralisation and decentralisation.

(d) **Decision support tools** allow decisions to be made by a larger number of staff.

(e) **Wireless** communication technology allows staff 'in the field' to send and receive information wherever they are.

(f) **Interactive websites** allow personalised contact with many customers (or at least the appearance of personalised contact).

(g) Automatic identification and **tracking technology** allows the whereabouts of objects or people to be monitored.

(h) High performance computing allows **instant** revision of plans rather than periodic updates.

Why focus on processes?

5.17 Many businesses recognise that value is delivered **through processes,** but still define themselves in terms of their functional roles. To properly harness the resources within a business a clear agreement of the management and implementation of processes is needed. **Without this focus** on processes:

(a) It is **unclear how value is achieved** or can continue to be achieved.

(b) The **effects of change** on the operation of the business are **hard to predict**.

(c) There is no basis to achieve **consistent** business improvement.

(d) **Knowledge is lost** as people move around or out of the business.

(e) Cross-functional interaction is not encouraged.

(f) It is **difficult to align the strategy** of an organisation with the people, systems resources through which that strategy will be accomplished.

5.18 One way of portraying the relationship between organisation strategy, process, people and technology is shown below.

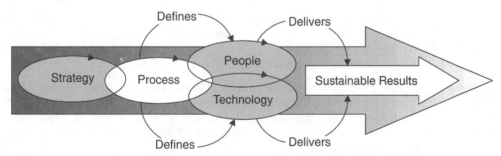

Problems with BPR

5.19 There are concerns that BPR has become misunderstood. According to an independent study of 100 European companies, BPR has become allied in managers' minds with narrow targets such as reductions in staff numbers and other **cost-cutting** measures.

5.20 *Champy* suggests that management itself should be re-engineered. Managers are not used to thinking in systems terms, so, instead of looking at the **whole picture** (which might affect their own jobs), they tend to **seize on individual aspects** of the organisation.

5.21 It is argued that process re-engineering is really only a part of the **wider picture**. A report in the *Financial Times* (see below) on an unnamed company suggested four sets of changes as important to the transformation from a company which **satisfies** customers, to a company that **delights** them - and from a company which is **competent** to a company which is the **best** in its industry. Extracts from the report follow.

'... **first, breaking down barriers** between its different disciplinary specialists and national units by a series of procedural and structural steps, of which the re-engineering of cross-unit processes is only one;

second, developing an explicit set of values and behaviour guidelines which are subscribed to (or 'shared') by everyone in the organisation;

third, redefining the role of management in order to foster much more empowerment, responsibility and decisiveness at every level.

All this requires the creation of the **fourth factor: an unprecedented degree of openness** and trust among managers and employees'.

Case example

Workflow systems / process re-engineering

Work design, whether it is related to work in the factory or at the desk, is a process of arriving at the most **efficient** way of completing tasks and activities that minimises effort and reduces the possibility of mistakes. It is involved in increasing productivity and efficiency whilst maintaining or improving quality standards.

Today work design is often referred to as process re-engineering and has a bad press because the perceived outcome is reduced employee numbers or downsizing. As we move increasingly to a computerised workplace the use of workflow systems is growing and changing the nature of work from one of social contact to service to the system.

A **workflow system** is a system that organises work and allocates it to particular workstations for the attention of the person operating the workstation. The system usually also incorporates a document-management facility. There are three main forms in which workflow systems operate. These are on the **casework basis**, the **flowline basis** or an **ad hoc basis**.

The **casework** basis functions by knowing the individual caseload of staff and directs existing cases to the appropriate caseworker and new cases or customers are allocated on the basis of equalising caseload.

The **flowline** approach allocates a small number of tasks to each operator and the case flows along the line from screen to screen. The **ad hoc** system works on the basis of equalising workload, regardless of who may have dealt with the case previously. The choice depends on the particular circumstances of the business and the approach taken to customer service.

Workflow management provides supervisors with information on screen about the workloads of individuals and information on their processing capabilities with statistics for average time taken to deal with a case, errors detected by the system as a percentage of cases, and so on. This information is intended to ensure that staff receive appropriate support and training, but can be and is used for bonus payments and league tables of performance.

In one organisation where workflow has been used in sales-order processing, the use of the management statistics has become quite draconian and the average period of employment of sales-order staff is three months.

The **advantages** and benefits of workflow systems come mainly from improvements in productivity and efficiency and better or speedier services to customers.

Offset against these benefits are the **disadvantages** stemming from the way that workflow systems are implemented and managed.

A list of the **benefits from the employer's point of view** would be:

- More efficient office procedures
- Providing workflow management
- Equalising of workloads
- Monitoring of operator performance
- Better security
- Ensuring work gets done when it should get done

The **dangers** lie in the segmentation or specialisation in a small number of tasks before passing the work on to the next person's screen, almost like a production line. This **de-skilling** of work increases boredom and leads to high staff turnover. It also reduces social contact to a minimum and the contact that does exist takes place via the system.

So far the casework approach, where staff deal with cases as a 'one stop shop', is the most empowering and beneficial for staff. The skills needed are high and there is a greater sense of completion and satisfaction for operators. In the flowline approach people are demoralised at the repetitive nature of the work. Ad hoc approaches seem to fall between two stools - there is work satisfaction to a degree and no sense of continuing customer contact.

Adapted from: 'Computer talk' - Workflow systems Trevor Bentley - CIMA Articles database

6 PROCESS INNOVATION 5/02

6.1 The writer Davenport introduced the theory of Process Innovation (PI) in 1993.

KEY TERM

Process innovation (PI) combines the adoption of a process view of the business with the application of innovation to key processes. What is new and distinctive about this combination is its enormous potential for helping any organisation achieve major reductions in process cost or time, or major improvements in flexibility, service levels, or other business objectives.

6.2 Process Innovation is similar to BPR. PI does however focus to a greater extent on the **creation of new processes**. For this reason, PI is seen by some as being an even more radical approach.

6.3 Davenport identifies five steps of PI.

Step 1. Identify business areas or processes suitable for innovation.

Step 2. Identify the tools that can be used to innovate (change levers).

Step 3. Develop statements of purpose for the process ('process vision').

Step 4 Understand existing processes and prepare for new systems and processes.

Step 5. Design and prototype new processes.

Chapter roundup

- A **strategy** is a general statement of long-term objectives and goals and the ways by which these will be achieved.

- Information systems strategy is an example of a functional/operational strategy, although it often has **strategic implications**.

- A **strategy for information systems** and information technology is justified on the grounds that IS/IT:

  - Involves high costs
  - Is critical to the success of many organisations
  - Is now used as part of the commercial strategy in the battle for competitive advantage
  - Impacts on customer service
  - Affects all levels of management
  - Affects the way management information is created and presented
  - Requires effective management to obtain the maximum benefit
  - Involves many stakeholders inside and outside the organisation

- **Enterprise analysis** involves examining the entire organisation in terms of structure, processes, functions and data elements to identify the key elements and attributes of organisational data and information.

- **Critical success factors** are a small number of key operational goals vital to the success of an organisation.

- **Cost-benefit analysis** is a key part of a business case justification. Cost-benefit analysis of information systems is complicated by the fact that many of the system cost elements are poorly defined and that benefits are **subjective** in nature.

- An **information audit** aims to establish the information needs of users and decide how these needs could be met.

- An information system **resource analysis**, or Current Situation Analysis (**CSA**), reviews all aspects of IS/IT in the context of the organisation's overall strategy and the IS/IT strategy.

- **Earl's grid** and Peppard's **strategic grid** can be used to evaluate an organisation's use of IT.

- A **business case** is a justification for a project or particular course of action (an investment) to be undertaken.

- A **centralised architecture** involves all computer processing being carried out on a single central processor. **Distributed architectures** spread the processing power throughout the organisation at several different locations.

- With a **client-server** architecture each computer or process on the network is either a 'client' or a 'server'.

- The **general** framework for business case development has four stages:

  1 Where are we now?
  2 Where do we want to be?
  3 How are we going to get there?
  4 Justification

- When selecting information systems another relevant consideration is determining the **best fit** with existing systems.

- **Business process re-engineering** is concerned with how business processes can be redesigned to improve efficiency.

- Simply using technology to automate an existing process does not cause it to be re-engineered.

- **Process innovation** focuses on the creation of new processes to achieve business objectives.

Quick quiz

1   List five reasons why a strategy for information systems and information technology is justified.

✔   1   ....HIGH COST.....................................
    2   ...COMPETITIVE ADVANTAGE................
    3   ...CRITICAL TO SUCCESS...................
    4   ...AFFECTS MIS...............................
    5   ...INVOLVES MANY STAKEHOLDERS......

2   List four reasons why an information system may fail to provide the benefits expected.

    1   ....IRRELEVENT................................
    2   ...INCOMPLETE...............................
    3   ...STAFF RESISTANCE/LACK OF KNOWLEDGE IE POORLY MAINTAINED
    4   ...INSUFFICIENT HARDWARE/SOFTWARE/INVESTMENT

3   List three issues an IS/IT strategy should deal with.   OVERALL NEEDS/CURRENT IT USE/OPP @ THREATS

4   List four general sources of CSFs.

    1   ......CUSTOMERS.............................
    2   ....EMPLOYEES..............................
    3   ....~~MANAGERS~~ INDUSTRY FACTORS........
    4   ......ECONOMY..............................

5   List the four roles IT could play in an organisation identified on Peppard's modified version of McFarlan's strategic grid.

    1   H.H. ~~KEL OP~~ STRATEGY.......   i)   STRATEGIC IMPORTANCE IN FUTURE
    2   H.L. HIGH POTENTIAL.............   ii)   ✔   ✔   CURRENT
    3   LH KEY OPERATIONAL...........
    4   LL   SUPPORT..................

6   What does IRM stand for?   INFO. RESOURCE MANAGEMENT

7   List five categories of costs related to the implementation of an information system.

    1   ⎧ CAPITAL EXP   ⎫   HARDWARE
    2   ⎨ ONE OFF COSTS ⎬   SOFTWARE
    3   ⎩ ONGOING COSTS ⎭   PERSONNEL
    4   ....   OPERATING
    5   ....   INSTALLATION

8   List three approaches to quantifying the intangible benefits a new information system may provide.

    1   ......GUESSTIMATE...........................
    2   ......IGNORE TOO INTANGIBLE...............
    3   ......QUALITATIVE APPROACH................

9   'Automating an existing process means the process has been re-engineered.'

    True   ☐
    False   ☒

10   List two possible limitations of BPR.

    1   ...ASSOC. NARROW TARGETS EG STAFF REDUCTION.
    2   ....

Answers to quick quiz

1   Some reasons follow – you may have thought of others. IS/IT involves high costs, is critical to the success of many organisations, is a source of competitive advantage, impacts on customer service, affects all levels of management, affects the way management information is created and presented, requires effective management to obtain the maximum benefit and involves many stakeholders both inside and outside the organisation.

2   Possible reasons include: IT may be used to tackle the 'wrong' problem (ie the use of IT has not been thought through in the context of the wider organisational context), senior management may not support the implementation, users are ignored in design and/or development and insufficient attention is given to behavioural factors in design and operation.

3   An IS/IT strategy must deal with three general issues; the organisation's overall business needs, the organisation's current use of IS/IT and the potential opportunities and threats that IS/IT can bring.

4   The industry that the business is in; the company itself and its situation within the industry; the environment, for example consumer trends; the economy; political factors; temporal organisational factors (areas of corporate activity which are causing concern).

5   Support applications (not critical to business success), key operational applications (support established core business activities), strategic applications (vital to the organisation's future success) and high potential applications (applications likely to have a significant impact in the future environment).

6   Information Resource Management. (Ensure you have read the *Case example* at the end of section 2.)

7   Examples include; hardware, installation, development costs, personnel costs, operating costs and intangible costs.

8   Three approaches are; calculate a value for the benefits, ignore the 'too intangible' benefits or adopt a qualitative approach.

9   False.

10 Possible limitations include: BPR has become associated with narrow targets such as reductions in staff numbers and other cost-cutting measures. Managers may not look at the whole picture and focus on individual aspects of the organisation. Some believe greater emphasis should be on new processing, eg PI.

Questions to try	Level	Marks	Time
1(a)	Examination	10	18 mins
2	Examination	25	45 mins
15	Examination	20	36 mins

Chapter 4

USING IS/IT COMPETITIVELY

Topic list	Syllabus reference	Ability required
1 Using SWOT analysis for information systems strategy development	(ii)	Evaluation
2 Integrating IS/IT and business objectives	(ii)	Evaluation
3 The effect of IS/IT on an industry	(ii)	Evaluation
4 Using IS/IT for competitive advantage	(ii)	Evaluation

Introduction

The vast majority of organisations now utilise **Information Systems** that rely on **Information Technology**. Most of these organisations are more efficient as a result.

However, to translate these efficiency gains into improved profitability, an organisation must obtain a **competitive advantage** - that is they must do something better than their competitors (or at least give the appearance of doing so).

In this chapter we turn our attention to how organisations can use Information Systems and Information Technology to **gain an advantage over their competitors.**

Learning outcomes covered in this chapter

- **Evaluate** the use of IS/IT to gain competitive advantage and **recommend** appropriate strategies

- **Evaluate** the strategic benefits of IT and **advise** managers on the development of an IS/IT/IM strategy

Syllabus content covered in this chapter

- How organisations can compete through better use of information as opposed to technology, e.g. using a database to identify potential customers or market segments as opposed to creating a barrier to entry through investment in IT

- The link between IS/IT and business strategies and how one supports the other whilst, at the same time, potentially using IT as the key element of the strategies in a positive way

- The way IT can impact upon an industry by utilising frameworks such as Porter's Five Forces and Value Chain, and how organisations can use IT to enhance their competitive position

- The concept of business integration - links between strategy, people, technology and operations in determining the role of IS/IT *(Also see Chapter 3)*

1 USING SWOT ANALYSIS FOR INFORMATION SYSTEMS STRATEGY DEVELOPMENT

1.1 The general management technique of **SWOT analysis** can be applied to the development of information systems strategy.

> ### KEY TERM
>
> **SWOT analysis,** when used as a technique for identifying opportunities in information systems development, aims to determine:
>
> What **Strengths** does our (overall) information system have? (How can we take advantage of them?)
>
> What **Weaknesses** does the system have? (How can we minimise them?)
>
> What **Opportunities**, outside the information system, are there in the organisation or beyond? (How can we capitalise on them?)
>
> What **Threats**, outside the information system, might prevent us operating or improving the information system? (How can we protect ourselves from them?)

1.2 The **strengths** and **weaknesses** analysis has an **internal** focus. The identification of shortcomings in a system could lead to a decision to enhance the current system or to purchase a new system.

1.3 Opportunities and threats are considered as part of an **external appraisal,** or **environmental scan**.

1.4 The internal and external appraisals of SWOT analysis will be brought together. The analysis aims to ensure that a strategy is not followed without considering the wider implications.

    (a) Major **strengths** and profitable opportunities can be **exploited** especially if strengths and opportunities are matched with each other.

    (b) Major **weaknesses** and threats should be **countered,** or a contingency strategy or corrective strategy developed.

1.5 The elements of the SWOT analysis can be summarised and shown on a **cruciform chart**. The following chart relates to a proposal to install a new computerised accounting system.

1.6   EXAMPLE: NEW COMPUTERISED ACCOUNTING SYSTEM

STRENGTHS	WEAKNESSES
£1 million of funds allocated	Workforce has very limited experience of computerised systems
Willing and experienced workforce	Seems to be an expectation that the new system will 'do everything'

THREATS	OPPORTUNITIES
The software vendor is rumoured to be in financial trouble and may 'disappear'	Chance to introduce compatible systems in other departments at a later date
System failure, particularly at month- or year-end, would be costly	Later integration with e-commerce functions is possible

Potential strategy

Significant benefits could be obtained from implementing the system, which should be able to achieve its aims within the £1 million budgeted.

Assurances should be sought from the software vendor as to their future plans and profitability. Contractual obligations should be obtained in regard to this. If the rumours are justified, either another supplier should be approached or the possibility of employing the original vendor's staff on a contract basis could be explored. (*This is an example of an alternative strategy coming out of the SWOT analysis.*)

The end users of the system must be involved in all aspects of system design. Training of staff must be thorough and completed before the system 'goes live'. Management and users must be educated as to what the system will and will not be able to do.

A contingency plan should be in place for repairing or even replacing hardware at short notice.

1.7   The application of SWOT analysis to an information systems scenario is shown in the following question.

Question 1

Scenario

Bargos plc operates 150 retail stores nation-wide. Each store sells a wide variety of consumer goods including kitchenware, clothing, electrical appliances, computers and peripherals, sporting goods, toys and hardware.

Very few goods are displayed in Bargos stores. Customers choose items they wish to purchase from copies of the Bargos catalogue. Customers write the product code on order slips and take completed slips to sales counter staff to complete the sale.

Most goods are held at the back of the service area, enabling customers to take their items with them when leaving the store. Larger, or out-of-stock items are delivered within 48 hours to the customer's address.

Bargos has been established for over 50 years and has developed a reputation as an efficient, reputable retailer of good quality goods.

However, sales have stagnated over the last three years. Senior management believe sales are being lost to competitors, particularly those that offer customers on-line purchasing using an Internet website.

Bargos are now considering an investment of £10 million pounds in a system that would provide on-line purchasing to customers over the Internet. Much of the £10 million is necessary to replace existing back-office systems that would not be able to integrate with the web-based system.

Required

Produce a brief SWOT analysis relevant to the proposed new system at Bargos plc.

Answer

Strengths

- **£10 million** is available for the new system
- **Existing** warehouses and delivery infrastructure could be used with the new system
- Although Bargos has no experience of web technology, the organisation is **IT-literate**

Weaknesses

- The amount of extra sales the site will generate is **unclear**
- Bargos has no in-house **web expertise**
- **Stockholding levels** may need to be higher to ensure prompt delivery
- The **on-going costs** of staff time and expertise to keep the site operational and up-to-date

Opportunities

- E-commerce provides a **new sales channel** and revenue stream
- **Partnerships with suppliers** may be forged allowing delivery direct from the factory
- The use of 'cookies', database and data mining technology to establish more profitable **customer relationships**

Threats

- The **security** implications of establishing Internet links
- Timing – Bargos has missed 'first-mover' advantage
- Consumer **resistance** to on-line purchasing

The possibility of losing Bargos' **distinct** catalogue-based market position (becoming just another retailer with a web-site).

1.8 The following general points may be of use when applying SWOT analysis to a particular information systems scenario.

Economic/industry context

1.9 IT is an **enabling technology**, and can produce dramatic changes in individual businesses and whole industries, especially where there are other major forces for change.

Stakeholders

1.10 Stakeholders are affected by an organisation's use of IT.

(a) **Customers and suppliers** have preferences as to how IT should be used (eg electronic data interchange, extranet).

(b) **Governments** have an interest in the legal aspects of copyright, data protection, security and e-commence.

(c) **IT manufacturers** pioneer the development and use of new technology.

(d) **Consumers:** both their expectations of IT and their willingness to use it are important for its success.

(e) **Employees** and other internal users are interested as IT affects work practices.

Technical issues

1.11 A strategic view of IT must take detailed **technical issues** into account. For example, two UK building societies abandoned a merger because of incompatibility between their computer systems.

1.12 The **security** of IT-based systems must be considered.

The importance of management

1.13 Success or failure in implementing IS/IT depends on the systems themselves and the management effort behind them. An implementation or strategy will fail if:

(a) The system is designed to tackle the wrong problem; that is, the use of IT has not been thought through in the wider organisational context.

(b) Senior management are not interested in, and do not appreciate the significance of, IT based choices.

(c) Users are ignored in design and development.

(d) When no attention is given to behavioural factors in design and operation.

Case example

An example of the importance of the wider organisational processes for the success of information technology is provided by the *Taurus project.*

This was a project, funded by various institutions in the City of London and managed by the Stock Exchange, to computerise certain aspects of share trading and registration. There was an existing computer system, Talisman, but for various reasons it was regarded as being no longer suitable.

(a) A new system was felt to be necessary to cope with increased trading volumes.

(b) Stock markets and bourses elsewhere in Europe already used computerised settlement systems, giving increased competition to London as a financial centre.

However, the plans to develop a computer system failed, at a substantial cost to City institutions and damage to London's reputation as a financial centre. What went wrong? There was nothing inherently impossible about the task: automated settlement has been achieved in other financial centres. A number of reasons were suggested.

(a) Poor project management with inadequate control.

(b) The system was designed to *replicate* existing structures. Rather than use *one* central database, it was decided to use a system of separate but linked databases. Not to do so would have taken away business (and profits) from *share registrar* companies. The design was made unnecessarily complex in order to cater for all the vested interests. This then is an instance of the neutralisation of technology's possible benefits by wider social and organisational choices.

---

2 INTEGRATING IS/IT AND BUSINESS OBJECTIVES 5/01

2.1 A firm's IS/IT strategy should support the overall strategy of the business. We explained why an organisation should have an IS/IT strategy, and the development of an IS/IT strategy in Chapter 3.

2.2   IS/IT can be considered a functional strategy, but might also be viewed as an aspect of **corporate or business strategy**: The strategy for information systems deals with the deployment of a crucial resource throughout the whole business.

2.3   A representation of IS/IT strategy development is given in the following diagram.

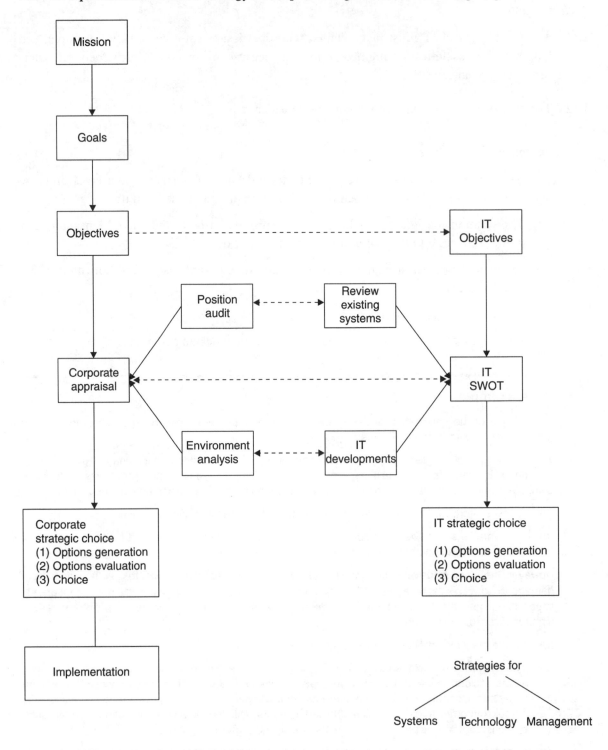

Business objectives and IS/IT resources

2.4   The **identification of business needs** and the information technology framework to satisfy them is at the **heart of a strategy for information systems** and information technology. This is not always feasible, especially if an organisation's use of IS/IT has grown in a haphazard fashion. The purpose of the strategy in this situation may be to impose some sort of order on a disorganised situation.

2.5 The ability to use information and/or information systems to provide better quality information, or to facilitate more efficient processes and therefore establish competitive advantage, is referred to as **information leadership**.

2.6 We discussed **critical success factors** (CSFs) in Chapter 3. CSFs can translate business objectives into IS/IT objectives - they function as linking pins between IS/IT and business planning. The process is as follows.

(a) **Define business objectives** (eg raise earnings per share, develop new businesses).

(b) **Identify the CSFs** whose success is necessary for the organisation to flourish (eg new markets, new products, core activities).

(c) **Develop the information systems to support the CSFs** (eg develop customer information systems, improve the financial control reporting system).

2.7 EXAMPLE

A bank hopes to persuade its customers to buy more of its products.

Step 1. Business objective: **increase profit.**

Step 2. Strategies to increase profit are cutting costs per customer and increasing revenue per customer.

Step 3. A critical success factor for increasing revenue per customer is **getting customers to buy other services.**

Step 4. A key task in getting customers to buy other services is to identify those customers who are most likely to be receptive to new products. A customer **database** could help here.

Evolution of IS/IT

2.8 Organisations that had previously paid little attention to IS/IT may be forced into radical changes in strategy and operations to enable them to embrace technology. On the other hand, organisations that keep up-to-date with IS/IT developments are able to implement changes more gradually.

2.9 *Richard Nolan's* **stage hypothesis,** outlined below, attempts to model the stages organisations go through in their use of IS/IT.

Stage 1: Initiation

2.10 The firm begins its involvement with IS/IT.

(a) **Applications.** The objective is to discover to identify suitable applications (eg **payroll**), and to **save money** on clerical processing. There are a number of separate IS/IT applications that carry out restricted, well-defined tasks.

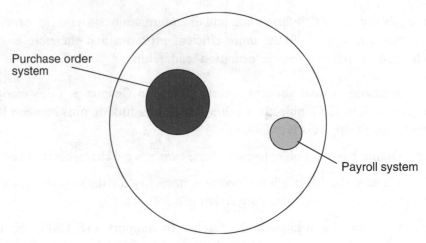

Purchase order system

Payroll system

(b) IS/IT is a distinctly separate department, for technical experts.

(c) **Control:** there are computer controls, but few management controls and little planning.

(d) **Users** have little involvement.

Stage 2: Contagion

2.11 The use of IS/IT spreads over time.

(a) **Applications.** Many more applications are developed, but a lot of time is spent updating old ones. This is a period of unplanned, haphazard growth.

(b) **Organisation.** The IS/IT department is still centralised, but end-users begin to influence what it does. Programmers become more sensitive to user needs.

(c) **Controls** are still very lax. IS/IT is a corporate overhead, and budgetary control over IS/IT expenditure is limited. Furthermore, there are few checks over requests for more applications.

(d) **User awareness.** Users are enthusiastic about IS/IT, but have little understanding as to its benefits and drawbacks.

Stage 3: Control

2.12 The excesses of the contagion stage (too many applications not providing value for money, overspend) lead to tight management controls.

(a) **Applications.** There are restrictions on the development of new systems; existing applications are consolidated. Users might feel frustrated.

(b) **Organisation.** The IS/IT function is properly organised and headed by a manager, who has to justify expenditure, just as is the case with other departments.

(c) **Control.** Financial, quality and other controls (eg steering committees) are introduced over projects and purchases. User departments begin to be charged for the IS/IT resource, as a way of controlling costs. However, controls are mainly exercised in and over the IS/IT department.

(d) **Users** begin to understand IS/IT.

Stage 4: Integration

2.13 The role of IS/IT in the business and the controls over it are greatly clarified. **IS/IT begins to be considered as integral to business issues.**

    (a) **Applications** begin to cross the boundaries of each business function (eg integrating sales order processing and stock control). However, data is often duplicated, so there is an attempt to integrate information and accounting systems. A **management information system** enables managers to get information about many of the firm's activities from a database.

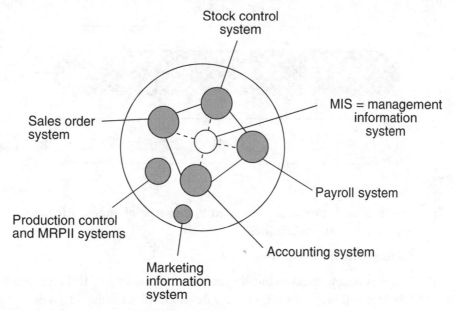

    (b) **Organisation:** perhaps a higher profile for IS/IT?

    (c) **Controls.** More planning is introduced to IS/IT.

    (d) **User involvement** in policy and project management increases.

Stage 5: Data administration

2.14 The organisation gains confidence in managing IS/IT. Information is seen as a resource. **Information requirements, not the technology** which supports it, is the focus of management attention.

    (a) **Applications.** The organisation seeks to develop a single integrated database serving organisational needs, and applications are devised to use the database.

    (b) **Organisation.** A database administrator is appointed.

    (c) **Control.** Data, rather than the systems which process it, is the subject of control. To avoid duplication, data definitions, coding systems, file layouts and so on are standardised.

    (d) **Users** become more accountable themselves for the integrity and correct use of information.

Stage 6: Maturity

2.15 **Information flows reflect the real-life requirements of the organisation.** An organisation's information systems and databases become a sort of mirror in which the workings of the organisation can be scrutinised, modelled and analysed, in a way that was not possible before.

(a) **Applications.** In theory, data about all the organisation's activities find their way into an information system, which can be interrogated in a variety of ways. If the information is analysed with sufficient rigour it may be possible to discover those areas in the organisation's **value chain** where savings can be made or advantages delivered.

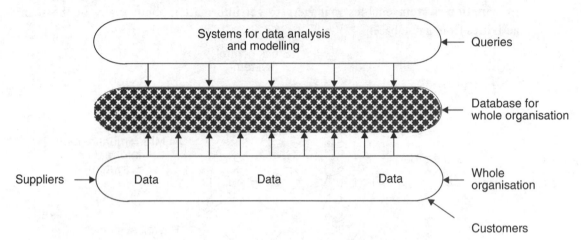

(b) Information is now able to be used as **a source of competitive advantage**. There is an emphasis on **strategic issues**.

(c) Control data is used flexibly.

(d) There is heavy involvement by **users** and management. IS/IT professionals act more as advisors and support staff: systems developments are user-driven.

Case example

The South Bank Arts Centre in London has used *Concentrics*, a system which covers 'everything from space allocation to the timely supply of fireworks for a performance of Tchaikovsky's 1812 Overture'.

At the same time, the planning system is used as a marketing tool. Customer details are entered into the system, so that the firm can tailor its direct mailshots, and thus save money on advertising.

The accounting system is also to be integrated with the other systems to enable 'open access to the accounting system to non-financial departments, giving them responsibility for their own budgeting and report writing'.

The electronic diary and scheduling system will streamline the production process. The aim is to control overheads so as to maintain artistic budgets.

2.16 The **value** of the stage hypothesis is that it is:

(a) **Diagnostic:** managers might be able to make sense of IS/IT's current position in the organisation and where it might be headed.

(b) **Prescriptive:** it suggests remedies which IS/IT managers in the business can prescribe to correct any problems.

2.17 **Problems** with the stage hypothesis include those described below.

(a) **Dated.** First developed in 1974, it preceded PCs, Windows, networks, the Internet, client/server architecture etc.

(b) **Linearity.** Some organisations' uses of IS/IT have the characteristics of several of the stages.

(c) **Size and cost.** IS/IT is now cheaper than when the hypothesis was developed. The management issues do not really arise for many of the smaller businesses running PC-based office automation software.

2.18 Key **lessons** of the stage hypothesis

- An organisation's use of IS/IT must be **planned** and **managed**
- **Users** are empowered by IS/IT

2.19 The stage model was 'born for the DP era'. (DP stands for data processing.) *Earl* describes the differences between the DP era and the IT era as follows.

	DP	IT
Money spent on IT is	... a cost	... an investment
The role of IT in business is	... support	... critical
IT applications are	... tactical	... strategic
The economic context of IT is	... neutral	... welcoming
IT's social impact is	... limited	... pervasive
Technologies	... computing	... multiple
Management of IT	... delegated	... leadership

2.20 The future management problems of IS/IT will no longer be those of control and cost-efficiency. Future management effort will concentrate on configuring IS/IT at those places in the value chain where it can **deal with weaknesses** and **enhance competitive performance;** and on ensuring that the firm manages the **risks** of IS/IT appropriately.

2.21 *Nolan's* stage hypothesis described what was essentially an **emergent strategy**.

(a) IS/IT was adopted by departments according to their operational needs without any real idea of what wider overall implications there might be.

(b) Organisations ended up with a number of different IS/IT systems which may or may not have been compatible.

2.22 With IS/IT, more than with other functional strategies, **conscious planning**, not crafting strategies after the event, is necessary to ensure that IS/IT's potential is maximised and that pitfalls are avoided. Issues of systems **compatibility** and **design** are at the heart of the overall value of the system to an organisation.

2.23 That said, it is short-sighted to go back to a planning model that ignores the value and **creativity** of emergent strategies.

- Opportunities for the use of IT cannot always be identified in advance
- Creative thinking should be encouraged.
- There should be many inputs as possible to the planning process
- End-user development is increasingly viable as IT literacy and technology develop

2.24 **Successful IT development tendencies**

- **User-driven**, with the active support of superiors in user departments
- **Evolutionary** developments of existing approaches, rather than revolutionary change
- Developed outside the information system function
- Marketed extensively throughout the organisation and to customers
- Developed in consultation with **customers**

3 THE EFFECT OF IS/IT ON AN INDUSTRY   Pilot paper

3.1 Porter and Millar state that IS/IT has the potential to change the **nature of competition** within an industry in three ways. IS/IT can:

- Change the industry structure
- Create new businesses and industries
- Be used to create competitive advantage

Sections three and four of this chapter look at these three areas.

Changing the industry structure

3.2 *Porter's* five forces model can be used to analyse the effect of IS/IT on an industry. **Porter** identified **five competitive forces** operating in a competitive environment.

(a) The threat of **new entrants**.
(b) The bargaining power of **suppliers**.
(c) The bargaining power of **customers**.
(d) The threat of **substitute** products/service.
(e) The **existing competitive rivalry** in the industry.

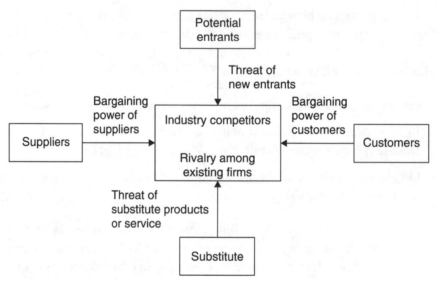

Source: adapted from Porter *(Competitive Strategy)*

New entrants

3.3 IS/IT can have two possible roles in relation to **barriers to entry**.

(a) **Defensively**, IS/IT can increase economies of scale, raise the capital cost of entry (by requiring a similar investment in IS/IT) or effectively colonising distribution channels by tying customers and suppliers into the supply chain or distribution chain.

(b) **Offensively**, IS/IT can leap over entry barriers. An example is the use of telephone banking, which sometimes obviates the need to establish a branch network.

Suppliers

3.4 **Supplier power** can derive from various factors such as geographical proximity and the fact that the organisation requires goods of a certain standard in a certain time. The bargaining power of suppliers can be **eroded** by IS/IT in three ways.

(a) By **increasing competition** between suppliers. IS/IT can provide a purchases database, which enables easy scanning of prices from a number of suppliers.

(b) Suppliers' power can be **shared**. An example is using CAD and so forth to **design components in tandem with suppliers**. Such relationships might be developed with a few key suppliers. The supplier and the organisation both benefit from performance improvement.

(c) Suppliers can be **integrated**, in purely administrative terms, by a system of **electronic data interchange**.

Case example

Some German companies have reported losing lucrative home markets because the Internet has made it easier for customers to access and compare prices from other suppliers.

Geographical price discrimination is becoming harder to sustain in an age where 'a shopper with a credit card and computer can sit at home and order from around the world'. The Internet has therefore increased competition, and is used by many organisations as a competitive weapon.

Customers

3.5 The bargaining power of **customers** can be affected by using IS/IT to '**lock them in**'.

(a) IS/IT can **raise switching costs** (in both cash terms, and in terms of operational inconvenience). An example is where IS/IT provides a distribution channel for certain services (eg airline tickets). Another example comes from the computer industry itself. Until the advent of the PC, most computers were run with proprietary software: in other words, you could not run ICL software, say, on IBM mainframes. This made any switch in supplier (of hardware or software) too much trouble to contemplate.

(b) Customer information systems can enable a **thorough analysis of marketing information** so that products and services can be **tailored to the needs** of certain segments.

Substitutes

3.6 IT has the following relationship to existing and substitute products and services.

(a) In some cases IT/IS itself **is the 'substitute'**. PC-based word processing packages are a substitute for typewriters, e-commerce is a substitute for a high street shop.

(b) IT is the basis for **new leisure activities** (eg computer games). Alternatively, IT-based systems can imitate existing goods (eg electronic keyboards imitating pianos).

(c) IT can **add value to existing services** by allowing **more detailed analysis** (as in a geographical information system), by generating **cost advantages,** or by **extending the market**.

(i) The **cost advantages** of microprocessors massively extended the market for computing.

(ii) *Earl* quotes the example of an econometrics firm, whose innovation enabled PC users to access its database, broadening the reach of the company's services.

Rivalry

3.7 IT can be used to compete – as a source of **competitive advantage**. This is covered later in this chapter.

3.8 Alternatively, IT can be used as a **collaborative venture**, perhaps to set up new communications networks. An example is the perceived threat that IT-based firms like Reuters pose to stock exchanges and commodities exchanges. A communications network soon becomes something that can be marketed. Some competitors in the financial services industry share the same ATM network. (Also see the following section.)

3.9 Porter's five forces model has come in for criticism in recent years.

(a) The model relies on a **static picture of the competition** and therefore plays down the role of innovation.

(b) It over-emphasises the importance of the **wider environment** and therefore ignores the significance of possible individual company advantages with regard to resources, capabilities and competence.

IT as a collaborative venture

3.10 Companies have been using computerised networks for many years to exchange information about ordering, invoicing and delivery with their main customers and suppliers. Until recently (ie before widespread use of the Internet - which we look at in Chapter 5) the main examples were **Electronic Data Interchange (EDI)** and **Value Added Network Services (VANS)**. Although these methods require close co-operation with other organisations, the ultimate aim is still to gain a competitive advantage.

Case example

Wickes, the timber, building materials and home improvement products group has made electronic trading a core part of the company's IT operations.

Wickes started by approaching larger suppliers to pilot the receipt of electronic orders and now uses EDI to send over 10,000 orders a month to over 75% of its suppliers. The retail sites provide order information on a daily basis for consolidation at the company's computer centre. The consolidated orders are then transmitted to suppliers overnight and are ready for processing the following morning. Order lead times are reduced, slower paper-based ordering is eliminated and accuracy is better.

Wickes also receives around 60% of its invoices electronically. Early receipt of invoices via EDI into the company's in-house invoice processing application allows prompt identification of problems and mismatches.

Creating new businesses and industries

3.11 There have been many examples in the last decade of IT affecting the competitive business environment by creating new businesses. This may take the form of a completely new business or a significant change to an existing business.

3.12 For example, the Internet Service Provider industry is a completely **new industry** resulting from technological change. The publishing industry provides a good example of an **existing industry** affected by IS/IT. Encyclopaedia publishers such as Encyclopaedia Britannica have moved in recent years from solely paper-based products to paper and CD-ROM, and then again to a hybrid CD-ROM/Web-based product.

3.13 The **nature of competitors** can also be influenced by developments in technology. For example, Encyclopaedia Britannica now has to compete not only against traditional encyclopaedia producers, but also against software companies such as Microsoft (with Microsoft Encarta).

3.14 Technology has increased the amount of information that can be collected. For example, the use of bar-code scanners in retail outlets means accurate sales data is available across all product ranges. This data is then available for further analysis, perhaps against customer profiles obtained under 'customer loyalty' schemes. This information could be **used internally,** and/or could be **offered for sale** to producers or other interested parties.

4 USING IS/IT FOR COMPETITIVE ADVANTAGE 5/01

4.1 As the importance of information has increased over the last two decades, organisations have realised that **Information Systems (IS)** and **Information Technology (IT)** can be used as a source of **competitive advantage**.

> **KEY TERM**
>
> **Competitive advantage** is a profitable and sustainable position. It exists in the minds of customers, who believe the value they will receive from a product or service is greater than both the price they will pay and the value offered by competitors.

Generic strategies for competitive advantage

4.2 *Porter* proposes **three generic strategies** for achieving competitive advantage.

(a) **Cost leadership** means being the lowest-cost producer in the industry as a whole. A cost leadership strategy seeks to achieve the position of lowest-cost producer in the industry.

(b) **Differentiation** is the exploitation of a product or service which the industry as a whole believes to be unique. A differentiation strategy assumes that competitive advantage can be gained through **particular characteristics** of a product or service.

(c) **Focus** involves a restriction of activities to only part of the market (a segment or niche) through:

(i) Providing goods and/or services at lower cost **to that segment** (**cost-focus**).

(ii) Providing a differentiated product or service to that segment (**differentiation-focus**).

4.3 Cost leadership and differentiation are **industry-wide** strategies. Focus involves segmentation - pursuing **within the segment** a strategy of cost leadership or differentiation.

4.4 Examples of how IS/IT can support each of these strategies are shown in the following table.

Strategy	How IS/IT can support the strategy
Cost-leadership	By facilitating reductions in cost levels, for example by reducing the number of administration staff required.
	Allowing better resource utilisation, for example by providing accurate stock information allowing lower 'buffer' inventories to be held.
	Using IT to support just-in-time and advanced manufacturing systems.
Differentiation	Differentiation can be suggested by IT, perhaps in the product itself or in the way it is marketed.
	The publishing example quoted earlier provides evidence of this – with the move from paper-based products to electronic.
Focus	IT may enable a more customised or specialised product/service to be produced.
	IT also facilitates the collection of sales and customer information that identifies targetable market segments.

Porter's value chain

4.5 *Michael Porter* analyses the various activities of an organisation into a **value chain**. This is a model of value activities (which procure inputs, process them and add value to them in some way, to generate outputs for customers) and the relationships between them.

4.6 The value chain can be used to design a competitive strategy, by deploying the various activities strategically. The two examples below are based on two different supermarkets.

(a)

	INBOUND LOGISTICS	OPERATIONS	OUTBOUND LOGISTICS	MARKETING & SALES	SERVICE
Firm infrastructure	Minimum corporate HQ				
Human resource management		De-skilled store-ops	Dismissal for checkout error		
Technology development	Computerised warehousing		Checkouts simple		
Procurement	Branded only purchases big discounts	Low cost sites			Use of concessions
	Bulk warehousing	1,000 lines only		Low price promotion	Nil
		Price points		Local focus	
		Basic store design			

(b)

	INBOUND LOGISTICS	OPERATIONS	OUTBOUND LOGISTICS	MARKETING & SALES	SERVICE
Firm infrastructure	Central control of operations and credit control				
Human resource management	Recruitment of mature staff	Client care training	Flexible staff to help with packing		
Technology development		Recipe research	Electronic point of sale	Consumer research & tests	Itemised bills
Procurement	Own label products	Prime retail positions	Adverts in quality mags & poster sites		
	Dedicated refrigerated transport	In-store food halls Modern store design Open front refrigerators Tight control of sell-by dates	Collect by car service	No price discounts on food past sell-by dates	No quibble refunds

---

Question 2

One of these chains is concentrating on low prices, the other differentiated on quality and service. Which is which?

Answer

The value chain in (a) is based on that of Kwik Save, a 'discount' chain which sells on price, pursuing a cost-focus strategy. The value chain in (b) is based on Marks and Spencer foods, which seeks to differentiate on quality and service.

4.7 Value chain analysis can be used to assess the impact of IS/IT, and to identify processes where IT could be used to **add value**.

4.8 IT can be used to **automate** and improve physical tasks in the **manufacturing** sector. It also provides **extra information** about the process.

(a) **Process** control. Computer systems enable tighter control over production processes.

   (i) It is possible to **measure** many aspects of the production process.

   (ii) A variety of control techniques are available.

(b) **Machine tool control.** Machine tools can be automated and, it is hoped, be made more precise.

   (i) **Numerical control**: information to operate the machine tool is prepared in advance to generate a set of instructions.

   (ii) **Computer numerical control** is where the computer produces the instructions.

   (iii) **Direct numerical control** is where the computer is linked directly to the machine tool.

(c) **Robots** can automate some of the process.

(d) **Computer-aided manufacturing** (CAM) involves a variety of software modules.

   • Production control, supervisory systems
   • Materials requirement planning (MRP) and MRP II
   • Capacity requirements planning

(e) **Computer-integrated manufacturing** (CIM) integrates all aspects of an organisation's manufacturing activities. IT cannot solve basic organisational problems, but the essence is the use of the IT to provide integration though communication, effectiveness and efficiency. Flexible manufacturing systems include:

- Machine tools
- Materials handling conveyor sets
- Automatic guided vehicles

(f) **Enterprise Resource Planning** (ERP) systems take MRP II systems a step further, and are not restricted to certain types of organisation. ERP systems are used for identifying and planning the **enterprise-wide** resources needed to record, produce, distribute, and account for customer orders.

4.9 In both **inbound** logistics and **outbound** logistics IT can have an impact.

(a) The use of IT in **inbound logistics** includes stock control systems such as MRP, MRP II, ERP and JIT systems.

(b) **Warehousing**. The use of barcodes can increase knowledge about the quantity and nature of stock in hand.

(c) It is possible to create computer models, or **virtual warehouses**, of stock actually held at **suppliers**. For example an organisation with several outlets might have each connected to a system which indicates the total amount of stock available at different sites.

4.10 **Marketing and services** can be made more effective by **customer databases** enabling market segmentation.

(a) Buying and analysing a mailing list is a more precise method of targeting particular groups of consumers than television advertising.

(b) A variety of market research companies use IT to **monitor consumers' buying habits**.

(c) Supermarkets can use automated **EPOS** systems to have a precise hour-by-hour idea of how products are selling to enable speedy ordering and replenishments.

4.11 **Customer relationship management (CRM)** describes the methodologies, software, and usually Internet capabilities that help an enterprise manage customer relationships.

4.12 For example, an enterprise might build a database about its customers that described relationships in sufficient detail so that individuals (management, salespeople, service staff, and maybe the customer), could access information, match customer needs with product plans, remind customers of service requirements and know what other products a customer had purchased.

CRM consists of:

(a) Helping an enterprise to identify and target their best customers, manage marketing campaigns with clear goals and objectives, and generate quality leads.

(b) Assisting the organisation to improve telesales, account, and sales management by **optimising information shared**, and streamlining existing processes (for example, taking orders using mobile devices).

(c) Allowing the formation of relationships with customers, with the aim of improving customer satisfaction and maximising profits; identifying the most profitable customers and providing them with the highest level of service.

(d) Providing employees with the information and processes necessary to know their customers, understand their needs, and effectively build relationships between the company, its customer base, and distribution partners.

4.13 As far as **support** activities are concerned IT has some impact.

(a) **Procurement.** IT can automate some purchasing decisions. Paperwork can be saved if the organisation's purchase systems are linked directly to the sales order systems of some suppliers (eg by electronic data interchange).

(b) **Technology development.** Computer aided design (**CAD**) is, in a number of areas, an important influence.

 (i) **Drafting.** CAD produces engineer's drawings, component design, layout (eg of stores, wiring and piping) and electronic circuit diagrams in complex systems.

 (ii) **Updating.** It is easy to change design in CAD systems and to assess ramifications of any changes. Some CAD systems have archive data (eg for reference).

 (iii) CAD enables modelling to be **checked** without the necessity of producing working prototypes. Some 'stress testing' can be carried out on the model.

(c) There is perhaps less impact on **human resources.** However, the HR applications include the maintenance of a skills database, staff planning (eg using network analysis), computer-based training, time attendance systems, payroll systems, pension systems.

Case example
Fast-growing firms say IT's their edge

The fastest-growing companies in the United States attribute their competitive advantage to an edge in IT. A PricewaterhouseCooper's survey found that 52% of the 436 CEOs interviewed said that their companies have a competitive edge in computer and information technology. The companies are identified as the fastest-growing U.S. businesses over the last five years.

The 'trendsetter' companies 'with an IT advantage are reaping the benefits,' Jim Atwell, global private equity director at Pricewaterhouse, said in a statement. 'Their composite revenues have grown 20-fold over the past 5 years, 45% faster growth than their counterparts without an IT edge. And they also tend to be larger - with 58% higher revenues and 56% more employees.'

The study found that service firms lead product vendors in claiming an IT advantage, 58% compared to 46%. 57% of the companies surveyed report having financial analysis/cash management systems; 52% have sales information systems; 37% have sales/customer service systems; 28% have marketing systems; and 24% have customer 'end user' systems. In addition, 47% report the Internet as being very important to their business. *(BPP note: This figure is likely to have increased significantly since the survey date - late 1998.)*

Nearly all of the CEOs of the companies studied (97%) rated computers and information technology as important to their company's profitable business growth over the past two years, with 80% rating them as extremely or very important.

Companies that rated IT as extremely important to their business have grown their revenues ten-fold over the past five years, or 72% faster than those who did not rate it as highly. Likewise, 96% of the CEOs said computers and IT have generally lived up to their expectations for increased business productivity. 60% rated IT as performing extremely or very well against their original expectation.

Although a majority of the companies studied praised IT as a business necessity, 84% of growing companies' CEOs now express concern about information security, an increase of 7 points from a similar study done two years ago. 31% say security is a major concern, with this high degree of discomfort more prevalent among service than product firms. To address this issue, more than half of the CEOs of these companies have documented disaster recovery plans in place for IT emergencies.

Looking ahead over the next year, 32% of the companies surveyed said they are planning to increase their levels of investment in computers and information technology, while only 11% are cutting back. About 55% expect to continue with current IT spending levels, and the remaining 2% are uncertain.

Adapted from an article posted on CNET News.com

IS/IT and competitive advantage - other writers   **5/01**

4.14 *Ward* and *Griffiths* suggested four ways that IS/IT could be used for competitive advantage:

   (a) **Linking the organisation to customers or suppliers,** eg EDI, website, VAN, extranet.

   (b) Creating **effective integration** of the use of information in a value-adding process, eg data-mining, ERM.

   (c) Enabling the organisation to **develop, produce, market and distribute new products or services,** eg CAD, CRM.

   (d) Giving **senior management information** to help develop and implement strategy, eg knowledge management.

4.15 *Moriarty* and *Swartz* provide an example of how the application of IS/IT can generate a competitive advantage in relation to the sales and marketing function. They explain how technology can **increase productivity** through providing better marketing information (eg databases), and more efficient sales and marketing tools (eg direct mail, websites).

4.16 To be classed as a competitive advantage the increased productivity **would not be available to others.** This is unlikely unless the technology is too expensive (entry barrier), or competitors are unaware of how to utilise it.

4.17 Increased productivity may lead to **reduced fixed costs.** For example, fewer sales and marketing staff may be required, allowing a move to smaller premises. The effect of reduced fixed costs is shown in the following diagram.

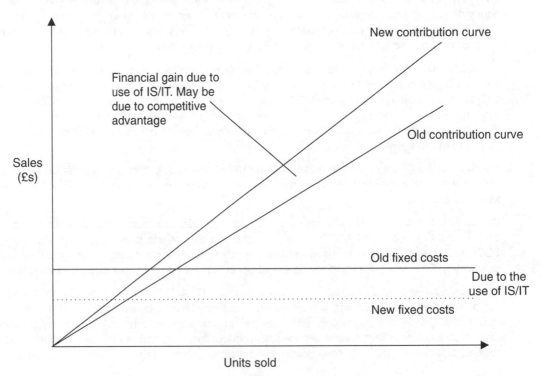

4.18 Peppard summarises the ways in which IS/IT can be used for competitive advantages as:

- Establishing entry barriers
- Affecting the cost of switching operations
- Differentiating products/services
- Limiting access to distribution channels
- Ensuring competitive pricing
- Decreasing supply costs
- Increasing cost efficiency
- Using information as a product
- Building closer relationships with supplies and customers

Case example

Competitive Advantage through IT - Information Technology at OTIS

Otis' competitive advantage stems from three main developments – OTISLINE, REM and the use of fuzzy logic.

OTISLINE

The 'freephone' OTISLINE, in addition to its original purpose of improving customer service, has helped in areas like elevator maintenance, new equipment sales, marketing of elevator services. Otis has used OTISLINE in foreign markets to **increase the barriers to entry for its competitors** seeking to enter those same markets.

Otis now possesses the ability to access service information from both independent service companies and its own regional offices. This serves as a **database for customer files** as well as a **depository for all maintenance activities** for elevators under service contracts.

REM

REM is a PC-based system designed to monitor elevator performance from a distant location, 24 hours a day, that controls selected standard functions in order to spot problems in advance and to **avoid breakdowns**.

It is a **preventive** system that is programmed with predefined parameters that when deviated from initiates a warning signal which if unattended, could lead to a breakdown. Otis is able to recognise potential problems without alerting the customer and perform the necessary maintenance quickly. Technicians **can access elevator maintenance information as they are working** upon the problem without having to completely shut down the elevator beforehand.

Fuzzy Logic

Neural networks and artificial intelligence are used to identify peak hours of usage and the elevator can respond accordingly. Using weight and frequency, **elevators decide for themselves** where they should be at certain times of the day, thus greatly **reducing waiting time** (2 minutes to 30 seconds).

As a technology-based development, fuzzy logic is **copied relatively easily by competitors**, thus effectively eliminating Otis' competitive advantage in this area.

Exam Focus Point
The examiner has a history of emphasising the use of information and technology for competitive advantage.

Case study link
The use of technology for competitive advantage, and the impact that technology can have on an organisation or an industry, could be relevant to the Final Level Case Study.

Chapter roundup

- The general management technique of **SWOT** analysis can be applied to the development of **information systems strategy**.

- The identification of **business needs** and the information **technology framework** to satisfy them is at the heart of a strategy for information systems and information technology.

- Critical success factors (**CSFs**) function as linking pins between IS/IT and business planning. The process is as follows.

    Step 1. Define business objectives.

    Step 2. Identify the CSFs whose success is necessary for the organisation to flourish.

    Step 3. Develop the information systems to support the CSFs.

- Richard Nolan's **stage hypothesis** attempts to model the stages organisations go through in their use of IS/IT. A key lesson of the stage hypothesis is that an organisation's use of IS/IT must be **planned** and **managed**.

- Porter and Millar state that IS/IT has the potential to change the **nature of competition** within an industry in three ways. IS/IT can:

    ° Change the industry structure
    ° Create new businesses and industries
    ° Be used to create competitive advantage

- Porter's **five forces model** can be used to analyse the effect of IS/IT on an industry. Porter identified five competitive forces operating in a competitive environment:

    ° The threat of new entrants
    ° The bargaining power of suppliers
    ° The bargaining power of customers
    ° The threat of substitute products/service
    ° The existing competitive rivalry in the industry

- Porter proposes three **generic strategies** for achieving competitive advantage:

    ° Cost leadership
    ° Differentiation
    ° Focus (either cost or differentiation)

- Michael Porter's **Value Chain** models activities (inputs, process and add value to generate outputs for customers) and the relationships between them. The value chain can be used to design a competitive strategy.

- Ways in which IS/IT can be **used for competitive advantage** include:

    ° Establishing entry barriers
    ° Differentiating products/services
    ° Ensuring competitive pricing
    ° Increasing cost efficiency
    ° Building closer relationships with supplies and customers
    ° Affecting the cost of switching operations
    ° Limiting access to distribution channels
    ° Decreasing supply costs
    ° Using information as a product

Quick quiz

1   What does SWOT analysis, when used as a technique for identifying opportunities in information systems development, aim to determine?

— INTERNAL / EXTERNAL
 SW   OT

2   List two key lessons of Nolan's stage hypothesis.

   1   PLANNED & MANAGED

   2   USERS EMPOWERED

3   List Porter's five competitive forces operating in a competitive environment.

   1   ENTRANTS

   2   CUSTOMERS

   3   SUPPLIERS

   4   SUBSTITUTES

   5   RIVALRY

4   List Porter's three generic strategies for achieving competitive advantage.

   1   COST – LEADERSHIP   — REDUCE OPERATING COSTS / INCREASE REV.

   2   DIFFERENTIATION   — INNOVATION / SPEED / QUALITY

   3   FOCUS   — NICHE MARKETING / MIS USE

5   Provide an example of how IS/IT can support each of Porter's generic strategies.

6   What does CRM stand for?

C. USTOMER   R. ELATION   M. ANAGEMENT

7   What does ERP stand for?

E. NTERPRISE   R. ESOURCE   P. LANNING

8   List five ways in which IS/IT could be used for competitive advantage.

   1   ESTABLISH ENTRY BARRIERS

   2   COST OF SWITCHING

   3   DIFFERENTIATING

   4   DECREASE COSTS

   5   BUILD RELATIONSHIPS

Answers to quick quiz

1   What Strengths does our (overall) information system have? (How can we take advantage of them?)

   What Weaknesses does the system have? (How can we minimise them?)

   What Opportunities, outside the information system, are there in the organisation or beyond? (How can we capitalise on them?)

   What Threats, outside the information system, might prevent us operating or improving the information system? (How can we protect ourselves from them?)

2   An organisation's use of IS/IT must be planned and managed.

   Users are empowered by IS/IT.

3   The threat of new entrants.

   The bargaining power of suppliers.

   The bargaining power of customers.

   The threat of substitute products/service.

   The existing competitive rivalry in the industry.

4   Cost leadership.

   Differentiation.

   Focus.

5   Some of the examples provided within this Chapter are reproduced here (try to think of your own). Cost-leadership - by facilitating better resource utilisation, for example by providing accurate stock information allowing lower 'buffer' inventories to be held. Differentiation – technology can allow changes to the nature of the product offered, for example changing from paper-based publishing products to electronic. Focus - IT facilitates the collection of sales and customer information that identifies targetable market segments.

6   Customer Relationship Management.

7   Enterprise Resource Planning.

8   Possibilities include: Establishing entry barriers, affecting the cost of switching operations, differentiating products/services, limiting access to distribution channels, ensuring competitive pricing, decreasing supply costs, increasing cost efficiency, using information as a product and building closer relationships with supplies and customers.

Questions to try	Level	Marks	Time
7	Examination	20	36 mins
11	Examination	25	45 mins

USING INFORMATION COMPETITIVELY

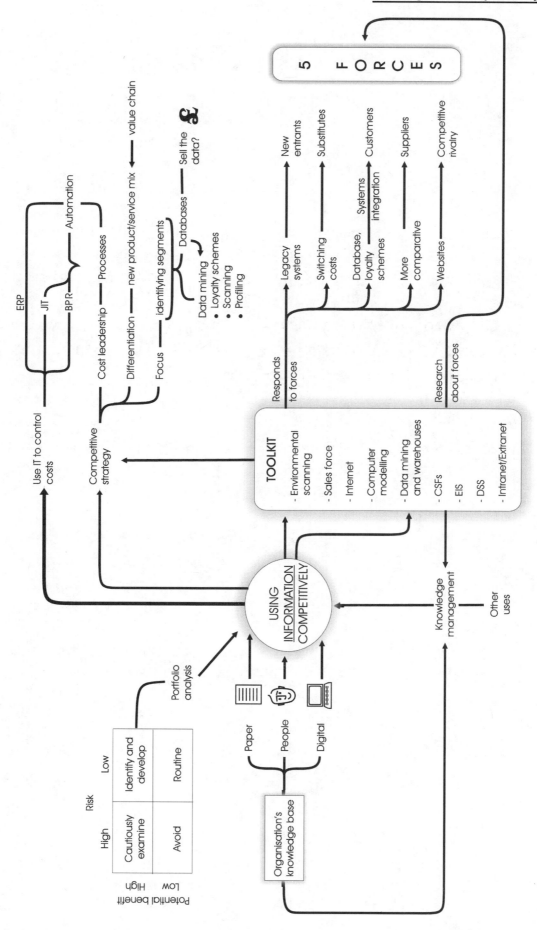

Chapter 5

THE INTERNET AS A STRATEGIC BUSINESS TOOL

Topic list	Syllabus reference	Ability required
1 The Internet – an overview	(i)	Evaluation
2 Internet security issues	(i)	Evaluation
3 Electronic commerce	(i), (ii)	Evaluation
4 Developing a strategy for e-commerce	(i), (ii)	Evaluation

Introduction

The Internet is potentially the most **significant business and social development** since the advent of the telephone.

As with any new technology the Internet provides both opportunities and risks. In this chapter we look at how the **Internet can be exploited** to provide enhanced value to businesses and their customers. We also cover the **security issues** associated with the Internet and e-commerce.

The Internet is a '**hot topic**' in both the academic and business worlds – so ensure you understand the issues raised in this chapter.

Learning outcomes covered in this chapter

- **Evaluate** the impact of electronic commerce on the way business is conducted and recommend an appropriate strategy

Syllabus content covered in this chapter

- The strategic business use of the Internet and WWW in terms of marketing and sales activities, and utilising the technology to provide enhanced value to customers and suppliers

- Potential benefits and drawbacks of Internet use by organisations for activities such as data collection and dissemination of information, including the security issues to be borne in mind

- Concept of electronic commerce and the potential impact it has on business strategy

1 THE INTERNET – AN OVERVIEW   Pilot paper

What is the Internet?

> ### KEY TERMS
>
> The **Internet** is a global network connecting millions of computers.
>
> The **World Wide Web** (WWW) is a system of Internet servers that support specially formatted documents. Most documents on the web are formatted in HTML (HyperText Markup Language) that supports links to other documents, as well as graphics, audio, and video files.
>
> A group of documents accessed from the same base web address is known as a **website**.

1.1 The Internet is the name given to the technology that allows any computer (or WAP phone, or other device) with a telecommunications link to **send and receive information** from any other suitably equipped device.

1.2 Connection is made via an **Internet Service Provider (ISP).** Many ISPs offer free access to the Internet, meaning users pay only the local telephone charges incurred during connection. 'Free' ISPs include Virgin Net and Freeserve. Other ISPs such as AOL charge a subscription fee, but offer unmetered access time (in effect 'free' calls).

1.3 The Internet is viewed through interface programs called **browsers**. The most widely used are Microsoft Internet Explorer and Netscape Navigator. Searching the web is done using a **search engine** such as Yahoo!, Lycos or Google.

1.4 Most organisations now have a **website** on the Internet. A website address will typically be given in the format of a **U**niversal **R**esource **L**ocator (**URL**). eg http://www.bbc.co.uk

URL element	Explanation
http://	'http' tells the browser to use the HyperText Transfer Protocol when retrieving the document from the Internet server. The two forward slashes after the colon introduce a 'host name' such as www.
www	This stands for **World Wide Web**. As noted before, to put it simply the web (via its use of HTML), is what makes the Internet user-friendly
bbc	This is the **domain name** of the organisation or individual whose site is located at this URL
co	This indicates the type of organisation concerned, in this case a company. Other designations include: .com — commercial .ac or .edu — educational and research .org — usually non-commercial institutions .net or .biz — inconsistent, an 'overflow' from .com and .org .mil — military .gov — government agencies
uk	This indicates that the organisation is located in the UK. For a full list of country codes used on the web visit; www.dundee.ac.uk/english/url-jav.htm

Current uses of the Internet

1.5 The scope and potential of the Internet are still developing. Its uses already embrace the following:

(a) **Dissemination of information**.

(b) Product/service development - through almost instantaneous **test marketing**.

(c) **Transaction processing** - both business-to-business (B2B) and business-to-consumer (B2C).

(d) **Relationship enhancement** - between various groups of stakeholders, but principally (for our purposes) between consumers and product/service suppliers.

(e) **Recruitment** and job search - involving organisations worldwide.

(f) **Entertainment** - including music, humour, games and some less wholesome pursuits!

Growth of the Internet

1.6 It is estimated that 60% of households in the USA and 50% of households in the UK will have Internet access by the end of 2002.

(a) Many households are now establishing multiple Internet access points eg Digital TV set, PCs, WAP phones.

(b) **Changes in the telecoms market** are likely to mean that Internet connection time will become cheaper.

(c) Digital television and WAP enabled mobile phones permit the Internet to be accessed without the necessity to use a personal computer.

(d) For many, the preferred Internet interface is not the PC but the **PDA (Personal Digital Assistant)**.

(e) Internet kiosks are becoming increasingly common in shopping centres and cafes.

1.7 A critical factor in the long-run expansion of the Internet is its use today by children, the adult consumers of tomorrow.

1.8 The Internet is not expanding at the same rate in every sphere of business. The rate of growth is influenced by:

(a) The degree to which the customer can be persuaded to believe that using the Internet will **deliver some added-value** - in terms of quickness, simplicity and price.

(b) Whether there are 'costs' which the **customer** has to bear - not exclusively 'costs' in the financial sense, but also such psychological 'costs' as the isolated on-line shopping experience.

(c) The **market segment** to which the individual belongs. The Internet is largely the preserve of younger, more affluent, more technologically competent individuals with above-average amounts of disposable income.

(d) The frequency of supplier/customer contact required.

(e) The availability of **incentives** which might stimulate Internet acceptance. For example, interest rates on bank accounts which are higher than those available through conventional banks (Egg), the absence of any charges (Freeserve), the creation of penalties for over-the-counter transactions (Abbey National), and the expectations of important customers (IBM's relationships with its suppliers).

Case example

In many areas, users are proactively switching to the Internet. When Lloyds TSB first developed Internet banking facilities, they were not publicised but customers were seeking it out and joining at the rate of 380 accounts per day. At the same time, customers are not yet ready to abandon the channels they used in the past: even with Internet and telephone banking, many still visit their bank branches regularly.

1.9 Arguably, the most profitable pure Internet companies, as well as the most influential, will be **business-to-business 'infomediaries'** (the term coined by John Hagel of McKinsey), because they can exploit the Internet's most salient characteristics.

(a) **The Internet shifts power from sellers to buyers by reducing switching costs**. Buyers may feel overwhelmed by this power, but they typically want one-stop shopping, with information they believe and advice they can trust.

(b) **The Internet reduces transaction costs and thus stimulates economic activity**. According to one US calculation, a banking transaction via the Internet costs 1 cent, 27 cents at an ATM (automated teller machine) and 52 cents over the telephone. Infomediaries can enable significant savings to be enjoyed by small-scale or even single customers.

(c) **The speed, range and accessibility of information on the Internet, and the low cost of capturing and distributing it, create new commercial possibilities.** Infomediaries can focus on particular product/service supply issues; by doing so, they attract specialised buyers and sellers; in turn they acquire more expertise which generates continued customer loyalty and participation.

1.10 The major growth so far in the field of e-commerce has concentrated on the **Business to Business** (B2B) sector.

(a) **Major companies** are setting themselves up as e-businesses. In November 1999, both Ford and General Motors announced that they were switching a major portion of their procurement and supply chain management to the web.

(b) IBM now requires **all its suppliers to quote and invoice electronically** - no paper documentation is permitted.

(c) Many firms are using the Internet to exploit the **transparency of supplier prices,** and to maximise their purchasing benefits from the availability of world-wide sourcing. Robert Bosch, the German kitchen appliance manufacturer, **requires all its suppliers to have web-based catalogues** and prices.

(d) Companies are also increasing their customer service through the web. Dell, the computer company, has created **extranets for its major business customers,** enabling them to receive personalised customer support, their own price lists, and some free value-added services.

Case example

Business and the Internet

The Internet has the potential to turn business upside down and inside out, to fundamentally change the way companies operate, whether in high-tech or metal-bashing. This goes far beyond buying and selling over the Internet, or e-commerce, and deep into the processes and culture of an enterprise.

Some companies are using the Internet to make direct connections with their customers for the first time. Others are using secure Internet connections to intensify relations with some of their trading partners, and using the Internet's reach and ubiquity to request quotes or sell off perishable stocks of goods or services by auction.

The Internet is helping companies to lower costs dramatically across their supply and demand chains, take their customer service into a different league, enter new markets, create additional revenue streams and redefine their business relationships.

Some writers argue that companies can be either **'brick' or 'click'** businesses, but they can't be both: if they are a 'brick' operation - ie they have real premises, real shops, real factories and warehouses - then their culture will make it impossible for them fully to assimilate the drastic changes required in order to operate successfully in a 'click' environment. It is no accident, therefore, that companies like Prudential Assurance have initiated their Internet activities through stand-alone enterprises, using newly-recruited people situated in geographically-distinctive locations.

1.11 The Internet provides opportunities to automate tasks which would previously have required more costly interaction with the organisation. These have often been called low-touch or zero-touch approaches.

1.12 Tasks which a website may automate include:

(a) **Frequently-Asked Questions (FAQs)**: carefully-structured sets of answers can deal with many customer interactions.

(b) **Status checking**: major service enquiries (Where is my order? When will the engineer arrive? What is my bank balance?) can also be automated, replacing high-cost human service processes, and also providing the opportunity to proactively offer better service and new services.

(c) **Keyword search**: the ability to search provides web users with opportunities to find information in large and complex websites.

(d) **Wizards (interview style interface) and intelligent algorithms**: these can help diagnosis, which is one of the major elements of service support.

(e) **E-mail and systems to route and track inbound e-mail**: the ability to route and/or to provide automatic responses will enable organisations to deal with high volumes of e-mail from actual and potential customers.

(f) **Bulletin boards**: these enable customers to interact with each other, thus facilitating self-activated customer service and also the opportunity for product/service referral. Cisco in particular has created communities of Cisco users who help each other - thus reducing the service costs for Cisco itself.

(g) **Call-back buttons**: these enable customers to speak to someone in order to deal with and resolve a problem; the more sophisticated systems allow the call-centre operator to know which web pages the users were consulting at the time.

(h) **Transaction processing**: the taking of orders and payment on-line.

BPP PUBLISHING

Problems with the Internet

1.13 To a large extent the Internet has grown **without any formal organisation**. There are specific communication rules, but it is not **owned** by any one body and there are no clear guidelines on how it should develop.

1.14 Inevitably, the **quality** of much of the information on the Internet leaves much to be desired.

1.15 Speed is a major issue. Data only downloads onto the user's PC at the speed of the slowest telecommunications link - downloading data can be a time-consuming procedure. However, future developments will mean that speeds will improve.

1.16 A number of **faster services** have recently become available, but cost is preventing widespread installation of these technologies by consumers.

  (a) **Integrated Services Digital Network (ISDN)** is an international communications standard for sending voice, video, and data over digital telephone lines or normal telephone wires. ISDN supports data transfer rates three times faster than modems.

  (b) **ADSL** (Asymmetric Digital Subscriber Line) offers data transfer rates of up to **8 Mbps,** considerably faster than ISDN. ADSL allows information to be sent out over ordinary copper wires and simultaneous use of the normal telephone service.

1.17 So much information and entertainment is available that employers worry that their **staff will spend too much time** browsing through non-work-related sites.

1.18 **Security** is perhaps the biggest worry of all; this is covered in the next section.

1.19 The following diagram shows how the different elements of the Internet fit together.

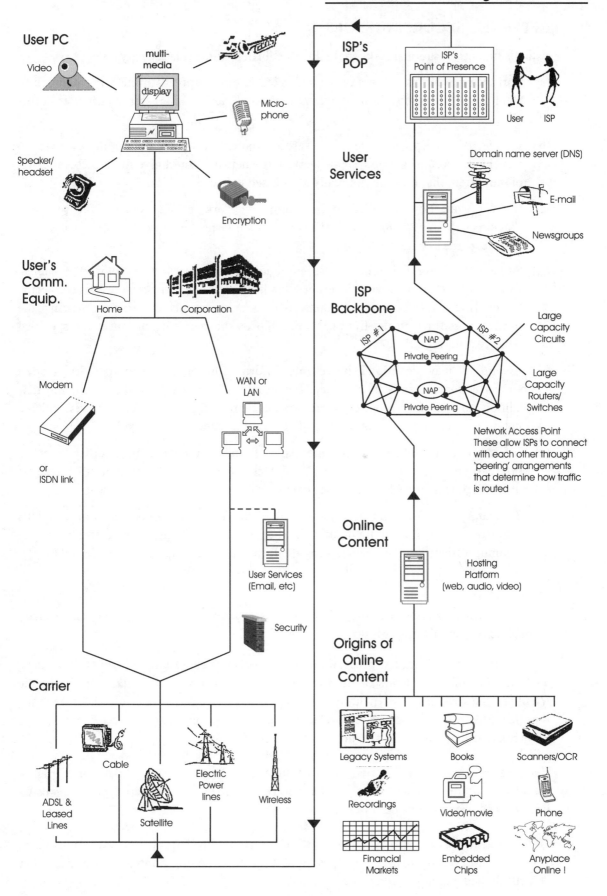

BPP PUBLISHING

2   INTERNET SECURITY ISSUES

2.1   Establishing organisational links to the Internet brings numerous security risks.

(a)   Corruptions such as **viruses** on a single computer can spread through the network to all of the organisation's computers. (Viruses are described at greater length later in this chapter.)

(b)   Disaffected employees have much greater potential to do **deliberate damage** to valuable corporate data or systems because the network could give them access to parts of the system that they are not really authorised to use.

(c)   If the organisation is linked to an external network, persons outside the company (**hackers**) may be able to get into the company's internal network, either to steal data or to damage the system.

Systems can have **firewalls** to prevent unauthorised access into company systems. Firewalls are used to prevent Internet users from accessing private networks connected to the Internet, especially intranets. All communications entering or leaving the intranet pass through the firewall, which blocks those that do not meet the specified security criteria.

(d)   Employees may **download inaccurate information** or imperfect or **virus-ridden software** from an external network. For example 'beta' versions of forthcoming new editions of many major packages are often available on the Internet. Beta versions are not fully tested and may contain bugs that could disrupt an entire system.

(e)   Information transmitted from one part of an organisation to another may be **intercepted**. Data can be 'encrypted' (scrambled) in an attempt to make it unintelligible to eavesdroppers. (See below.)

(f)   The communications link itself may break down. The worldwide telecommunications infrastructure is improving thanks to the use of new technologies, and there are communications 'protocols' governing the format of data and signals transferred.

Hacking

2.2   Hacking involves attempting to gain unauthorised access to a computer system, usually through telecommunications links.

2.3   Hackers require only limited programming knowledge to cause large amounts of damage. The fact that billions of bits of information can be transmitted in bulk over the public telephone network has made it **hard to trace** individual hackers, who can therefore make repeated attempts to invade systems. Hackers, in the past, have mainly been concerned to **copy** information, but a recent trend has been their desire to **corrupt it**.

2.4   Phone numbers and passwords can be guessed by hackers using **electronic phone directories** or number generators and by software which enables **rapid guessing** using hundreds of permutations per minute.

2.5   **Default passwords** are also available on some electronic bulletin boards and sophisticated hackers could even try to 'tap' messages being transmitted along phone wires (the number actually dialled will not be scrambled).

Viruses

> **KEY TERM**
>
> A **virus** is a piece of software which infects programs and data and possibly damages them, and which replicates itself.

2.6 Viruses need an **opportunity to spread**. The programmers of viruses therefore place viruses in the kind of software which is most likely to be copied. This includes:

(a) **Free software** (for example from the Internet).
(b) **Pirated software** (cheaper than original versions).
(c) **Games software** (wide appeal).
(d) **E-mail attachments** (often with instructions to send the message on to others).

2.7 The problem has been exacerbated by the portability of computers and disks and the increased availability and use of e-mail.

2.8 Whilst it is possible to disable floppy disk drives to prevent files entering the organisation via floppy disk, this can severely disrupt work processes. At the very least, organisations should ensure all files received via floppy disk and e-mail are virus checked.

2.9 Very new viruses may go undetected by anti-virus software (until the anti-virus software vendor updates their package - and the organisation installs the update). Two destructive viruses of recent times are:

- **Melissa** - which corrupts Microsoft Office documents
- **Love bug** – which attacks the operating system

2.10 Viruses can spread via floppy disk, but the most destructive viruses utilise e-mail links – **travelling as attachments to e-mail messages**. When the file attachment is opened or executed, the virus infects that system. Recent viruses have been programmed to send themselves to all addresses in the user's electronic address book.

Type of virus	Explanation/Example
File viruses	File viruses infect program files. When you run an infected program the virus runs first, then passes control to the original program. While it has control, the virus code copies itself to another file or to another disk, replicating itself.
Boot sector viruses	The boot sector is the part of every hard disk and diskette which is read by the computer when it starts up. If the boot sector is infected, the virus runs when the machine starts.
Overwriting viruses	An overwriting virus overwrites each file it infects with itself, so the program no longer functions. Since this is very easy to spot these viruses do not spread very well.
Worms	A worm is a program which spreads (usually) over network connections. It does not attach itself to a host program.
Dropper	A dropper is a program, not a virus itself, that installs a virus on the PC while performing another function.

BPP
PUBLISHING

Type of virus	Explanation/Example
Macro viruses	A macro virus is a piece of self-replicating code written in an application's 'macro' language. Many applications have macro capabilities including all the programs in **Microsoft Office**. The distinguishing factor which makes it possible to create a virus with a macro is the existence of **auto-execute events**. Auto-execute events are opening a file, closing a file, and starting an application. Once a macro is running, it can copy itself to other documents, delete files, and create general havoc. Melissa was a well publicised macro virus.

Encryption and other safety measures

2.11 **Encryption** aims to ensure the security of data during transmission. It involves the translation of data into secret code. To read an encrypted file, you must have access to a secret key or password that enables you to decrypt it. Unencrypted data is called plain text; encrypted data is referred to as cipher text.

KEY TERM

Encryption involves scrambling the data at one end of the line, transmitting the scrambled data, and unscrambling it at the receiver's end of the line.

2.12 **Authentication** is a technique of making sure that a message has come from an authorised sender. Authentication involves adding an extra field to a record, with the contents of this field derived from the remainder of the record by applying an algorithm that has previously been agreed between the senders and recipients of data.

2.13 Systems can have **firewalls** (which disable part of the telecoms technology) to prevent unwelcome intrusions into company systems, but a determined hacker may well be able to bypass even these.

2.14 **Dial-back security** operates by requiring the person wanting access to the network to dial into it and identify themselves first. The system then dials the person back on their authorised number before allowing them access.

2.15 All attempted **violations of security** should be automatically **logged** and the log checked regularly. In a multi-user system, the terminal attempting the violation may be automatically disconnected.

Case example

Love bug virus creates worldwide chaos

A computer virus which exploits office workers' yearnings for love shut down computer systems from Hong Kong to the Houses of Parliament yesterday and caused untold millions of pounds worth of delays and damage to stored files across the world. The virus, nicknamed 'the love bug' and 'the killer from Manila' after its apparent Philippine origins, is **carried in an e-mail** with the heading 'ILOVEYOU'. The text of the message reads: 'Kindly check the attached love letter from me!' A **click on the attached file launches the virus**, which promptly spreads by sending itself to everyone in the recipient's e-mail address book, overloading e-mail systems.

Once embedded in a host computer, the virus can download more dangerous software from a remote website, rename files and redirect Internet browsers. 'It's a very effective virus. It's one of the most aggressive and nastiest I've ever seen,' said Kieran Fitzsimmons of MessageLabs, which screens millions of company e-mails for viruses. 'It manifests itself almost everywhere in the computer.' One tenth of the world's mail servers were down as a result of the love bug, he said. Estimates suggested that between 10% and 30% of UK businesses were hit.

IT specialists described the love bug as '**a visual basic worm**' far **more dangerous** and fast-spreading than the similar **Melissa virus, which also replicated itself by e-mail**. Melissa infected about a million computers and caused £50m of damage. ILOVEYOU is eight times bigger, sends itself to everyone in a recipient's address book instead of just the first 50 (and then deletes the address book), and, unlike Melissa, **tampers with operating systems**.

Last night a virus tracker, TrendMicro, was reporting more than 800,000 infected files around the world. One expert said the love bug spread 'like wild fire' in Britain after 11.30am. 'It's taking out computers right, left and centre,' he said.

The Guardian May 5, 2000

Trojans

2.16 A Trojan or Trojan Horse is a program intended to perform some covert and usually malicious act which the victim did not expect or want. It differs from a virus in that it doesn't reproduce (though this distinction is by no means universally accepted).

  (a) A **logic bomb** is a type of trojan that is triggered by certain events. A program will behave normally until a certain event occurs, for example when disk utilisation reaches a certain percentage.

  (b) A **time bomb** is triggered at a certain time or date such as April 1 or Friday 13th.

Jokes and hoaxes

2.17 Some messages or programs falsely claim to warn you of something destructive happening (or going to happen) to your system. For example, a message may appear suggesting that your hard disk is about to be reformatted.

2.18 There are a number of common hoaxes, the most common of these is **Good Times**. This hoax has been around for a few years, and usually takes the form of a virus warning about viruses contained in e-mail. People pass along the warning because they are trying to be helpful, but they are wasting the time of all concerned.

2.19 The security issues surrounding e-commerce, particularly regarding making payment over the Internet are covered later in this chapter.

3 ELECTRONIC COMMERCE   5/02

> **KEY TERM**
>
> **Electronic commerce** means conducting business electronically via a communications link.

3.1 An older technology that is covered under the electronic commerce umbrella is Electronic Data Interchange (EDI).

Electronic Data Interchange (EDI)

3.2 EDI is a form of computer-to-computer data transfer. For instance instead of sending a customer a paper invoice through the post the data is sent over telecommunications links. This offers savings and **benefits** to organisations that use it.

(a) It reduces the **delays** caused by postal paper chains.

(b) It avoids the need to **re-key** data and therefore saves time and reduces errors.

(c) It provides the opportunity to reduce administrative **costs** eg the costs associated with the creation, recording and storage of paper documents.

(d) It facilitates shorter **lead times** and reduced stock holdings which allow reductions in working capital requirements (eg Just-In-Time policies).

(e) It provides the opportunity to improve **customer service**.

3.3 The general concept of having one computer talk directly to another might seem straightforward enough in principle, but **difficulties** may arise.

(a) Businesses hold records in computer files to their own **file structure** specifications. A translation mechanism may be required to allow transfer between the systems.

(b) The problem of **compatibility** between different makes or types of computer was a serious one in the past, and some form of interface between the computers had to be devised to enable data interchange to take place.

(c) Businesses often work to differing **time** schedules and time-zones. Organisations may conduct system maintenance late at night thinking this will not affect business. However, an overseas company in a different time zone, may need to access the system.

(d) As the number of trading partners grows the number of one-to-one links eventually becomes **unmanageable**.

E-commerce and the web

3.4 Over the last few years, electronic commerce or **e-commerce** has increasingly been used to describe the use of the Internet and websites in the sale of products or services. A simple definition is that 'e-commerce is the process of trading on the Internet'.

3.5 The Internet allows businesses to reach potentially millions of consumers worldwide and extends trading time to seven days, around the clock. Electronic commerce worldwide is valued at US$12 billion, and is set to reach US$350-500 billion by 2002. The OECD forecasts global e-commerce to be worth $1 trillion by 2003-05.

3.6 An e-business **start-up** has a considerable advantage over more established companies working in the same business area, because it does not have to take existing systems into account. This gives the start-up the agility and flexibility to launch new services far more quickly and cheaply than established rivals.

3.7 For established companies e-commerce reduces expensive sales and distribution workforces, and offers new marketing opportunities.

Distribution

3.8 The Internet can be used to get certain products **directly into people's homes**. Anything that can be converted into **digital form** can simply be uploaded onto the seller's site and then **downloaded** onto the customer's PC at home. The Internet thus offers huge opportunities to producers of text, graphics/video, and sound-based products. Much computer software is now distributed in this way.

Electronic marketing

3.9 Besides its usefulness for tapping into worldwide information resources businesses are also using it to **provide information** about their own products and services.

3.10 For **customers** the Internet offers a **speedy and impersonal** way of getting to know about the services that a company provides. For **businesses** the advantage is that it is much cheaper to provide the information in electronic form than it would be to employ staff to man the phones on an enquiry desk, and much more effective than sending out mailshots that people would either throw away or forget about when they needed the information.

3.11 Companies will need to develop new means of promoting their wares through the medium of the Internet, as opposed to shop displays or motionless graphics. Websites can provide **sound and movement** and allow **interactivity**, so that the user can, say, drill down to obtain further information or watch a video of the product in use, or get a virtual reality experience of the product or service.

3.12 For many companies this will involve a rethink of current promotional activity.

Case example

Peapod.com is an online supermarket and one of the more sophisticated recorders and users of customers' personal data and shopping behaviour. With over 200,000 customers in various US cities, Peapod's website sells groceries that are then delivered to customer's homes. a list of previous purchases (including brand, pack size and quantity purchased) is kept on the site, so the customer can make minor changes from week to week, saving time and effort.

Peapod creates a database on each shopper that includes their purchase history (what they bought), their online shopping patterns (how they bought it), questionnaires about their attitudes and opinions, and demographic data (which Peapod buys from third parties). A shopper's profile is used by the company to determine which advertisement to show and which promotions/electronic coupons to offer. Demographically identical neighbours are thus treated differently based on what Peapod has learned about their preferences and behaviours over time.

Shoppers seem to like this high-tech relationship marketing, with 94% of all sales coming from repeat customers. Manufacturers like it too. the more detailed customer information enables them to target promotions at customers who have repeatedly bought another brand, thereby not giving away promotion dollars to loyal customers.

Collecting information about customers

3.13 People who visit a site for the first time may be asked to **register**, which typically involves giving a name, physical address and post code, e-mail address and possibly other demographic data such as age, job title and income bracket.

3.14 When customers come to the site on subsequent occasions they either type their (self-chosen) username and password or more usually now, if they are using the same computer, the website recognises them using a **cookie**, which is a small and **harmless** file containing a string of characters that uniquely identify the computer.

3.15 From the initial registration details the user record may show, say, that the user is male, aged 20 to 30 and British. The **website can respond** to this by displaying products or services likely to appeal to this segment of the market.

Clickstreams

3.16 As users visit the site more often, more is learned about them by **recording what they click on,** since this shows what they are really interested in. On a news site for instance, one user may always go to the sports pages first, while another looks at the TV listings. In a retail sense this is akin to physically following somebody about the store recording everything they do (including products they pick up and put back) and everything they look at, whether or not they buy it.

Virtual companies and virtual supply chains (VSC)

> ### KEY TERMS
>
> A **virtual company** is a collection of separate companies, each with a specific expertise, who work together, sharing their expertise to compete for bigger contracts/projects than would be possible if they worked alone.
>
> A traditional **supply chain** is made up of the physical entities linked together to facilitate the supply of goods and services to the final consumer.
>
> A **Virtual Supply Chain (VSC)** is a supply chain that is enabled through e-business links (eg the web, extranets or EDI).

3.17 The **virtual company** concept has been around since the mid-1990s. Initially, companies attempted to work together using fax and phone links. The concept only really became a reality when technology such as extranets came into common usage. Companies are now able to work together and exchange information on-line. For example, engineers from five companies could design a product together on the Internet.

3.18 Many companies have become, or are becoming, more 'virtual'. They are developing into looser affiliations of companies, organised as a supply network.

3.19 Virtual Supply Chain networks have two types of organisation: producers and integrators.

    (a) **Producers** produce goods and services. They have core competencies in production schedule execution. Producers must focus on delivery to schedule and within cost. The sales driver within these companies is on ensuring that their capacity is fully sold through their networking with co-ordinators. Producer are often servicing multiple chains, so managing and avoiding capacity and commercial conflicts becomes key.

    (b) **Integrators** manage the supply network and effectively 'own' the end customer contact. The focus of the integrating firms is on managing the end customer relationship. Their core competence is in integrating and controlling the response of the company to customer requirements. This includes the difficult task of synchronising the responses and performance of multi-tiered networks, where the leverage of direct ownership is no longer available, and of often outsourced services such as warehousing and delivery.

3.20 Many of the most popular Internet companies are integrators in virtual company's eg Amazon.com and Lastminute.com. These organisations 'own' customer contact and manage customer relationships for a range of producers.

How does the Internet and e-commerce challenge traditional business thinking?

3.21 There are several features of the Internet which make it radically different from what has gone before.

(a) It **challenges traditional business models** - because, for example, it enables product/service suppliers to interact directly with their customers, instead of using intermediaries (like retail shops, travel agents, insurance brokers, and conventional banks).

(b) Although the Internet is global in its operation, its benefits are not confined to large (or global) organisations. **Small companies** can move instantly into a global market place, either on their own initiative or as part of what is known as a 'consumer portal'. For example, Ede and Ravenscroft is a small outfitting and tailoring business in Oxford: it could easily promote itself within a much larger 'portal' called OxfordHighStreet.com, embracing a comprehensive mixture of other Oxford retailers.

(c) It offers a **new economics of information** - because, with the Internet, much information is free. Those with Internet access can view all the world's major newspapers and periodicals without charge.

(d) It supplies an almost incredible **level of speed** - virtually instant access to organisations, plus the capacity to complete purchasing transactions within seconds. This velocity, of course, is only truly impressive if it is accompanied by equal speed so far as the delivery of tangible goods is concerned.

(e) It has created **new networks of communication** - between organisations and their customers (either individually or collectively), between customers themselves (through mutual support groups), and between organisations and their suppliers.

(f) It stimulates the appearance of **new intermediaries** and the disappearance of some existing ones. Businesses are finding that they can cut out the middle man, with electronic banking, insurance, publishing and printing as primary examples.

(g) It has led to **new business partnerships** through which small enterprises can gain access to customers on a scale which would have been viewed as impossible a few years ago. For example, a university can put its reading list on a website and students wishing to purchase any given book can click directly through to an on-line bookseller such as Amazon.com. The university gets a commission; the on-line bookseller gets increased business; the student gets a discount. Everyone benefits except the traditional bookshop.

(h) It promotes **transparent pricing** - because potential customers can readily compare prices not only from suppliers within any given country, but also from suppliers across the world.

(i) It facilitates **personalised attention** - even if such attention is actually administered through impersonal, yet highly sophisticated IT systems and customer database manipulation.

(j) It provides sophisticated **market segmentation** opportunities. Approaching such segments may be one of the few ways in which e-commerce entrepreneurs can create **competitive advantage**. As **Management Today** (March 2000) puts it:

'The starting point must be a neat niche, a funky few, a global tribe. You need to understand your particular tribe better than anyone else. The tribe is the basic unit of business... The good news is that there are lots of tribes out there - and some are enormous. It's just a question of identifying them, understanding them and meeting their needs better than anyone else.'

(k) The web can either be a **separate** or a **complementary** channel.

(l) A new phenomenon is emerging called **dynamic pricing**. Companies can rapidly change their prices to reflect the current state of demand and supply.

3.22 These new trends are creating **pressure** for companies. The main threat facing companies is that **prices will be driven down by consumers' ability to shop around.**

Case example

(1) Airlines

The impact of the web is seen clearly in the transportation industry. Airlines now have a more effective way of bypassing intermediaries (ie travel agents) because they can give their customers immediate access to flight reservation systems. British Airways aims to sell at least half of its tickets on-line by the year 2003; one of the new low-cost airlines in the UK, EasyJet, has become the first airline to have over half of its bookings made on-line.

(2) Travel agents

The web has also produced a new set of on-line travel agents who have lower costs because of their ability to operate without a High Street branch network. Their low-cost structure makes them a particularly good choice for selling low margin, cheap tickets for flights, package holidays, cruises and so forth.

These low-cost travel agents have been joined, furthermore, by non-travel-agents who simply specialise in opportunistic purchasing (eg lastminute.com).

(3) Tesco

In another arena, Tesco is already the UK's largest Internet grocery business, but other companies are rapidly developing new initiatives. Waitrose@work allows people to order their groceries in the morning (typically through their employer's Intranet communication system) and then have them delivered to the workplace in the afternoon: this approach achieves significant distribution economies of scale so far as Waitrose is concerned.

(4) Financial services

The impact of the Internet is especially profound in the field of financial services. New intermediaries enable prospective customers to compare the interest rates and prices charged by different organisations for pensions, mortgages and other financial services. This means that the delivering companies are losing control of the marketing of their services, and there is a downward pressure on prices, especially for services which can legitimately be seen as mere commodities (eg house and contents insurance).

Disadvantages of e-commerce

3.23 E-commerce involves an unusual mix of people – security people, web technology people, designers, marketing people – and this can be very difficult to manage. The e-business needs supervision by expensive specialists.

3.24 In spite of phenomenal growth the market is still fuzzy and undefined. Many e-businesses have only recently reported making any **profit**, the best-known example being **Amazon.com** the Internet book-seller.

3.25 Unless the e-business is one started completely from scratch, any new technology installed will **need to link up with existing business systems,** which could potentially take years of programming. Under-estimating the time and effort involved is a common obstacle.

3.26 The international availability of a website means that the laws of all countries that transactions may be conducted from have to be considered. The legal issues surrounding e-commerce are complex and still developing.

Lack of trust

3.27 Above all, however, the problem with e-commerce is one of **trust**. In most cultures, consumers grant their trust to business parties that have a close **physical presence**: buildings, facilities and people to talk to. On the Internet these familiar elements are simply not there. The seller's reputation, the size of his business, and the level of customisation in product and service also engender trust.

3.28 Internet merchants need to elicit consumer trust when the level of **perceived risk** in a transaction is high. However, research has found that once consumers have built up trust in an Internet merchant such concerns are reduced.

3.29 Internet merchants need to address issues such as fear of **invasion of privacy** and abuse of customer information (about their **credit cards**, for example) because they stop people even considering the Internet as a shopping medium.

Cryptography, keys and signatures

3.30 The parties involved in e-commerce need to have confidence that any communication sent gets to its target destination **unchanged**, and **without being read by anyone else**.

3.31 One way of providing electronic signatures is to make use of what is known as **public key** (or asymmetric) **cryptography.** Public key cryptography uses **two keys – public and private**. The **private key** is only known to its owner, and is used to scramble the data contained in a file.

3.32 The 'scrambled' data is the electronic signature, and can be checked against the original file using the **public key** of the person who signed it. This confirms that it could only have been signed by someone with access to the private key. If a third party altered the message, the fact that they had done so would be easily detectable.

3.33 An alternative is the use of encryption products which support **key recovery,** also known as **key encapsulation.** Such commercial encryption products can incorporate the public key of an agent known as a **Key Recovery Agent (KRA).** This allows the user to recover their (stored or communicated) data by approaching the KRA with an encrypted portion of the message. In both cases the KRA neither holds the user's private keys, nor has access to the plain text of their data.

Case example

E-commerce dangers and benefits

For some the Internet is a necessary evil - others browse and surf the net with that obsessive drive that is peculiar to any new technology. But the Internet is not just any new technology. It is the most important communications development since the advent of the telephone, and like the telephone it has created its own culture and given birth to new businesses and new possibilities.

Early confusion about the Internet meant that many companies came to us having built their own websites after learning the rudiments of HTML. They had registered their company name and done everything by the book. The website went on-line and they all waited with baited breath. Nothing happened. No new business arrived and nothing changed, and they couldn't understand why.

E-commerce is a tidal wave; if you choose to participate you either 'sink or swim'. You must be daring enough in design to achieve something quite different from the ways things have been done in the past.

A website is a shopfront that must be located in the centre of town in the full gaze of everyone. A good one can make a small business as powerful and competitive as some of the largest players. It just needs flair and commitment to succeed. But to do so there are some measures that must be used. Marketing outside the web, in the press or even on the radio can alert the market to the website. The site itself should be properly identified by name, registered competently with the appropriate search engines and it must look good.

> **WEBSITE ESSENTIALS**
>
> - Integration with all company systems (ie back office)
> - Speedy implementation
> - Quick and easy updating by own staff to retain topicality
> - Self producing audit records
> - Promotion via the internet
> - Press and PR for website
> - Attractive design but appropriate for the web
> - Scope to interact with visitors
> - Planned structure to include profitable business concept
> - Control and maintenance by owner, without developer involvement

The appearance of a website is extremely important. Attractive and easy to fill interactive forms can lure a sales prospect into being a buyer. One has seconds in which to achieve this end. Too many graphics slow down the procedure. The experience of visiting and browsing through the shop and responding to the goods on offer must be clever, intriguing, quick and efficient. Millions of pounds worth of business is lost on the Internet every day as a result of so-called interactive websites that are difficult to operate and dull.

The **key to success**, and the true working system is to be found in the **back office**. This invisible component is frequently overlooked. You can have the most seductive website in the world, but without a robust, secure, integrated back office system it's worth nothing. The website designer makes the shop window look good but cannot be expected to address the back office system.

Installing e-commerce can bring about overall improvements in accounting and management systems across the board. One bookseller never realised that he had fundamental problems in terms of dispatching stock and warehouse management. This is now being solved by the introduction of an integrated website that will interact with his financial and accounting system.

There are so many new possibilities and ventures created by this new technology, and the most inspired e-commerce enterprises will empower small and medium sized concerns to compete as never before.

Adapted from Management Accounting, February 2000

Customer service on the web

3.34 Effective, competent and acceptable customer service through the web is a combination of the following factors:

(a) **Rapid response time**. If the website is not fast, the transient potential shopper will simply click on to another. These 'fickle' visitors to a website will only allow around five to eight seconds: if the site has not captured their attention in that time-frame, they will move elsewhere.

(b) **Response quality**. The website must be legible, with appropriate graphics and meaningful, relevant information supplied. Generally speaking, website visitors are not interested in the company's history and size: they are much more concerned about what the company can offer them.

(c) **Navigability**. It is important to create a website which caters for every conceivable customer interest and question. Headings and category-titles should be straightforward and meaningful, not obscure and ambiguous.

(d) **Download times**. Again, these need to be rapid, given that many Internet shoppers regard themselves (rightly or otherwise) as cash-rich and time-poor.

(e) **Security/Trust**. One of the biggest barriers to the willingness of potential Internet customers actually to finalise a transaction is their fear that information they provide about themselves (such as credit card details) can be 'stolen' or used as the basis for fraud.

(f) **Fulfilment**. Customers must believe that if they order goods and services, the items in question will arrive, and will do so within acceptable time limits (which will generally be much faster than the time limits normally associated with conventional mail order). Equally, customers need to be convinced that if there is a subsequent need for service recovery, then speedy and efficient responses can be secured either to rectify the matter or to enable unsatisfactory goods to be returned without penalty.

(g) **Up-to-date**. Just as window displays need to be constantly refreshed, so do websites require frequent repackaging and redesign.

(h) **Availability**. Can the user reach the site 24 hours a day, seven days a week? Is the down-time minimal? Can the site always be accessed?

(i) **Site effectiveness and functionality**. Is the web site intuitive and easy to use? Is the content written in a language which will be meaningful even to the first-time browser (ie the potential customer)?

Question 1

Up to now, many companies have ignored e-commerce. They have watched as a succession of much-publicised ventures have failed to get off the ground and even the best have struggled to translate success into profits. This has created an impression that the Internet is a confusing and dangerous sales channel that can, for now, be left to others.

Why, do you think, is this view increasingly untenable?

Answer

Relevant points include:

(a) The likely scale and speed of development is immense: by the end of 2002, Internet business between, for example, US businesses, is thought likely to exceed $300bn, rising from only $4.5bn in 1997.

(b) Every part of the value chain is up for grabs. Any participant in the value chain could usurp the role of any other participant.

    (i) The free flow of information about buyers and sellers undermines the role of intermediaries.

    (ii) A book publisher could bypass retailers or distributors and sell directly.

    (iii) A book seller could decide to publish books, based on the information it has obtained about readers' interests.

3.35 Net pioneers can secure important advantages over latecomers. They can use information about their customers to tailor their offerings and they may even be able to foster a sense of community among users. For example, part of the appeal of Amazon.co.uk (the Internet bookseller) is the book reviews posted by other readers.

4 DEVELOPING A STRATEGY FOR THE INTERNET AND E-COMMERCE

Pilot paper, 5/01, 11/01, 5/02

4.1 Four broad approaches a company may adopt towards the Internet are:

(a) Do not sell products through the Internet at all, and if distribution is conducted through resellers, prevent them from doing so. Provide only product **information** on the Internet. This may be an appropriate strategy where products are **large, complex and highly customised,** such as aircraft manufacturing.

(b) **Leave the Internet business to resellers** and do not sell directly through the Internet (ie do not compete with resellers). This can be appropriate, for instance, where manufacturers have already assigned exclusive territories to resellers.

(c) The manufacturer can **restrict Internet sales exclusively to itself.** The problem with this is that most large manufacturers do not have systems that are geared to dealing with sales to end users who place numerous, irregular small orders.

(d) Open up Internet sales to everybody and **let the market decide** who it prefers to buy from.

4.2 On a more detailed level, in an article for *IT Consultancy* magazine, *Laurence Holt* offered 18 potential strategies for e-commerce.

Strategy	Comment
Outsource to your customers	What do we do for our customers that they would rather do for themselves and could probably do better? Examples: *www.cisco.com, www.dell.com.*
Cannibalise your own business	If there were an Amazon.com in our market, what would it be doing? Examples: *www.egghead.com.*
Host your competitors	How can we create a marketplace that includes our competitors, but that we own? Examples: *www.sabre.com, www.jewellery.com.*
Build one-to-one customer relationships	How can we make each customer feel that we built our organisation just for them? Examples: *www.My.yahoo.com, www.firefly.com, www.netgrocer.com.*
Make first contact	What is the first step our customers take in the chain of events that leads them to buy from us? How can we make contact with them? Examples: *www.autobytel.com.*
Be a process integrator	What other things do customers need or do when they buy from us? Examples: *www.autobytel.com.*
Catch rites of passage	What major life changes are customers going through when they come into contact with us? How can we help? Examples: *www.usnews.com, www.citibank.com.*
Create a community	What interests do our customers share? How can we create a place that people with those interests will keep coming back to? Examples: *www.yahoo.com.*
Create a niche portal	How can we make our site the portal our customers go to first? Examples: *www.ft.com.*
Pirate your value chain	How can we take over the roles of others in our value chain? Examples: *www.dell.com.*
Re-intermediate on information value	How can we boost the value we add through information? Examples: *www.britannica.com.*

Strategy	Comment
Go pure cyberspace	What if we made the digital world our first priority and the physical world second? Examples: *www.tiscali.com*.
Be a fast follower	What are our competitors doing that looks likely to be successful? How can we do the same thing faster? Examples: *www.barnesandnoble.com*.
Think dream not transaction	What dream do our customers start with that leads them to buy from us? How can we realise that dream? Examples: *www.expedia.com*.
Beat the physical world	What can we do in the digital world that would be impossible or not feasible in the physical world? Examples: *www.benjerry.com*.
Leverage the froth	What simple ideas would capture most media and public attention, even if short-lived? Examples: *www.travelocity.com*, *www.lastminute.com*.
Change the pricing model	Would our customers benefit from a different way of pricing, perhaps micro-payments or auctions? Examples: *www.priceline.com*.
Convert atoms to bits	What physical world core competencies do we have that could be applied to the digital world? Examples: *www.ups.com*.

4.3 If the decision is made to enter into e-commerce, an e-business venture needs **support and long-term commitment from high-level management**. Ideally such a project should be 'sponsored' by the chief executive or a board-level director.

Guidelines for establishing an Internet sales/marketing capability

4.4 An organisation's sales/marketing Internet capability may, at the outset, solely **dispense information** (operating like a product catalogue), but may eventually become **transactional** (so that individuals can place orders) and/or **interactive** (dealing with queries, complaints and other kinds of customer communications).

The context

4.5 To put these guidelines into context, a survey in 2000 by Booz Allen & Hamilton and the Economist Intelligence Unit, involving 600 executives, sought views on the strategic significance of the Internet.

(a) 61 per cent believed the Internet would help them to achieve business goals.

(b) 30 per cent said the Internet had already forced them to overhaul their existing business strategies.

(c) On the other hand, only 28 per cent had generated income from the Internet.

4.6 The same survey highlighted seven **megatrends** which, coupled with the Internet, are changing the face of organisations:

(a) New **distribution channels**, revolutionising sales and brand management.

(b) The continued **shift of power** towards the consumer.

(c) **Growing competition** locally, nationally, internationally and globally.

(d) An acceleration in the **pace of business**.

(e) The **transformation of companies** into 'extended enterprises' involving 'virtual teams of business, customer and supplier' working in collaborative partnerships.

(f)   A re-evaluation of how companies, their partners and competitors **add value** not only to themselves but in the wider environmental and social setting.

(g)   Recognition of **'knowledge'** as a strategic asset.

4.7   Most observers and experts agree that a successful strategy for e-commerce cannot simply be bolted on to existing processes, systems, delivery routes and business models. Instead, management groups have, in effect, to start again, by asking themselves such **fundamental questions** as:

(a)   What do customers want to buy from us?
(b)   What business should we be in?
(c)   What kind of partners might we need?
(d)   What categories of customer do we want to attract and retain?

4.8   In turn, organisations can visualise the necessary changes at three interconnected levels.

Level 1   The simple **introduction of new technology** to connect electronically with employees, customers and suppliers (eg through an intranet, extranet or website).

Level 2   **Re-organisation** of the workforce, processes, systems and strategy - in order to make best use of the new technology.

Level 3   **Re-positioning** of the organisation to fit it into the emerging e-economy.

4.9   So far, very few companies have gone beyond levels (1) and (2). Instead, pure Internet businesses such as Amazon.com and AOL have emerged from these new rules: unburdened by physical assets, their competitive advantage lies in knowledge management and customer relationships.

Ten key steps to constructing an effective strategy for e-commerce

Step 1. Upgrade customer interaction

4.10   The first thing for the organisation to do is to **upgrade the interaction with its existing customers**.

(a)   Create automated responses for the FAQs (Frequently Asked Questions) posed by customers, so that customers become conditioned to electronic communication. Automated responses, perhaps surprisingly in view of their impersonal nature, can help to improve customer confidence and trust.

(b)   Set fast response standards, at least to match anything offered by the competition.

(c)   Use e-mail in order to confirm actions, check understanding, and reassure the customer that their business is being taken forward.

(d)   Establish ease of navigation around your website and enhance the site's 'stickiness' so that there is a measurably reduced likelihood that actual or potential customers will migrate elsewhere.

4.11   A study conducted by Rubic Inc in the USA ('Evaluating the 'Sticky' Factor of E-Commerce Sites') found that the majority of websites fail to communicate effectively with customers. Only 40 per cent had a strategy of personalisation for their e-mail messages to customers; when customers responded to follow-up offers, only one quarter of websites recognised the fact that they were dealing with a repeat customer; 40 per cent of e-mail enquiries went unanswered despite promises of replies within two days.

Step 2. Understand customer segments

4.12 The organisation preparing its e-commerce strategy should **understand its customer segments** and classify each segment against the likelihood that it will be receptive to an Internet business route.

(a) Some will be eager to transfer to the new technology, others will do so if persuaded (or incentivised), and residual groups will prefer to remain as they are.

(b) Once the degree of profitability-per-customer has been established, efforts should be made to automate the provision of customer service and transaction capability so far as low-value customers are concerned.

(c) The organisation may establish personalised service relationships with key (ie high profit-generating) customers.

Step 3. Understand service processes

4.13 The organisation must **understand its customer service processes** in order to disentangle those processes which can safely be put on to the Web and those which have to be delivered in other ways.

(a) Typically, organisations serving customers may find that there are between five and ten generic transaction types which describe their relationships with these customers (eg information query, complaint, and so forth).

(b) This analysis is essential for addressing such questions as: Which of these processes is appropriate for automation? Which of these processes will work better, from the customer's standpoint, if put on the web?

(c) Transaction costs also need to be investigated, again from the perspective of the organisation and its overheads, and also taking into account the transaction costs incurred by the customer. These may involve money, but customers are often more conscious about time and timeliness. Getting on to the Internet takes longer than a telephone call (though this may not always be the case), so the customer, behaving rationally, will want more value from the process.

(d) On the other hand, a short simple transaction is often better conducted over the telephone.

Step 4. Define the role

4.14 The organisation needs to **define the role for live interaction with its customers**.

(a) Live interaction may be very useful if there is scope for cross-selling and the conversion of enquiries into sales.

(b) The availability of service supplied by human intervention can also be appropriate if the organisation needs to build trust (eg it is a new brand which must work hard to establish confidence) and secure diagnostic information from the customer before any product or service can be delivered.

(c) E-mail may not be sufficient as a communications route, especially if it involves a delay before replies or acknowledgements are forthcoming.

(d) Live interaction can be essential for customers who have a strong preference for human contact.

Step 5. Decide technology

4.15 **Making the key technology decisions** involves some tough choices. Given the pace of change and innovation in this arena, it is difficult to know whether to initiate a pilot programme immediately, with the full IT and people investment scheduled for later, or whether to go for full integration at once. The risk with a pilot programme is that the organisation can be overtaken by pioneering competitors; the risk with full integration is that new systems can be inadequate or may even collapse completely, causing irretrievable havoc with customers.

Step 6. Deal with the tidal wave

4.16 There is much evidence that offering an Internet-based service can lead to a major increase in customer interaction, and so organisations need to develop strategies for **dealing with the tidal wave**. This might involve:

(a) Ensuring sufficient capacity is available for worst-case scenarios.
(b) Using user-friendly technologies and system design.
(c) Setting targets for low-touch interaction.
(d) Ensuring facilities are scaleable if demand rapidly outstrips supply.

Step 7. Create incentives

4.17 The organisation may have to **create incentives for use of the lowest-cost channels**, with savings passed on the customer through discounts. The alternatives are:

(a) To create **incentives** to switch to the lowest-cost channels, through financial inducements, training and additional benefits.

(b) To introduce **disincentives** for continuing to use existing channels. Thus Abbey National has implemented a £5 charge for customers who pursue over-the-counter cash transactions in their branches. Such tactics almost invariably generate very hostile reactions from customers themselves and from consumer groups.

Step 8. Decide on channel choices

4.18 The eighth consideration involves the decision about **which channel choices to offer**, and whether, for instance, to confine operations to the 'click' route or whether to simultaneously maintain the 'brick' presence through a branch network. There are two crucial questions:

(a) **Whether to offer the customer a choice of channels**, eg face-to-face, post, phone and Internet. Many banks offer all four; some have single-channel accounts (phone or Internet only), whilst others (like **egg**) allow constrained choice: **egg** (the Internet and telephone banking arm of the Prudential Assurance Company) will allow telephone and Internet customer interaction, but only permits new customers to enrol via the web.

(b) **How to balance the costs of different channels whilst managing the Customer Relationship Management (CRM) database**. In most customer service environments, the quality and scope of the CRM database is central to the successful delivery of service, so it becomes desirable not to operate each customer-communication channel separately, but to integrate existing channels around a single CRM database.

(c) One reason why Charles Schwab (specialists in stock and share dealing) is able to charge much bigger fees than some of its rivals is that it combines an on-line service with a low-cost branch network and a telephone service. They have recognised the web has certain virtues and weaknesses. The web is lousy if you have a complex question. Likewise, it does not allow for people's need for relationships. Not everyone feels happy about sending a cheque to a broker they have never seen.

Step 9. Exploit the Internet

4.19 The organisation should **exploit the Internet in order to create new relationships and experience**.

(a) It is desirable to create **tailor-made service** sites for significant customers.

(b) Proactive **product/service offerings** should be regularly incorporated into the website architecture.

(c) **Communities of users** and/or customers (depending on whichever is appropriate) should be facilitated, since these generate additional business through referral and may well undertake a large proportion of the customer-service activity among themselves. Such communities may also stimulate product/service innovation, new uses for existing products and services, and product/service extensions.

(d) Deliberate mechanisms need to be developed in order to **turn browsers into buyers**, and transform one-off customers into repeat purchasers.

(e) Any successful e-commerce strategy presupposes the likelihood that the product/service supplier can engage the potential customer **emotionally** despite the technology which surrounds Internet availability.

4.20 It is necessary for the strategist to visualise the **extended experience** that customers encounter when they carry an Internet transaction through from initiation to completion. It is vital for organisations to place themselves in the shoes of customers and ask the question: what are our customers really buying? The answer, 99 times out of 100, is that customers are buying benefits whilst companies are selling features. Further, if the transaction lacks any emotional commitment, then it also lacks any real likelihood of voluntary customer retention.

Step 10. Implement

4.21 No strategy is worth the paper is written on if it simply remains a document, gathering dust: as *Peter Drucker* once pointed out, 'Strategy is nothing until it degenerates into work'.

Important aspects of strategy implementation for e-commerce

4.22 **Organisation and culture**. When organisations move into an electronic age, some people (and functions) increase their corporate influence, whilst others move into the shadows. The increasing use of technology is unsettling, especially for senior people (ironically, employees lower down the hierarchy are likely to be much more comfortable about technological innovation). The Internet promotes freedom of information, both upwards and downwards; this, for some managers, is equated with a loss of authority.

4.23 **Systems and infrastructure**. Implementation of e-commerce often requires integration of service systems, particularly call centres, the web, and CRM processes. This in turn may require a company to review its whole decision-making patterns and make some difficult choices about existing 'legacy' procedures.

4.24 **Training**. Effective e-commerce implementation requires both staff and customers to be trained. Dealing with electronic interaction demands different skills from those which are appropriate to staff who focus on voice communications. Dealing simultaneously with written and verbal interaction is likely to call for a new skill set.

4.25 **Looking to the customers**. This is well summarised by Mike Harris, Chief Executive of Egg, explaining the need to avoid rehearsed, scripted and bureaucratic approaches which give the impression that technology is driving the interaction rather than the need to relate to people.

4.26 Conventional thinking says that a company should pay no more to bring in a customer than the net present value of the stream of profits that the customer will subsequently generate. Yet in the e-commerce context, investors have often rewarded companies for customer acquisition without asking any questions about how quickly those customers may disappear.

4.27 Similar turbulence is affecting the B2B world. Traditional manufacturing companies around the world, sensing the potential benefits from automating transactions with suppliers and customers, have rushed into e-commerce. Many have formed alliances to create their own on-line market place, especially in the automobile, aerospace and chemicals industries. By pooling their buying power, the organisations behind these alliances hope to have more control over their activities - and this leaves the small, purely Internet-based commodity/component exchanges struggling to attract the volume of transactions needed to make them viable.

Case example

E-technology - fuelling or fooling customer strategies?

One of the most important challenges the modern enterprise has is to find ways to increase value from its customers, rather than from its products, so as to get long-lasting growth rather than short-term gains. Research and practice forcefully demonstrate that e-technology can facilitate this - but not if e-technology is simply used to cut costs in order to drive market share of core products or services and so perpetuate past strategies.

Increased and sustained growth from customers can only come to firms that know how to 'lock-in' their customers. This means customers want them as their dominant or sole choice because they get ongoing superior value at low cost.

Enterprises get this lifelong customer value when they push boundaries to create new 'market spaces' which link benefits otherwise separated by industry or companies providing users with results or outcomes rather than just what they happen to make, have in stock, or be promoting at a moment in time. Contrast for instance: cars v personal mobility; books v information and knowledge discovery; PCs v global networking capability; audio-visual equipment v integrated home 'edutainment' - to see the difference.

In new market spaces, working together with a network of partners, the object is to provide an integrated experience for customers over their activity cycles: 'pre' the experience, when customers are deciding what to do; 'during' the experience, when they are doing it, and 'post' the experience, when they are keeping it going, reviewing, updating, and renewing. If value gaps or discontinuities happen in the customer activity cycle, companies (even industries) become vulnerable: other players (usually outsiders) get in, build relationships and capture the new wealth. Which is what happened to IBM in the late 1980s and why Amazon took the book retailers by storm.

There are four levels for which e-technology is currently being used.

Level 1: Tell. At its most basic, the object here is to create presence on the web for customers who come to the site in search of information about the company and its products or services. The result is a website catalogue or brochure..

Level 2: Sell. Here the Internet is used as an alternative channel or tool to promote and sell a firm's wares on-line, typically what food retailers are doing, or alternatively to sell others' wares. The problem here is that the enterprise is playing the same game: frequently what is delivered is just what is kept in stock, and emphasis often goes to supply management to save costs. When combined with savings on conventional infrastructures, price competition is created - resulting in a commodity spiral which inevitably ends up in poor service where no-one gains, including customers.

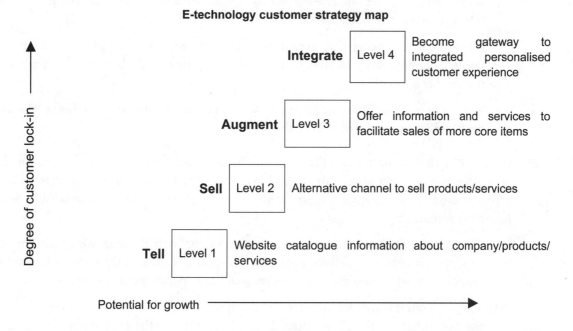

E-technology customer strategy map

Level 3: Augment. At a more advanced level, through e-technology a firm can offer information, choice or services like remote diagnostics, as Dyson Appliances is doing. But the goal is still transactional - sell more core items, either directly or through distributors or retailers. The offering is augmented to differentiate the company in order to get customer loyalty and retention, to increase transactions and decrease transactional costs. This is often accompanied by customer relationship management tools: using databases to learn about what customers buy, in what quantities, where, and how often, as well as promotional devices like loyalty cards, typical of banks and airlines, but all too easy to emulate. Such CRM approaches do not really consider who these customers are, or interact with them to deliver ongoing, superior, personalised value.

Level 4: Integrate. In order to achieve that value, we need to move to level 4 on the e-technology customer strategy map. Here the enterprise becomes the gateway to customers, providing them with an integrated experience across product, industry, company, country and even brand, over time - sometimes lifetime. Customer relationships are managed interactively in a highly personalised way so as to achieve the 'lock-in', which happens because the enterprise knows more about the customer than anyone else and uses this information and knowledge to build offerings which are proactive and precise.

The intangibles - ideas, information and knowledge - which become the key component of the offering - are easy to assimilate, codify and disseminate using e-technology. And while the internet is a mass medium, customers can be handled in a highly personalised way at extremely low, if not zero, marginal cost.

What protects the enterprise here is that, once Level 4 has been reached, customer lock-in becomes self-reinforcing: the more information and knowledge customers share with the firm, the more proactive and precise offerings become, the more customers lock-in, and the more ideas, information and knowledge they share.

With its powerful and pervasive effects, e-technology allows the enterprise to excel with customers in ways never before imagined. The e-technology strategy map may help managers position themselves and make better decisions so that e-technology can fuel, rather than fool, their customer strategy.

Strategy Magazine, May 2000

Building an investment case for e-commerce

4.28 There is still opposition in some organisations to the necessary investment required for e-commerce. Reasons for this opposition often include:

(a) Straightforward **resistance to change**, coupled with **fear of the unknown**. Even stories about Internet successes elsewhere may be viewed with caution on the grounds that they may not easily be transferable.

(b) Existence of the belief that even if new entrants were able to take advantage of the fashionable popularity of the Internet, others coming along behind - 'laggards' - will not be able to do so.

(c) The evidence that many 'dot.com' enterprises remain **unable to achieve sustained profitability** or indeed any profitability at all.

4.29 On the other hand, companies still experiencing doubts should put themselves in the shoes of a potential Internet competitor - and ask themselves: *How might they attack us?* The evidence from experience gained so far in the field of electronic commerce suggests the following scenarios:

(a) They would ignore the unattractive, expensive channels through which your product or service is currently delivered. If your business is banking, they will not establish a branch network; if you are a retailer, they will not operate a chain of shops.

(b) They will **cherry-pick** the more profitable customer segments. Again, if you are a bank, the new entrant will seek to entice away your credit-worthy customers with expensive tastes and unrestricted consumption habits.

(c) They will create highly **differentiated customer segments**, possibly customised for specific individuals. In other words, they will offer a degree of personalised attention which you may find difficult to match.

(d) They will deliberately choose to supply products and services where their presence on the World Wide Web will **add value** - both for themselves and for their customers.

(e) They will offer **shared services** - so that they operate, in effect, as a one-stop shop for, say, a whole repertoire of financial services or in-home entertainment products.

(f) They will capture **intermediary roles** - and benefit from the savings because their costs will not include commission paid to travel agents.

(g) They can use the strength of their website as a **portal** - generating even more business for themselves through the provision of allied, complementary or even virtually identical services.

(h) They can create **affiliate programmes** - equipping them with the capacity for organising comprehensive options. Thus, for example, an on-line grocer may develop relationships with up-market catering companies which cook and serve meals for dinner parties in customers' own homes.

(i) They may **offer incentives** - in the form of reduced prices, discounts, cashback offers, lower interest rates, or higher investment returns. Some of these incentives may be tax-free if they are operated outside any given country's tax regime.

Case example

E-business and what it means for accountants

Electronic business refers to aspects of business being conducted electronically throughout the entire value chain. Figures suggest companies that have commenced trading electronically with their supplies are experiencing a 20% reduction in costs.

In today's business environment, organisations are looking for accountants to act as business partners in delivering value to shareholders, manage financial risks, while still maintaining financial control. We speculate that tomorrow's winners will be those companies that possess accountants who have full understanding of their industry's long-term growth patterns, corporate profiles, together with an understanding of the most appropriate business model(s) necessary to achieve corporate objectives.

E-business

Businesses around the world are on the verge of a revolution, as the web shifts the power from the firm to the customer. Products and services are now being purchased by consumers who are able to obtain more information, and thereby becoming more discerning.

The electronic communication revolution will mean that distance will no longer determine the price of communicating electronically. Adept use of e-commerce will become arguably the most important form of competitive advantage for businesses. It has the potential to create new business models and to find new ways of doing things. The benefits of e-commerce come not only from speeding up and automating a firm's internal processes but also from its ability to spread the benefits to other members of its supply chain.

E-business will eventually be deployed throughout an entire industry's supply chain, linking manufacturers, assemblers, distributors, marketers and customers. A single press of a button will trigger many processes throughout the chain. Table 1 provides a summary of the strategic implications of e-business. The provision of services will increasingly become more important than mere products. Web pages will deliver bespoke services, such as help for consumers in making their choices or stock management for business partners. Fixed prices will give way to reflect true market worth, and firms will join together to make convenient packages for the customer.

Table 1 Strategic implications for e-business

	E-commerce	Strategic implications
Communication	The falling costs and increases in capacity of communications	Death of distance. Virtual firms can become a reality.
Business model	The traditional business model is inappropriate for e-business.	Virtual organisations will be used to capture cost savings and overthrow established practices.
IT	Existing IT systems have not adequately dealt with the customer.	Traditional IT systems will have to complement the Internet.
E-revolution	Commoditisation will make it extremely difficult for firms to differentiate their products.	Need to refine and implement new e-business strategies.
Value	The finance function does not currently provide much added value in the current e-business environment.	Redesign traditional financial planning, control and evaluation techniques.

King and Clift assert that most businesses will migrate to e-business in four stages.

- *Website:* Organisations make their presence in e-business. Attempts will be made to integrate their site's buying and selling processes into the organisation's back office, customer and marketing systems.

- *Connect website to supply chain:* Involves connecting the web site's capabilities to supply chains. For example, it is anticipated that the reduction in paperwork will reduce costs.

- *Form alliances:* Alliances will be formed to operationalise the new business model. Electronic share dealing on the internet is an example of this.

- *Industrial convergence:* E-business makes it possible for industries to combine expertise and produce package solutions.

The massive scale changes taking place in global markets now make it imperative that organisations (private and public sector) fully understand the business applications of e-commerce and are able to formulate, implement and evaluate corporate, business and operational strategies. We speculate whether accountants are well positing to influence strategic direction in these e-business times.

The e-business accountant: fact or fiction?

It is interesting to note that, despite budgetary control being the genesis of strategic management, accountants still focus on budgets for strategic planning.

This has been highlighted by Gluek *et al*, who observed four phases of strategic management. This has been echoed by Phillips and Moutinho, who, applying Gluek *et al*'s model to the service sector, see the evolution of strategic management consisting of our phases: first, budgetary control, where the main focus is the setting and achievement of budgets; second, long-range planning, which focuses on medium-term forecasting; third, strategic planning, where the main emphasis is to think strategically; and then, strategic management, where there is an attempt to alter and create the future for the organisation. Moreover, in the age of one-to-one relationship marketing, e-business has now arguably helped to create a fifth phase, which involves understanding customer needs and customer values.

Table 2 Evolution of strategic management

Phase I	Phase II	Phase III	Phase IV
Budgetary control	Long-range planning	Strategic planning	Strategic management
Operational control	Planning for growth	Strategic control at HQ	Strategic control at SBU
Annual budget	Extrapolation of budgets	Strategic plans	Implementation barrier
Internal focus	External focus	Systematic external audit	Suitable planning framework
Attain budget	Forward planning	Strategic vision	Competitive advantage

For many accountants, e-business requires new skills and a fresh mindset. A single push of a button means that e-commerce can operate in real time. We speculate that the challenge for accountants is to provide timely and meaningful information through strategic financial analysis which support their firm's decision to invest in e-business.

Pitturro highlights three critical areas that impact the effectiveness of the e-business accountant:

- The cost of the investment in e-commerce can be hard to evaluate, and costs can escalate as the technology is implemented.

- Accountants should weigh the costs, risks and benefits of e-commerce investments.

- Accountants should integrate e-commerce financial planning with IT and other functional processes.

According to Ray Lane, president and chief operating officer of Oracle, the economic structure of companies is changing. Existing financial statements can cope with physical assets. However, they cannot cope with intellectual capital or knowledge, which is the difference between real tangible value and market value. Lane asserts that the real value of a company in the future will be how fast information can be gathered throughout the world, analysed, have value added to it, and then be redistributed back into the value chain. The faster the cycle, the more value that is added to the company.

Many organisations still believe that e-business can be ignored until it is more fully developed. However, according to recent research, e-business will become commonplace, in years, rather than decades, which may be too late for the current non-adopters or those companies that are unable to design and implement the business models adopted by companies like Cisco.

Adapted from *Management Accounting*, February 2000

Chapter roundup

- The **Internet** is a global network linking millions of computers. The World Wide Web (**WWW**) is a system of Internet servers that support specially formatted documents. A group of documents accessed from the same base web address is known as a **website**.

- Most organisations now have a **website**, and some conduct **transactions** over the Internet.

- The major growth of **e-commerce** so far has been in the Business to Business (B2B) sector.

- The Internet provides opportunities to **automate tasks** which would previously have required human intervention.

- Establishing links to the Internet brings **security risks**. Suitable systems, policies and procedures should be implemented to minimise these risks.

- **Hacking** involves attempting to gain unauthorised access to a computer system, usually through telecommunications links. A **virus** is a piece of software which infects programs and data and possibly damages them, and which replicates itself. Viruses often use e-mail links to spread.

- **Encryption** aims to ensure the security of data during transmission. Encryption involves scrambling the data at one end of the line, transmitting the scrambled data, and unscrambling it at the receiver's end of the line.

- **Firewalls** are used to prevent Internet users from accessing private networks connected to the Internet, especially intranets. All communications entering or leaving the intranet pass through the firewall, which blocks those that do not meet the specified security criteria.

- **Electronic commerce** means conducting business electronically via a communications link. An older technology that is covered under the electronic commerce umbrella is **Electronic Data Interchange** (EDI).

- The Internet and e-commerce **challenges traditional business models**.

- Ensuring **'back-office' operations complement web-based operations** is vital.

- When developing **a strategy for e-commerce** consider:

  ○ Organisation and culture
  ○ Systems and infrastructure
  ○ Training
  ○ Customers

Quick quiz

1   List five current uses of the Internet.

1   ENTERTAINMENT ✓
2   COLLECT INFORMATION / GOV ✓
3   TRADE ✓
4   COMMUNICATE ✓
5   SEARCH EG JOBS ✓

2   List five tasks typically automated by a website.

1   DOWNLOAD
2   TRANSFER / SEND
3   LINK
4   OPEN / CLOSE
5   FAQ's

3   How do ISDN and ADSL technologies improve Internet efficiency?

- FASTER TRANSFER OF DATA,

BPP
PUBLISHING

4 Distinguish between encryption and authentication. *SCRAMBLING DATA / ALLOWSED*

5 What is a virus? *MANMADE PROGRAM WITH INTENT TO CORRUPT/DELETE/DAMAGE DATA OR DOS.*

6 Define the term 'virtual supply chain'. *VIA E-BUSINESS*

7 List five ways in which the Internet and e-commerce differ from normal business practices.

1 *RESPONSE TIME*

2 *SWITCHING SUPPLER*

3 *WIDER RANGE OF GOODS*

4 *NO MIDDLE MAN*

5 *ALL SIZES*

8 An organisation's reaction to the opportunities offered by e-commerce may be classified into one of three levels. What are these levels?

Answers to quick quiz

1 [Five of]
Dissemination of information
Product/service development (test marketing)
Transaction processing (B2B and B2C)
Relationship enhancement
Recruitment and job search
Entertainment

2 Frequently-Asked-Questions, order status checking, keyword search, interview style information gathering, e-mail, bulletin boards and requests for personal contact.

3 Through allowing faster transfer of data.

4 Encryption involves scrambling and unscrambling data to prevent unauthorised 'eavesdroppers' obtaining useful data. Authentication ensures a message has come from an authorised sender.

5 A small program that infects systems and possibly damages them.

6 A virtual supply chain (VSC) is a supply chain that is enabled through e-business links such as websites, extranets or EDI.

7 It challenges traditional business models.
Benefits are available to organisations of all sizes.
It challenges the need to pay for some information.
It encourages speed of product/service delivery.
It creates new communication networks and business alliances.

8 Level 1 - the simple introduction of a website, intranet or extranet.

Level 2 - reorganise the workforce, processes, systems and strategy to best utilise the new technology.

Level 3 - reposition the company to enable it to best fit into the emerging e-economy.

Questions to try	Level	Marks	Time
13	Examination	25	45 mins
16	Examination	25	45 mins

Part C
Planning and implementing IS/IT strategies

Chapter 6

PLANNING AND IMPLEMENTING INFORMATION STRATEGIES

Topic list		Syllabus reference	Ability required
1	Developing an information technology plan	(iii)	Analysis
2	Phases involved in establishing the IT plan	(iii)	Analysis
3	The systems development life-cycle	(iii)	Evaluation
4	Other system building tools and techniques	(iii)	Evaluation

Introduction

In this chapter we explore the main considerations when **devising** or **analysing information strategies**.

The second part of the chapter includes an overview of the **systems development life-cycle** and other **system development tools and techniques**. In particular, we examine how **users** and other non-technical staff are included in the planning and implementation process.

Learning outcomes covered in this chapter

- **Analyse** the contents of IS, IT and IM strategies and **recommend** improvements thereto *(Also see Chapter 3)*

- **Recommend** strategies for achieving the integration of technical and business staff *(Also see Chapter 7)*

- **Evaluate** and **recommend** strategies for change in an IT context *(also see Chapter 8)*

Syllabus content covered in this chapter

- The purpose and contents of IS, IT and IM strategies *(Also see Chapter 3)*

- How to develop a plan and implement the various strategies in a positive way *(Also see Chapter 7)*

1   DEVELOPING AN INFORMATION TECHNOLOGY PLAN   5/01

1.1   An organisation's information technology strategy and plan should reflect its business strategy, and match its information technology needs. The International Federation of Accountants, through its Information Technology Committee, identifies **ten principles an information technology management plan should be based on.** The approach outlined in the following paragraphs is based on those principles.

Ten principles to follow when establishing an IT management plan

1.2   1   **Alignment**

The IT strategy must be **consistent** with the needs and direction of the organisation. To achieve this alignment, the key drivers of the information technology strategy should be the targets identified in the overall organisation strategic plan.

2   **Scope**

The scope of the information technology plan has a major impact on the effort required to prepare it, as well as the plan's acceptance and ultimate success. Issues to consider include the extent to which the plan should address the business needs of geographically dispersed units or autonomous business units; **linkages with other business or functional strategies** - for example, a business process re-engineering program may require extensive dovetailing with human resource and workplace redesign strategies; and requirements to incorporate **linkages to third parties** (customers, suppliers, partners, etc.) and the manner in which joint plans should be established.

3   **Time frame**

Information technology initiatives can take a long period to implement. The timeframe will vary according to the **type of the industry** and an organisation's **circumstances**. Issues to consider include recognition of the planning horizon of the business plan and business cycle; anticipated life cycle of the technology infrastructure, impact of business objectives on the timeframe for an information technology initiative and if a consecutive series of projects is required to achieve the end result, a longer timeframe may be required.

4   **Cost-benefit justification**

Costs of implementation must be less than the combined **tangible** and **intangible** benefits expected to be realised. The implementation of information technologies can lead to considerable cost savings or other strategic benefits, for example, **increased market share** through better service delivery. These benefits, both tangible and intangible, must be realised if an organisation is to receive value-for-money from its information technology investments. Issues to consider include:

(a)   The manner in which the benefits stated in the plan will be realised. For instance, if the expenditure in a particular area is justified on efficiency grounds, then the plan must specify the amount, nature, and timing of cost savings.

(b)   The extent to which the proposed expenditures **necessary to maintain current operations**. This should be differentiated from other incremental expenditures.

(c)   The **degree of uncertainty** that applies to the benefits. For example, if the primary benefit from the strategy is to provide information for improved decision-making, then this intangible benefit may be both difficult to assess and realise.

(d)   The **return on capital provided** by the investment and the impact of not pursuing or delaying the implementation of specific strategies.

5   **Achievability**

Information technology related initiatives can require **major investments** in terms of capital and people. It is essential that the plan is **realistic** given the resources available. At times, this limitation may necessitate adoption of a **less than ideal solution**, or a **delayed implementation** of the ideal solution. Issues to consider include:

(a)   **Availability of additional resources** (capital, technology infrastructure, people) required to implement the plan - for example, if the plan is based on a significant increase in capital expenditure on information technology, then the source of such capital must be considered before the plan is fully developed.

(b)   Compatibility of proposed information technology-related initiatives with the **organisational culture** - for example, if a given initiative requires a high level of user experience in information technology, then this requirement must be compared to the user skill level within the organisation.

6   **Monitoring and control**

The plan should provide a basis for **measuring and monitoring performance**. A successful plan must provide a **yardstick** for measuring progress and serve as a **benchmark** for modifying objectives to improve and provide input for corrective action - either to improve performance or revise the plan. Typically, an information technology plan will provide performance **milestones** against which performance can be measured. Issues to consider include:

(a)   Setting **realistic and specific performance milestones** that facilitate periodic review of performance against the plan.

(b)   Formalising a **process for the periodic review** of progress against established milestones.

(c)   Assessing **benefits realised against benefits anticipated** on completion of the projects.

(d)   Providing for **progress reporting** against plans on an on-going basis, including early warning of any problem areas.

(e)   **Linking the IT plan deliverables to business targets** and budgets so that the impact of any delay is apparent and leads to a corresponding revision of the business plan.

7   **Reassessment**

Plans are based on business and information technology assumptions. If these **assumptions change**, the existing initiatives and projects may be inappropriate, or more effective alternatives may have emerged. An effective plan must be **flexible** and provide for **periodic reassessment** of the validity and effectiveness of both strategies and tactics. Issues to consider include:

(a)   Establish a **checklist of business and information technology assumptions** on which the plan is formulated.

(b)   Incorporate a mechanism to periodically **confirm validity of planning assumptions** (against the above checklist) **and critical success factors**. For example, if a selected technology becomes obsolete, the plan should be revised.

(c)   The **volatility of the business environment** and its impact on project priorities - for example, if a new business line is to be launched, then the information technology plan may need to be changed to reflect this business imperative.

8   **Awareness**

Once the information technology plan has been approved, it should be **disseminated** to all concerned parties to **ensure there is broad understanding** of the direction and strategy. Issues to consider include:

(a)   Elements of the plan which contain **sensitive information** - for example, competitive strategy should not be disclosed beyond those who need to know.

(b)   Providing relevant information to third-parties with an interest in the information technology strategies - without compromising the competitive needs or other sensitivities of the organisation.

9   **Accountability**

All plans require **translation into action**. **Responsibility** for the implementation, execution and monitoring of the plan should be explicit. Issues to consider include:

(a)   Identifying **sponsors** for each planned project - usually a senior executive for the business area most affected by the project.

(b)   Specifying the **technical and business team leaders** together with other appropriately skilled team members for each project and establishing clear areas of responsibility of key team members with agreed dates for delivery.

10   **Commitment**

The implementation of the projects contained in the plan may require significant resources. These resources are only likely to be available on a timely basis if there is **strong support for the plan** and its objectives from senior management. Issues to consider include:

(a)   **Management participation** in the formulation of key strategies - for example through **interviews** and **workshops**, to both contribute to the planning process and develop a progressive buy-in to the plan.

(b)   Progressive **executive management approvals and endorsements** are needed at the end of each phase of the planning process.

2   PHASES INVOLVED IN ESTABLISHING THE IT PLAN

2.1   We will now look at how the planning process should be approached. Some of the ideas referred to in this section echo those mentioned in the previous section. This is to be expected as the IT plan should incorporate the principles we have already identified.

2.2   Organisations develop information technology plans **specific** to their needs. However, the planning process used to develop the information technology plan will be **similar** across a wide range of organisations. The process can be broken down into four phases:

- Orientation
- Assessment
- Strategic
- Tactical

Phase I: Orientation

2.3   The first phase establishes the scope of the information technology planning process, the methodology and techniques to be applied, and identifies the planning team and reporting lines for the planning process. The planning process may have been initiated in response to a major change in the business strategy or as a reaction to changes in the business or information technology assumptions of the existing plan.

2.4   The key activities of the **orientation phase** are described below.

Step 1.   **Establish scope.**

(a)   Determining if the plan incorporates all business units or if separate plans will be developed for selected business units.

(b)   Assessing the impact of **organisational structure** and policies on the scope.

(c)   Evaluating the extent of **third-party involvement** in the planning process.

(d)   Establishing an overall **timeframe** for the strategic and tactical plans.

Step 2.   **Establish techniques and mobilise resources.**

(a)   Gathering **background information** on the organisation's information technology profile and capabilities.

(b)   Selecting a **proven methodology** to support the planning activities.

(c)   Determining **techniques** that will be used for collecting and analysing information (questionnaires, interviews, workshops etc).

(d)   Developing a **timetable** for the completion of the plan.

(e)   Establishing an **information technology project team**. This should be a multidisciplinary team possessing both information technology and business skills, and user representation.

(f)   Formalising the **reporting mechanism**. Generally, the team reports to a steering committee which is headed by a member of senior management.

Phase II: Assessment

2.5   In the second phase, data is **collected and analysed** to describe the **existing usage** and management of information technology and the extent to which they are unable, or may be unable, to support business objectives.

2.6   This phase also provides an opportunity to identify other **potential uses** of information technologies which may assist in meeting business objectives.

2.7   The key activities of the **assessment phase** are described below.

Step 3.   **Confirm business direction and drivers** to ensure the key driver for the information technology plan is the business direction of the organisation.

(a)   Identifying **core business goals**, strategies and priorities.

(b)   Identifying **critical success factors**, business and information technology assumptions and relevant external relationships.

(c)   Identifying current or **changing regulatory requirements, major business opportunities** and threats.

(d)   Developing a **competitive profile** of the business with respect to strengths, weaknesses, opportunities and threats.

(e)   Developing a competitive profile of the business in the use of information technology, preferably by reference to available **benchmarks,** such as expenditure on information technology as a percentage of total expenditure or total assets, service delivery times or customer satisfaction levels.

(f) Analysing the current and future **organisational structures** of the business and determining the impact of these structures on the information system.

Step 4. **Review technology trends**.

(a) Establishing the cost, complexity, applicability and practicality of each major technology.

(b) Assessing, at a high level, the **benefits, costs and risks** from leading the technology direction for the industry compared to established practice within the industry.

Step 5. **Outline future requirements**.

(a) Identifying the **information and related data** needs of an organisation through high-level data modelling and business process analysis.

(b) Determining the **broad applications areas** that are required to support the information needs.

(c) Determining current and future **service-level requirements**, such as security, response times, and problem resolution procedures.

Step 6. **Inventory existing information systems**.

(a) Documenting **existing information flows** to support operations and decision making.

(b) Describing **current applications** - nature, scope, source, language and hardware requirements, functionality, interfaces, dependencies, age, operating cost, complexity and known limitations.

(c) Documenting **linkages and interfaces** between internal information systems and external information systems.

(d) Listing **technology infrastructure** - processors, peripheral and storage devices, communications and network equipment, terminals and personal computers and the associated operating system software, protocols and communications software.

(e) The nature, use, age, cost, residual life and limitation of each group should also be identified.

(f) Identify organisational resources including skills, experiences, methodologies and tools.

Step 7. **Develop an assessment**.

(a) Comparing what information technology is **required** by the business against what **exists.**

(b) Evaluating each major area of the existing information systems to identify areas where there are significant **deficiencies.**

(c) Identifying business areas or practices where significant **new or improved information systems are required.**

(d) Preparing a **list of major issues** that need to be addressed in the formulation of the strategies - for example, capital constraints, infrastructure development, change management, exploitation of new technologies, business and information technology assumptions, improved service levels, risks and other obstacles to successful completion.

2.8 By the end of the assessment phase there should be:

(a) A **well-developed assessment** of the current and future business needs and the benefits available from implementing technologies.

172

(b) An **appreciation of the gap** between what is desired and what is required.

(c) A **list of the key issues** to be considered in the formulation of the information technology strategies.

Phase III: Strategic plan

2.9 In the third phase of the information technology planning process, appropriate **strategies are formulated**. These strategies are founded on the assessment of the business needs and priorities, information technology direction and other related issues considered in the assessment phase. Major steps in the phase and the corresponding activities are described below.

Step 8. **Develop a vision.**

(a) Determining the **information technology critical success factors** and related business and information technology assumptions.

(b) Identifying areas of **emphasis in developing the strategies** - for example to out-perform the competition in the provision of a state-of-the-art website may be an important objective, or to meet agreed service levels.

(c) Developing a realistic **vision and supporting goals** for the plan which recognise both the critical success factors and areas of emphasis.

Step 9. **Conduct option analysis.**

(a) Developing **alternate models** for assessing and delivering the data and information requirements of the organisation - what, why, when and where information is required.

(b) Identifying **alternative application approaches** for meeting the information needs of the organisation - for example, custom develop, retain existing information system, acquire a package, or a hybrid solution.

(c) Assessing alternate approaches and associated risks for **meeting the technology infrastructure** needs which satisfy the service level requirements of the organisation.

(d) **Evaluating** alternate **approaches** for meeting the communication needs - for example, a centralised communications network management model against a distributed network model.

(e) Identifying **organisational processes and policies** needed to support the acquisition, development, implementation, operation and maintenance of the information systems and the various ways that these needs may be met. For example, defining new policies, re-engineering business processes, recruitment of additional personnel; and outsourcing of implementation and/or delivery of new functionality.

Step 10. **Develop a strategic plan.**

(a) Selecting a **strategy that fits the business needs,** is compatible with other strategies, flexible to adapt to changing circumstances and adheres to industry standards.

(b) **Speed and method of implementation** (overview only), organisational capability and learning curve required, and relative costs and benefits.

(c) Developing an **integrated planning framework** to bring together individual strategies into a cohesive overall strategy covering information, applications, technology infrastructure, and organisation perspectives in a manner that meets business objectives.

Phase IV: Tactical plan

2.10 In the last phase of the planning process, the tactical (or implementation) **plan is developed**. In the tactical plan, the focus is on the projects that need to be undertaken to implement each of the strategies. Major steps in this phase and corresponding activities are described below.

Step 11. **Identify and specify projects.**

(a) Each strategy is **broken into specific projects** - to facilitate control, implementation and matching to the resource capability of the organisation.

(b) Specifying the nature, functionality, and scope of each project.

(c) Establishing **interdependencies** between projects.

(d) Identifying the **costs and benefits** of individual projects.

(e) Estimating the **implementation timeframe** for each project.

Step 12. **Prioritise projects.**

Criteria to consider include:

(a) Strategic impact of the project in supporting the business strategy.

(b) Dependencies on other projects - for example, a communication network may be the foundation project for a new service.

(c) **Business imperatives** - for example, the launch date of a new product or changes to regulatory requirements or meeting competitive or customer needs.

(d) **Benefits** that can be realised - projects with **high benefits or quick results should be fast-tracked.**

(e) **Resource requirements** - for example, funding may constrain the concurrent implementation of major projects.

Step 13. **Develop the tactical plan.**

(a) Schedule all projects, specifying **who does what and when.**

(b) Identify the **critical path** and **performance milestones** for key deliverables.

(c) Provide the underlying **assumptions** and **constraints.**

(d) Develop financial, resource allocation, and benefit realisation plans to support the implementation of the projects.

Step 14. **Establish monitoring and control mechanisms.**

(a) Develop a monitoring and control mechanism that will ensure that the plan implementation and business/IT assumptions are periodically reviewed, and where appropriate, corrective action taken.

(b) Assigning accountabilities for the implementation of specific projects within the plan - for example, a project sponsor and project manager.

(c) Assigning responsibilities for delivering estimated benefits from those parts of the information technology plan that have been implemented - for example, the senior business executives responsible for areas where the new or enhanced system is being used.

2.11 The establishment of monitoring and control mechanisms marks the **conclusion of the information technology planning process.**

3   THE SYSTEMS DEVELOPMENT LIFE-CYCLE (SDLC)   5/01

3.1   We now move away from the IT planning process for a fairly brief look at the range of approaches available when implementing an IT system. (The SDLC is covered in greater detail in Paper 10 - Systems and Project Management.)

3.2   There are a range of approaches that can be taken to the implementation of IT systems. In the early days of computing, systems development was piecemeal, involving automation of existing procedures rather than forming part of a planned strategy. The development of systems was not properly planned. The consequences were often poorly designed systems, which cost too much and which were not suited to users' needs.

3.3   In the 1960s the National Computing Centre developed a more disciplined approach to systems development, which could be applied almost anywhere. This approach became known as the Systems Development Life-Cycle (SDLC).

3.4   The Systems Development Life-cycle approach (sometimes referred to simply as the life-cycle approach) is a traditional method of building information systems. It prescribes a disciplined or 'hard' approach to systems development.

> ## KEY TERM
>
> The term **'systems life-cycle'** describes the stages a system moves through from inception until it is discarded or replaced.

Stage	Comment
Project definition	Involves an **investigation** and analysis of the organisation's information requirements to decide if a new or modified information system is required. If a new project is identified its **objectives**, **scope** and **project plan** are developed.
Feasibility study	This involves a review of the existing system and the identification of a range of possible alternative solutions. A feasible (technical, operational, economic, social) solution will be selected – or a decision not to proceed made. Findings are usually contained in a **feasibility study report** which describes the activities required in the remaining life-cycle phases.
Design	The logical and physical design specifications are produced in a **detailed specification** of the new system.
Programming or software selection	If bespoke software is to be produced, analysts work with programmers to prepare **program specifications** and then the **programs**. If off-the-shelf software is suitable, packages are evaluated (perhaps in a report) and **selected**.
Installation	Steps are taken to put the system into operation. **Testing**, file conversion and user **training** are carried out. A **formal conversion plan** is developed.
Post-implementation	The system is used and evaluated. A formal **post-implementation audit** determines how well the system has met its objectives and whether any modifications are required.

BPP PUBLISHING

Drawbacks of the lifecycle approach

3.5 The systems lifecycle is considered a hard systems approach as it has a narrow focus, and tends to ignore 'people issues'. The approach efficiently automates existing procedures within easily defined processing requirements. The resulting systems are modelled on the manual systems they are replacing.

3.6 Sequential models (such as the lifecycle model) restrict user input throughout much of the process. (A sequential model is one where a stage is not started until the previous stage is complete.) This often results in substantial and costly modifications late in the development process. It becomes increasingly difficult and expensive to change system requirements the further a system is developed.

3.7 Time overruns are common. The sequential nature of the process meant a hold-up on one stage would stop development completely – contributing to time overruns. Time pressures and lack of user involvement often resulted in a poor quality system.

3.8 Because of these drawbacks the lifecycle approach is not as widely used today as in the past. However, it is still used with success for building systems where requirements are highly structured and well-defined eg large transaction processing systems.

4 OTHER SYSTEM BUILDING TOOLS AND TECHNIQUES

The spiral model

4.1 When developing systems where requirements are difficult to specify it is unrealistic to follow a sequential process (such as the SDLC) which relies on getting things correct at each stage of development before starting subsequent activities. In these more complex situations the spiral approach is appropriate.

4.2 The spiral model represents an **evolutionary approach** to systems development. It involves carrying out the same activities over a number of cycles in order to clarify requirements and solutions.

4.3 The first spiral model was developed by *Boehm*. The model is shown below.

Boehm's spiral model

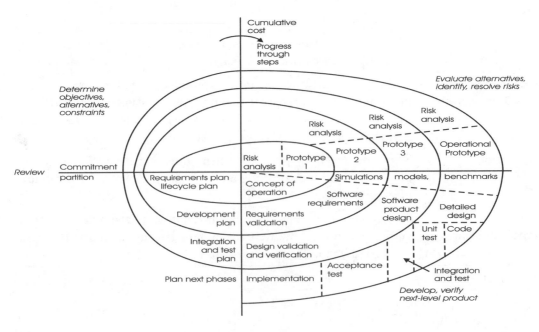

4.4 The development process starts at the centre of the spiral. At the centre requirements are not well-defined. System requirements are refined with each rotation around the spiral. The longer the spiral, the more complex the system and the greater the cost.

4.5 The model is divided into four quadrants.

(a) Top left

- Objectives determined
- Alternatives and constraints identified

(b) Top right

- Alternatives evaluated
- Risks identified and resolved

(c) Bottom right

- System development and implementation

(d) Bottom left

- The next phase in the overall development plan is planned

4.6 The spiral approach aims to avoid the problems of the life-cycle model (lack of user involvement, long delays). It is a 'softer' more flexible approach, usually used in conjunction with prototyping (which we look at later in this chapter).

Methodologies

4.7 Another way to facilitate systems development is to use a systems development methodology.

> **KEY TERM**
>
> A systems development '**methodology**' is a collection of procedures, techniques, tools and documentation aids which will help systems developers in their efforts to implement a new information system.

Characteristics of methodologies

Characteristic	Comment
Separation of logical and physical	The initial focus is on business benefits – on what the system will achieve (the logical design).
User involvement	User's information requirements determine the type of data collected or captured by the system. Users are involved throughout the development process.
Diagrammatic documentation	Diagrams rather than text-based documentation are used as much as possible to ensure the focus is on what the system is trying to achieve – and to aid user understanding of the process.

Characteristic	Comment
Data driven	Most structured methods focus on data items regardless of the processes they are related to. The type of data within an organisation is less likely to change than either the processes which operate on it or the output information required of it.
Defined structure	Most methodologies prescribe a consistent structure to ensure a consistent and complete approach to the work. For example, the Structured Systems Analysis and Design Method (**SSDAM**) suggests five modules: Feasibility, Requirements Analysis, Requirements Specification, Logical Systems Specification and Physical Design.

4.8 *Jayaratna* (*Understanding and Evaluating Methodologies*, 1994) estimates that there are over 1,000 branded methodologies in use. A popular systems development methodology is the Structured Systems Analysis and Design Method (**SSDAM**). This was originally designed for use by the UK Government – but is now widely used in many areas of business.

4.9 All methodologies seek to facilitate the '**best**' solution. But 'best' may be interpreted in a number of ways, such as **most rapid** or **least cost**. Some methodologies are highly **prescriptive** and require rigid adherence to stages whilst others are highly **adaptive** allowing for creative use of their components.

4.10 In choosing the **most appropriate methodology**, an organisation must consider the following questions.

- To what extent does the methodology facilitate **participation**?
- Does it generate **alternative solutions**?
- Is it well documented, **tried and tested**?
- Can component tools be selected and used as required?
- Will it facilitate the use of computer-aided tools and prototyping?

Advantages and disadvantages of methodologies

4.11 The **advantages** of using a methodology are as follows.

(a) Detailed **documentation** is produced.

(b) **Standard methods** allow less qualified staff to carry out some of the analysis work, thus **cutting the cost** of the exercise.

(c) Using a standard development process leads to **improved system specifications**.

(d) Systems developed in this way are **easier to maintain and improve**.

(e) **Users are involved** with development work from an early stage and are required to sign off each stage.

(f) The emphasis on **diagramming** makes it easier for relevant parties, including users, to **understand** the system than if purely narrative descriptions were used.

(g) The structured framework of a methodology **helps with planning**. It defines the tasks to be performed, sets out when they should be done and identifies an end product. This allows control by reference to actual achievements rather than to estimates of progress.

(h) A logical design is produced that is **independent of hardware and software**.

(i)   Techniques such as data flow diagrams, logical data structures and entity life histories **allow information to be cross-checked** between diagrams and ensure that the system delivered does what is required.

4.12   The use of a methodology in systems development also has **disadvantages**.

(a)   It has been argued that methodologies are ideal for analysing and documenting processes and data items at an operational level, but are perhaps **inappropriate for information of a strategic nature** that is collected on an ad hoc basis.

(b)   Some are a little **too limited in scope,** being too concerned with systems design, and not with their impact on actual work processes or social context of the system.

(c)   Arguably, methodologies encourage excessive documentation and **bureaucracy** and are just as suitable for documenting bad design as good.

Computer Aided Software Engineering (CASE)

4.13   Computer Aided Software Engineering tools are used in systems development to automate some development tasks, such as the production of documentation, and to provide an efficient tool to control developmental activities.

KEY TERM

CASE tools are software tools used to automate some tasks in the development of information systems eg generating documentation and diagrams. The more sophisticated tools facilitate software prototyping and code generation.

4.14   There are a range of CASE tools available. Some focus on certain phases of development such as analysis and design, others may be used throughout the complete development lifecycle.

4.15   The range of facilities offered by CASE tools are shown in the following table.

Stage of system development project	Possible use of CASE tools
Project initiation	• Generate project schedules in various formats
Analysis and design	• Produce diagrams eg flowcharts, DFDs, ERMs, ELHs • Generate data dictionary
Design (logical and physical)	• Produce system model diagrams • Data structures • Automate screen and report design
Implementation	• Installation schedule • Program code generator
Maintenance	• Version control • Change specification and tracking

BPP PUBLISHING

4.16 CASE tools can be grouped into Upper CASE tools (sometimes referred to as analysts' workbenches) and Lower CASE tools (sometimes referred to as programmers' workbenches).

Upper CASE tools (analysts' workbenches)

4.17 Upper CASE tools are geared towards automating tasks associated with systems analysis. They include:

(a) **Diagramming tools** that automate the production of diagrams using a range of modelling techniques.

(b) **Analysis tools** that check the logic, consistency and completeness of system diagrams, forms and reports.

(c) A **CASE repository** that holds all data and information relating to the system. The **Data dictionary** records all data items held in the system and controls access to the repository. The dictionary will list all data entities, data flows, data stores, processes, external entities and individual data items.

Lower CASE tools (programmers workbenches)

4.18 Lower CASE tools are geared towards automating tasks later in the development process (after analysis and design). They include:

(a) **Document generators** that automate the production of diagrams using a range of modelling techniques.

(b) **Screen and report layout generators** that allow prototyping of the user-interface to be produced and amended quickly.

(c) **Code generators** that automate the production of code based on the processing logic input to the generator.

Advantages of using CASE tools

4.19 Advantages of CASE include the following.

(a) **Document/diagram preparation** and amendment is quicker and more efficient.

(b) **Accuracy of diagrams** is improved. Diagram drawers can ensure consistency of terminology and maintain certain standards of documentation.

(c) **Prototyping** (see later in this section) is made easier, as re-design can be effected very quickly.

(d) **Blocks of code can be re-used**. Many applications incorporate similar functions and processes; blocks of software can be retained in a library and used (or modified) as appropriate.

Examples of CASE tools

4.20   Examples of CASE tools include Select's SSADM Professional, Rational's ClearCase and
AxiomSys from STG.

Example 1: Automated diagram production

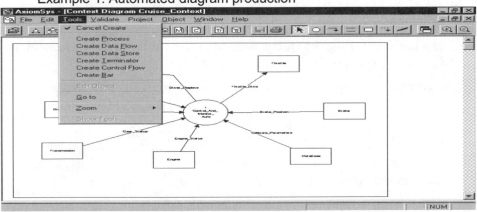

Example 2: Code generating and checking

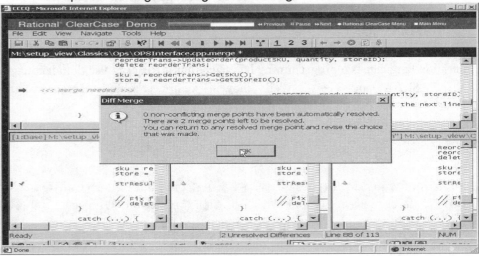

Example 3: Version/change control

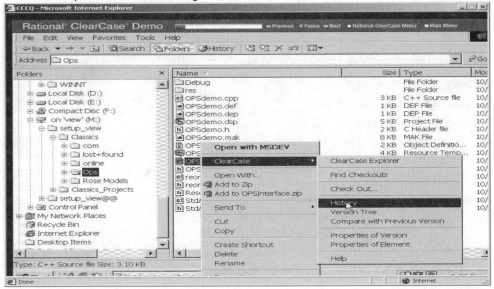

Fourth generation languages (4GLs)

4.21 As computer languages have developed over time, certain types of computer languages have become identified with a generation of languages. The four generations are explained in the following table.

Generation	Comment
First	Machine code. Program instructions were written for individual machines in binary form (a series of 1s and 0s).
Second	Assembly languages. Still machine specific, programs were written using symbolic code which made them easier to understand and maintain.
Third	High-level languages such as COBOL, BASIC and FORTRAN. These languages have a wider vocabulary of words, enabling commands to be closer to everyday language. Programs produced are able to be moved between similar computers.
Fourth	There is no formal definition of a Fourth Generation Language (4GL). Fourth-generation languages are programming languages closer to human languages than typical high-level or third generation languages. Most 4GLs use simple query language such as 'FIND ALL RECORDS WHERE NAME IS 'JONES'

4.22 A fourth generation language is a programming language that is easier to use than languages like COBOL, PASCAL and C++. Well known examples include **Informix** and **Powerhouse**.

> **KEY TERM**
>
> A **Fourth Generation Language (4GL)** is a high-level computer language that uses commands that are closer to everyday speech than previous languages. 4GLs usually also include a range of features intended to automate software production.

4.23 Most fourth generation languages use a graphical user interface. Icons, objects, help facilities, pull down menus and templates present programmers with the options for building the software. Sections of code are often treated as components, which may be used (maybe with slight modifications) in a variety of applications. A 4GL will often include the following features (many of these features could also be provided by a CASE tool).

- Relatively easy to learn and use
- Often centred around a database
- Includes a data dictionary
- Uses a relatively simple query language
- Includes facilities for screen design and dialogue box design
- Includes a report generator
- Code generation is often automated
- Documenting and diagramming tools

4.24 4GLs are often used to facilitate **object-oriented programming**. With object-oriented programming, programmers define the types of operations (functions) that can be applied to data structures (in programming, a data structure refers to a scheme for organising related pieces of information). In this way, the data structure becomes an object that includes both data and functions. In addition, programmers can create relationships between one object and another. For example, objects can inherit characteristics from other objects.

4.25   One of the principal advantages of object-oriented programming techniques over procedural programming techniques is that they enable programmers to create modules that do not need to be changed when a new type of object is added. A programmer can simply create a new object that inherits many of its features from existing objects. This makes object-oriented programs easier to modify (a group of objects with some common properties may be referred to as a **class**).

4.26   4GLs enable a more flexible approach to be taken to software production than under the traditional Systems Development Lifecycle. Using a 4GL, changes to the program design and to the code itself can be made relatively easily and quickly. This allows development to follow a pattern like the Spiral model, with users able to make amendments based on prototypes.

Examples taken from 4GLs

4.27   The following screenshots are taken from the Metamill 4GL.

Example 1: Automated diagram production

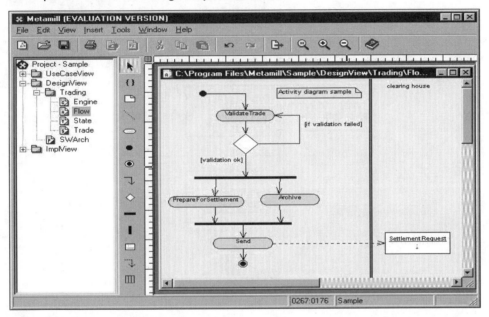

Example 2: Class properties window

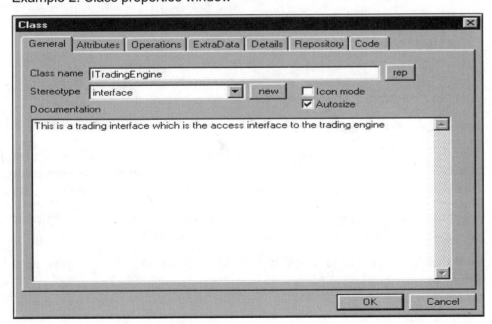

Prototyping

4.28 The use of 4GLs, together with the realisation that users need to see how a system will look and feel to assess its suitability, have contributed to the increased use of **prototyping**.

> ### KEY TERM
>
> A **prototype** is a model of all or part of a system, built to show users early in the design process how it will appear.

4.29 As a simple example, a prototype of a formatted screen output from a system could be prepared using a graphics package, or even a spreadsheet model. This would describe how the screen output would appear to the user. The user could make suggested amendments, which would be incorporated into the next model.

The prototyping process

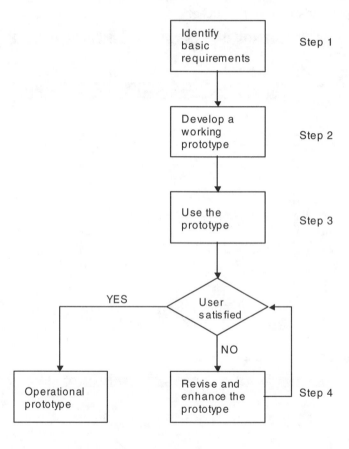

Advantages and disadvantages of prototyping

4.30 The **advantages** of prototyping.

(a) It makes it possible for programmers to present a 'mock-up' version of a proposed system to users before a substantial amount of time and money have been committed. The user can judge the prototype before things have gone too far to be changed.

(b) The process facilitates the production of 'custom built' (bespoke) software rather than off-the-shelf packages which may or may not suit user needs.

(c) It makes efficient use of programmer time by helping programmers to develop programs more quickly.

4.31 **Disadvantages** of prototyping.

(a) Many prototyping tools are tied to a particular software product.

(b) It is sometimes argued that prototyping tools are **inefficient** in the program codes they produce, so that programs are bigger and require more memory than a more efficiently coded program.

(c) Prototyping may help users to steer the development of a new system towards an **existing system**.

(d) As prototyping encourages the attitude that changes and amendments are likely, some believe prototyping tools encourage programmers to produce programs quickly, but to neglect program quality.

Structured walkthroughs

4.32 Structured walkthroughs are a technique used by those responsible for the design of some aspect of a system (particularly analysts and programmers) to present their design to user representatives – in other words to 'walk' them through the design. Structured walkthroughs are formal meetings, in which the documentation produced during development is reviewed and checked.

4.33 These presentations are used both to explain the new systems to users and also to offer the users the opportunity of making constructive criticism of the proposed system and suggestions for further amendments/improvements.

Question 1

What other benefits, besides identification of mistakes (errors, omission, inconsistencies etc), could a walkthrough provide?

Answer

(a) Users become involved in the systems analysis process. Since this process is a critical appraisal of their work, they should have the opportunity to provide feedback on the appraisal itself.

(b) The output from the development is shown to people who are not systems development personnel. This encourages its originators to prepare it to a higher quality and in user-friendly form.

(c) Because the onus is on users to approve design, they are more likely to become committed to the new system and less likely to 'rubbish' it.

(d) The process focuses on quality of, and good practice in, operations generally.

(e) It avoids disputes about who is responsible for what.

Joint Applications Development

4.34 Joint Applications Development (JAD) describes the partnership between users and system developers.

4.35 JAD was originally developed by *IBM* to promote a more **participative** approach to systems development. The **potential benefits** to an organisation include the following.

(a) JAD creates a pool of expertise comprising interested parties from all relevant functions.

(b) Reduced risk of systems being imposed by systems personnel.

(c) This increases user ownership and responsibility for systems solutions.

(d) Emphasises the information needs of users and their relationship to business needs and decision making.

4.36 There are a number of possible **risks** affecting the potential value of JAD.

(a) The relative inexperience of many users may lead to misunderstandings and possibly unreasonable expectations/demands on the system performance.

(b) The danger of lack of co-ordination leading to fragmented, individual, possibly esoteric information systems.

4.37 The shift of emphasis to applications development by end-users must be well managed and controlled. An organisation may wish to set up an **information centre** to provide the necessary support and co-ordination.

4.38 Achieving change requires a commitment to change by the people affected by the change. Getting commitment is expensive, and calls for an investment of time, effort and money.

Rapid Applications Development

4.39 **Rapid Applications Development (RAD)** can be described as a quick way of building software. It combines a managed approach to systems development with the use of modern software tools such as **prototyping**. RAD also involves the end-user heavily in the development process.

4.40 RAD has become increasingly popular as the pace of change in business has increased. To develop systems that provide competitive advantage it is often necessary to build and implement the system quickly.

4.41 RAD can create difficulties for the project manager as RAD relies to a certain extent on a lack of structure and control.

End-user development

4.42 End-user computing has been fuelled by the introduction of **PCs** to user departments, by **user-friendly software**, and by **greater awareness** of computers and what they can do.

> ### KEY TERM
>
> **End-user development** is the direct, hands-on development of computer systems by users.

4.43 Staff such as accountants often design and use complex **spreadsheet models** – this is an example of end-user computing.

4.44 Modern spreadsheet packages allow the use of macros and other 'programming' techniques which allow users to develop their own fairly complex applications. Often the people building these models have little or no formal training in programming and system design, and the methods used are personal to each user.

4.45 While these programs may work well, they are likely to be very **difficult to modify**. Often only the person who developed the model fully understands it. Such models are rarely documented. This is risky from the organisation's viewpoint: systems are developed with little control, and the organisation becomes dependant upon those individuals who developed the system.

4.46 Other disadvantages are as follows:

(a) The risk from the elimination of the **separation of the functions of user and analyst**.

(b) The risk from **limits on user ability** to identify correct and complete requirements for an application.

(c) The risk from **lack of user knowledge and acceptance of application quality assurance procedures** for development and operation.

(d) The risk from **unstable user systems**.

(e) The risk from encouraging **private information systems**.

(f) The risk from permitting **unstructured information systems development**.

User groups

> **KEY TERM**
>
> A **user group** is a forum for users of particular hardware or, more usually, software, so that they can **share ideas and experience**.

4.47 User groups are usually set up either by the software manufacturers themselves (who use them to **maintain contact** with customers and as a source of **new product ideas**) or by groups of users. The term is used most commonly with users of packaged software.

4.48 Users of a particular package can meet, or perhaps exchange views over the Internet, to discuss solutions, ideas or 'short cuts' to improve productivity. An (electronic) newsletter service might be appropriate, based on views exchanged by members, but also incorporating ideas culled from the wider environment by IT specialists.

4.49 Sometimes user groups are set up **within** individual organisations. Where an organisation has written its own application software, or is using tailor-made software, there will be a very **small knowledge base** initially, and there will obviously not be a national user group, because the application is unique.

4.50 'Interested parties', including, as a minimum, representatives from the **IT department** and **users** who are familiar with different parts of the system, can attend monthly or quarterly **meetings** to discuss the **operation** of the system, make **suggestions for improvements** (such as the production of new reports or time-tabling of processing) and raise any **queries**.

Question 2

Trends in IT such as distributed processing, increased use of PCs and wide availability of sophisticated general purpose packages have resulted in more responsibility for information systems being transferred to end-users. What problems may this result in for organisations?

Answer

Here are some suggestions.

(a) Lack of formal training could result in inefficient or even 'faulty' systems.

(b) User requests for assistance that overwhelm the IS/IT department.

(c) Lack of user knowledge or concern may lead to inadequate controls being built into the system.

(d)   Lack of integration across the organisation with many users developing systems to suit themselves.

(e)   Poor maintainability of user-developed systems as only the person that developed it understands it

(f)   Lack of centralised management of resources.

(g)   A lack of understanding of the organisation's use of IS/IT may develop – it becomes difficult to see the 'big picture'.

Chapter roundup

- An organisation's **IT strategy** should be driven by targets identified in the organisation's **overall strategy**.

- When establishing a strategy and **management plan for IT** ten considerations are:

° Alignment	° Monitoring and control
° Scope	° Reassessment
° Time-scale	° Awareness
° Cost/benefit	° Accountability
° Achievability	° Commitment

- Although organisations develop IT plans specific to their needs, the planning process followed will be similar across a range of organisations.

- **Four phases can be identified in the IT planning process.**

  ° Orientation
  ° Assessment
  ° Strategic
  ° Tactical

- **System building tools and techniques** include:

  ° The SDLC (sequential)
  ° The spiral model (evolutionary)
  ° Methodologies (consistent, structured)
  ° CASE tools (automate design and documentation)
  ° 4GLs (enable quicker programming)
  ° Prototyping (enables system to be 'seen' earlier, facilitates user involvement)
  ° Structured walkthroughs (involves users)
  ° JAD (user-developer partnership)
  ° RAD (combines JAD and tools such as prototyping)

Quick quiz

1   Fill in the missing word in the following statement. ' The key drivers of the information technology strategy should be the targets identified in the overall organisation .... plan. '

2   Give an example how the implementation of information technologies could lead to an organisation achieving increased market share.

3   The planning process used to develop an information technology plan may broken down into four phases. List them.

1   ....

2   ....

3   ....

4   ....

4   'The SDLC is a 'soft' approach to systems development'.

True   ☐

False   ☐

5   Define the term 'CASE tool'.

6   What is a fourth generation language?

7   List five features of a 4GL.

1   ....

2   ....

3   ....

4   ....

5   ....

8   List three advantages of prototyping.

1   ....

2   ....

3   ....

9   What does JAD stand for?

J........................... A........................... D...........................

10   What does RAD stand for?

R........................... A........................... D...........................

Answers to quick quiz

1 Strategic.

2 By enabling the organisation to provide better customer service.

3 Orientation, Assessment, Strategic, Tactical.

4 False.

5 CASE stands for computer aided software engineering. CASE tools are software tools used to automate some tasks in the development of information systems eg generating documentation and diagrams. The more sophisticated tools facilitate software prototyping and code generation.

6 There is no formal definition of a 4GL, but it is generally accepted that they are closer to human languages than typical high-level or third generation languages, and are therefore easier to use than previous generations of computer languages.

7 A 4GL will often include the following features: Relatively easy to learn and use, centred around a database, includes a data dictionary, uses a relatively simple query language, facilities for screen design and dialogue box design, a report generator, automated code generation and documenting and diagramming tools.

8 Prototyping allows programmers to present a 'mock-up' version of a proposed system to users before a substantial amount of time and money have been committed, so users can judge the prototype before things have gone too far to be changed. Prototyping facilitates the production of 'custom built' (bespoke) software rather than off-the-shelf packages which may or may not suit user needs. Prototyping allows programmers to develop programs quickly

9 Joint Applications Development.

10 Rapid Applications Development.

Question to try	Level	Marks	Time
9	Examination	5	9 mins
10	Examination	10	18 mins
14	Examination	15	27 mins

Chapter 7

ORGANISING THE INFORMATION TECHNOLOGY FUNCTION

Topic list		Syllabus reference	Ability required
1	Information systems department	(iii)	Evaluation
2	Centralisation and decentralisation	(iii)	Evaluation
3	Accounting issues	(iii)	Evaluation
4	Other organisational issues	(iii)	Evaluation
5	Outsourcing	(iii)	Evaluation

Introduction

As with any business function, the way in which the information technology function is organised will impact significantly on the service delivered.

We begin this chapter by looking at the different ways of structuring the information systems function. We then move on to explore wider organisational issues, including the options available to account for the costs associated with information systems.

The chapter concludes with the pros and cons of outsourcing.

Learning outcomes covered in this chapter

- **Evaluate** the organisation of the IS/IT function within a given organisation

- **Recommend** ways of achieving co-ordination of activities in a decentralised organisation

- **Evaluate** and **recommend** strategies for managing change in an IT context *(Also see Chapters 6 and 8)*

- **Recommend** strategies for achieving the integration of technical and business staff *(Also see Chapter 6)*

Syllabus content covered in this chapter

- The potential ways of organising the IT function involving the use of steering committees, support centres for advice and help desk facilities, end user participation *(Also see Chapter 6)*

- How to develop a plan and implement the various strategies in a positive way *(Also see Chapter 6)*

- The argument for and against outsourcing

- The criteria for selecting outsourcing / Facilities Management partners and for managing ongoing relationships, service level agreements, discontinuation change of supplier, hand-over considerations

BPP PUBLISHING

1 INFORMATION SYSTEMS DEPARTMENT

1.1 Most organisations choose have an information systems department, or team responsible for the tasks and responsibilities associated with information systems. In some organisations this department may be referred to as the information technology department – as information systems increasingly utilise information technology.

1.2 In a small company, information systems may be the responsibility of the finance director or the company secretary or simply an office manager. In larger organisations there may be an **information systems director** and/or an **information systems manager**.

1.3 The IS/IT director or manager would have responsibility for the following areas.

IS/IT director responsibility	Comment
IS/IT strategy development	The IS/IT strategy must compliment the overall strategy of the organisation. The strategy must also be achievable given budgetary constraints. Returns on investments in IS/IT should be monitored.
IS/IT risk management	This is a wide ranging area including legal risks, such as ensuring compliance with relevant data protection legislation, ensuring adequate IS/IT security measures and disaster recovery arrangements.
Steering committee	The IS/IT director should play a key role in a steering committee set up to oversee the role of IS/IT within the organisation. There is more on steering committees later in this chapter.
IS/IT infrastructure	Standards should be set for the purchase and use of hardware and software within the organisation.
Ensuring employees have the IS/IT support and tools the require	Efficient links are required between IS/IT staff and the rest of the organisation. Technical assistance should be easily obtainable.

1.4 An IS/IT director therefore requires a wide range of skills. The ideal person would possess technical know-how, excellent general management ability, a keen sense of business awareness and a good understanding of the organisations' operations.

1.5 In the following paragraphs we explain some of the key personnel and roles that may be present in an information systems department.

IS/IT steering committee

1.6 Organisations may set up a **steering committee** to oversee all information system development. A steering committee might also be set up for a 'one-off' computer-related project. The steering committee's tasks may include the following.

(a) To **approve (or reject) projects** whose total budgeted cost is below a certain limit and so within their authorisation limit.

(b) To **recommend projects** to the board of directors for acceptance when their cost is high enough to call for approval at board level.

(c) To establish **company guidelines** within the framework of the IT strategy for the development of computer-based processing and management information systems.

(d) The **co-ordination and control** of the work of the study group(s) and project development groups, in respect of the development time, the cost and the technical quality of the investigations.

(e) The **evaluation** of the feasibility study reports and system specifications. The steering committee must be satisfied that each new system has been properly justified.

(f) To monitor and **review each new system after implementation** to check whether the system has met its objectives. If it hasn't, to investigate the reasons for the system's failure, and take any suitable control or remedial measures.

(g) In an organisation which has a continuing programme of new DP projects, assessing the contribution of each project to the long-term **corporate objectives** of the organisation, ranking projects in order of **priority** and assigning resources to the most important projects first, and taking decisions to defer projects when insufficient resources are available.

1.7 The steering committee might include the following.

- The **information director,** or a senior IS staff member
- **Accountants** for advice relating to costs and benefits
- Senior **user management**

Database administrator

1.8 A key information systems role is that of database administrator. A database administrator is responsible for all data and information held within an organisation. Key tasks include:

- Preparing and maintaining a record of all data held within the organisation (the data dictionary)
- Co-ordinating data and information use to avoid duplication and maximise efficiency
- Analysing the data requirements of new applications
- Implementing and controlling procedures to protect data integrity
- Recording data ownership

Operations control

1.9 Operations control is concerned with ensuring IS/IT systems are working and available to users. Key tasks include:

- Maintaining the IS/IT infrastructure
- Monitoring network usage and managing network resources
- Keeping employees informed, eg advance warning of service interruptions
- Virus protection measures eg ensuring anti-virus software updates are loaded
- Fault fixing

Systems development staff

1.10 In medium to large organisations in is likely that the IS department will include staff with programming and systems analysis skills. Key tasks for staff involved in systems development include:

BPP PUBLISHING

- Systems analysis
- Systems design and specification
- Systems testing
- Systems evaluation and review

Data processing staff

1.11 Over the past two decades the traditional centralised data processing department has become less common. Most departments now process their own data using on-line systems, rather than batching up transactions and forwarding paper copies of them to a centralised department for processing.

1.12 Staff involved in data processing today are spread throughout the organisation, for example a call centre employee may input an order, an accounts clerk may process journal entries etc. Accurate data entry skills and an understanding of the task they are performing are key skills.

Information centre staff

KEY TERM

An **Information Centre (IC)** is a small unit of staff with a good technical awareness of computer systems, whose task is to provide a support function to computer users within the organisation.

1.13 Information centres, sometimes referred to as **support centres**, are particularly useful in organisations which use distributed systems and so are likely to have hardware, data and software scattered throughout the organisation.

Help

1.14 An IC usually offers a **Help Desk** to solve IT problems. Help may be via the telephone, e-mail, through a searchable knowledge base or in person.

1.15 **Remote diagnostic software** may be used which enables staff in the IC to take control of a computer and sort out the problem without leaving their desk.

1.16 The help desk needs sufficient staff and technical expertise to respond quickly and effectively to requests for help. IC staff should also maintain good relationships with hardware and software suppliers to ensure their maintenance staff are quickly on site when needed.

Problem solving

1.17 The IC will maintain a record of problems and identify those that occur most often. If the problem is that users do not know how to use the system, training is provided.

1.18 Training applications often contain analysis software, drawing attention to trainee progress and common problems. This information enables the IC to identify and address specific training needs more closely.

1.19 If the problem is with the system itself, a solution is found, either by modifying the system or by investment in new hardware or software.

Improvements

1.20 The IC may also be required to consider the viability of suggestions for improving the system, and to bring these improvements into effect.

Standards

1.21 The IC is also likely to be responsible for setting, and encouraging users to conform to, common **standards**.

(a) Hardware standards ensure that all of the equipment used in the organisation is compatible and can be put into use in different departments as needed.

(b) Software standards ensure that information generated by one department can easily be shared with and worked upon by other departments.

(c) Programming standards ensure that applications developed by individual end-users (for example complex spreadsheet macros) follow best practice and are easy to modify.

(d) Data processing standards ensure that certain conventions such as the format of file names are followed throughout the organisation. This facilitates sharing, storage and retrieval of information.

Security

1.22 The IC may help to preserve the security of data in various ways.

(a) It may develop utility programs and procedures to ensure that back-ups are made at regular intervals.

(b) The IC may help to preserve the company's systems from attack by computer viruses, for instance by ensuring that the latest versions of anti-virus software are available to all users, by reminding users regularly about the dangers of viruses, and by setting up and maintaining 'firewalls', which deny access to sensitive parts of the company's systems.

End-user applications development

1.23 An IC can help applications development by providing technical guidance to end-user developers and to encourage comprehensible and well-documented programs. Understandable programs can be maintained or modified more easily. Documentation provides a means of teaching others how the programs work. These efforts can greatly extend the usefulness and life of the programs that are developed.

2   CENTRALISATION AND DECENTRALISATION

2.1   We now look at how the IS/IT department could be structured. There are two main options - centralised or decentralised. (Note that in this section we are discussing the structure of a department – rather than the information system architecture structure we covered in Chapter 3.)

> **KEY TERMS**
>
> A **centralised** IS/IT department involves all IS/IT staff and functions being based out at a single central location, such as head office.
>
> A **decentralised** IS/IT department involves IS/IT staff and functions being spread out throughout the organisation.

2.2   There is no single 'best' structure for an IS/IT department – an organisation should consider its IS/IT requirements and the merits of each structure.

2.3   **Advantages** of a centralised IS/IT department.

(a)   Assuming centralised processing is used, there is only one set of files. Everyone uses the same data and information.

(b)   It gives better security/control over data and files. It is easier to enforce standards.

(c)   Head office is in a better position to know what is going on.

(d)   There may be economies of scale available in purchasing computer equipment and supplies.

(e)   Computer staff are in a single location, and more expert staff are likely to be employed. Career paths may be more clearly defined.

2.4   **Disadvantages** of a centralised IS/IT department.

(a)   Local offices might have to wait for IS/IT services and assistance.

(b)   Reliance on head office. Local offices are less elf-sufficient.

(c)   A system fault at head office will impact across the organisation.

2.5   **Advantages** of a decentralised IS/IT department.

(a)   IS/IT staff will be more aware of local business requirements.

(b)   Each office is more self-sufficient.

(c)   Offices are likely to have quicker access to IS/IT support/advice.

(d)   A decentralised structure is more likely to facilitate accurate IS/IT cost/overhead allocations.

2.6   **Disadvantages** of a decentralised IS/IT department.

(a)   Control may be more difficult - different and uncoordinated information systems may be introduced.

(b)   Self-sufficiency may encourage a lack of co-ordination between departments.

(c)   Increased risk of data duplication, with different offices holding the same data on their own separate files.

3   ACCOUNTING ISSUES

3.1   Providing and maintaining information systems to deliver good quality information involves significant expenditure. The costs incurred are summarised in the following table.

Capital costs	Revenue costs (one-off)	Revenue costs (ongoing)
• Hardware purchase • Cabling • System installation	• System development costs eg programmer and analyst fees, testing costs, file conversion costs etc • Initial training costs • Any redundancy costs attributable to the new system	• IS/IT staff costs • Communication and transmission costs • Power • Maintenance and support • Ongoing training • Consumables eg paper, printer ink, floppy disks, CDs

3.2   The organisation must account for the costs incurred providing and maintaining information systems. The IS charging system should encourage the efficient use of IS/IT resources. There are three broad possibilities when accounting for costs related to information systems.

- IS costs are treated as an **administrative overhead**
- IS costs are **charged out at cost**
- IS costs are **charged out at market rates**

Information technology as an administrative overhead

3.3   Under this system IT/IS costs are treated as a general administrative expense, and are not allocated to user departments.

3.4   **Advantages** of this approach are:

(a)   It is simple and cheap to administer, as there is no charge out system to operate.

(b)   May encourage innovation and experimentation as user-departments are more likely to demand better quality systems if they will not bear any cost.

(c)   The relationship between IS staff and user departments is not subject to conflict over costs.

3.5   **Disadvantages** of this approach are:

(a)   User departments may make unreasonable (and economically unjustifiable) demands.

(b)   Any inefficiencies within the IS/IT department are less likely to be exposed - as user departments will not be monitoring cost levels.

(c)   User departments may accept sub-standard service, as it is 'free'.

(d)   A true picture of user departments financial performance is not obtained - as significant costs attributable to that department are held in a central pool.

Information technology charged out at cost

3.6   A cost-based charge out involves IS/IT costs being allocated to user departments. Costs may be allocated according to methods such as: cost per transaction processed; cost per page; cost per hour of programmer's and/or analyst's time; cost per number of terminals/workstations; cost per unit of CPU time.

3.7 However, collecting and analysing the detailed information required to allocate costs using these indicators can be time-consuming, and therefore costly. For the sake of simplicity therefore, the allocation across user departments may be based on a relatively simple measure such as an estimate of IS/IT use.

3.8 The **advantages** of re-charging IS/IT costs to user departments, at cost, are:

(a) Simpler than charging at market value - the amount recharged is the total IS/IT costs incurred.

(b) User departments are encouraged to consider the cost of their usage of IT services.

(c) Encourages efficiency within the IS/IT department as excessive recharges are likely to result in complaints from other departments.

3.9 **Disadvantages** exist, too.

(a) Inefficiencies in the IS/IT department are merely passed on to users. This could be avoided if the department is only permitted to recharge budgeted or standard costs.

(b) The basis for recharging must be realistic - or users will feel that costs recharged are unfair which could lead to conflict.

(c) It may be difficult to choose a realistic basis to allocate the costs.

3.10 Under both the central overhead approach and the charge-out-at-cost approach the IS function is treated as a cost centre. This can influence the way in which information systems and technology are viewed within an organisation – it encourages the view that they are a drain on resources rather than tools in the quest for competitive advantage.

Market-based charge out methods

3.11 Under market-based methods, the IS/IT department acts as a profit centre. It sets its own prices and charges for its services with the aim of making a profit.

3.12 **Advantages** of the market-based charge out method include:

(a) User departments have the right to demand external standards of service. If the service provided by the IT department is sub-standard, it should be given the chance to improve - with the ultimate sanction of users choosing an outside supplier.

(b) It encourages an entrepreneurial attitude. IT managers are in charge of a department that could make a profit - this should help motivation.

(c) Efficiency and innovation within the IS/IT department is encouraged, as the more efficient the department is, and the more services users buy, the greater the profit will be. Bonuses for IT staff could be based on departmental profit.

(d) A true picture of user departments financial performance is able to be obtained - as the IS/IT costs charged to each department are based on market-rates.

3.13 **Disadvantages** of the market-based charge out method include:

(a) It can be difficult to decide on the charge out rate, particularly if there is no comparable service provider outside the organisation.

(b) If users feel rates are excessive, they may reduce their usage to below optimal levels, and relationships between the IS/IT department and user departments may become strained.

(c) Even if the service provided is poor, it may not be in the organisation's interest for user departments to buy from outsiders: the IS function's fixed costs still have to be covered, and there may result an under-use of resources available within the organisation. Also, a coherent approach to IS/IT should be taken - this would be difficult if a range of suppliers were used across the organisation.

Establishing the IS/IT function as a separate company

3.14 The concept of establishing the IS/IT department as a profit centre can be taken a step further - the IS/IT function could become a separate company, with a separate legal entity.

3.15 User departments within the 'main' company would purchase IS/IT services from the separate IS/IT company, and ideally should be free to change suppliers if service or value levels are sub-standard.

3.16 The new IS/IT company can also offer its services to other organisations - with the aim of increasing revenue and profit.

3.17 The advantages and disadvantages of market-based charge out methods covered earlier also apply to situations where a separate company has been set up.

3.18 Additional advantages include:

(a) The opportunity for increased revenue and profit.
(b) Increased career opportunities for IS/IT staff.
(c) Opportunities for economies of scale if the company grows.

3.19 Additional disadvantages include:

(a) IS/IT staff may lose touch with main company operations.
(b) Increased administration required for the additional company.
(c) The standard of service provided to the main company may suffer, as the focus switches to new clients.
(d) Setting appropriate prices for new clients may be difficult - tasks may not be similar to those undertaken within the original company.

4 OTHER ORGANISATIONAL ISSUES

Organisation structure

4.1 The structure of the organisation and the structure of the organisations information systems are related issues. Organisations that disperse decision making power to local offices will require an effective local management information system.

Constant change

4.2 A reliance on IS/IT commits an organisation to continual change. The pace of technological change is rapid. Computer systems - both hardware and software - are likely to be superseded after a few years.

Interoperability

4.3 Interoperability refers to the ability for systems to share and exchange information and facilities with other systems regardless of the technology platform or service provider. Interoperability implies an ability to cope with a variety of data structures, and the easy transfer of skills between applications and technologies.

BPP
PUBLISHING

Backward compatibility

4.4 A new version of a program is said to be backward compatible if it can use files and data created with an older version of the same program. Computer hardware is said to be backward compatible if it can run the same software as previous models.

4.5 Backward compatibility is important because it eliminates the need to start afresh when upgrading. In general, manufacturers try to keep their products backward compatible. Sometimes, however, it is necessary to sacrifice backward compatibility to take advantage of new technology.

Legacy system

4.6 A legacy system is an old outdated system which continues to be used, but no-longer meets the information requirements of the organisation. The main reason(s) legacy systems continue to be used often include the cost of replacing it, and the significant time and effort involved in introducing a new system.

4.7 Legacy systems often require specialised knowledge to maintain them in a condition suitable for operation. This may leave an organisation exposed should certain staff leave the organisation.

4.8 Legacy systems may also require data to be in a specific, maybe unusual format. This can cause compatibility problems if other systems are replaced throughout an organisation.

4.9 File conversion issues are common when replacing legacy systems, for example:

- Establishing the formats of data files held on the legacy system
- Assessing the data held for accuracy and completeness
- Automated file conversion procedures may not be applicable due to system compatibility and data issues
- Ensuring transferred data is available in the required format for all applications that access it

Open systems

4.10 Organisations develop computerised systems over a period of time, perhaps focusing on different functions at different times. The ease with which systems interact with each other is important for organisation efficiency. Examples of inefficiencies caused by systems incompatibility include:

(a) Hardware supplied by different manufacturers that can not interact.
(b) Data duplicated in different areas of the business as separate systems can not use the same source.
(c) Software that is unable to interact with other packages.

4.11 Open systems aim to ensure compatibility between different systems. An open systems infrastructure supports organisation-wide functions and allows interoperability of networks and systems. Authorised users are able to access applications and data from any part of the system.

5   **OUTSOURCING**   11/01, 5/02

> **KEY TERM**
>
> **Outsourcing** is the contracting out of specified operations or services to an external vendor.

Types of outsourcing

5.1   There are four **broad classifications** of outsourcing, as described in the following table.

Classification	Comment
Ad-hoc	The organisation has a short-term requirement for increased IS/IT skills. An example would be employing programmers on a short-term contract to help with the programming of bespoke software.
Project management	The development and installation of a particular IS/IT project is outsourced. For example, a new accounting system. (This approach is sometimes referred to as **systems integration.**)
Partial	Some IT/IS services are outsourced. Examples include hardware maintenance, network management or ongoing website management.
Total	An external supplier provides the vast majority of an organisation's IT/IS services; eg third party owns or is responsible for IT equipment, software and staff.

Levels of service provision

5.2   The degree to which the provision and management of IS/IT services are transferred to the third party varies according to the situation and the skills of both organisations.

(a)   **Time-share**. The vendor charges for access to an external processing system on a time-used basis. Software ownership may be with either the vendor or the client organisation.

(b)   **Service bureaux** usually focus on a specific function. Traditionally bureaux would provide the same type of service to many organisations eg payroll processing. As organisations have developed their own IT infrastructure, the use of bureaux has decreased.

(c)   **Facilities management (FM)**. The terms 'outsourcing' and 'facilities management' are sometimes confused. Facilities management traditionally involved contracts for premises-related services such as cleaning or site security.

In the context of IS/IT, facilities management involves an outside agency managing the organisation's IS/IT facilities. All equipment usually remains with the client, but the responsibility for providing and managing the specified services rests with the FM company. FM companies operating in the UK include Accenture and Cap Gemini.

5.3   The following table shows the main features of each of the outsourcing arrangements described above.

BPP
PUBLISHING

	Outsourcing arrangement		
Feature	**Timeshare**	**Service bureaux**	**Facilities Management (FM)**
Management responsibility	Mostly retained	Some retained	Very little retained
Focus	Operational	A function	Strategic
Timescale	Short-term	Medium-term	Long-term
Justification	Cost savings	More efficient	Access to expertise; higher quality service provision. Enables management to concentrate on the areas where they do possess expertise.

Organisations involved in outsourcing

Facilities management companies

5.4   FM arrangements have been covered in paragraph 5.2(c).

Software houses

5.5   Software houses concentrate on the provision of 'software services'. These services include feasibility studies, systems analysis and design, development of operating systems software, provision of application program packages, 'tailor-made' application programming, specialist systems advice, and so on. For example, a software house might be employed to write a computerised system for the London Stock Exchange.

Consultancy firms

5.6   Some consultancy firms work at a fairly high level, giving advice to management on the general approach to solving problems and on the types of system to use. Others specialise in giving more particular systems advice, carrying out feasibility studies and recommending computer manufacturers/software houses that will supply the right system. When a consultancy firm is used, the terms of the contract should be agreed at the outset.

5.7   The use of consultancy services enables management to learn directly or indirectly from the experience of others. Many larger consultancies are owned by big international accountancy firms; smaller consultancies may consist of one- or two-person outfits with a high level of specialist experience in one area.

5.8   The following categories of **consulting activity** have been identified by *Beaumont* and *Sutherland*.

   (a)   **Strategic studies,** involving the development of a business strategy or an IS strategy for an organisation.

   (b)   **Specialist studies,** where the consultant provides a high level of expertise in one area, for example Enterprise Resource Management software.

   (c)   **Project management,** involving supervision of internal and external parties in the completion of a particular project.

(d) **Body-shopping**, where the necessary staff, including consultants, project managers, systems analysts and programmers, for a project are identified.

(e) **Recruitment,** involving the supply of permanent or temporary staff.

Hardware manufacturers and suppliers

5.9 Computer manufacturers or their designated suppliers will provide the **equipment** necessary for a system. They will also provide, under a **maintenance contract,** engineers who will deal with any routine servicing and with any breakdown of the equipment.

Case example

The retailer Sears outsourced the management of its vast information technology and accounting functions to Accenture. First year *savings* were estimated to be £5 million per annum, growing to £14 million in the following year, and thereafter. This is clearly considerable, although re-organisation costs relating to redundancies, relocation and asset write-offs are thought to be in the region of £35 million. About 900 staff were involved: under the transfer of undertakings regulations (which protect employees when part or all of a company changes hands), Accenture was obliged to take on the existing Sears staff. This provided new opportunities for the staff who moved, while those who remained at Sears are free to concentrate on strategy development and management direction.

Developments in outsourcing

5.10 Outsourcing arrangements are becoming increasingly flexible to cope with the ever-changing nature of the modern business environment. Three trends are:

(a) **Multiple sourcing**. This involves outsourcing different functions or areas of the IS/IT function to a range of suppliers. Some suppliers may form alliances to present a stronger case for selection.

(b) **Incremental approach**. Organisations progressively outsource selected areas of their IT/IS function. Possible problems with outsourced services are solved before progressing to the next stage.

(c) **Joint venture sourcing**. This term is used to describe an organisation entering into a joint venture with a supplier. The costs (risks) and possible rewards are split on an agreed basis. Such an arrangement may be suitable when developing software that could be sold to other organisations.

(d) **Application Service Providers (ASP)**. ASPs are third parties that manage and distribute software services and solutions to customers across a Wide Area Network. ASPs could be considered the modern equivalent of the traditional computer bureaux.

Managing outsourcing arrangements   5/01

5.11 Managing outsourcing arrangements involves deciding what will be outsourced, choosing and negotiating with suppliers and managing the supplier relationship.

5.12 When considering whether to outsource a particular service the following questions are relevant.

(a) Is the system of strategic importance? Strategic IS are generally not suited to outsourcing as they require a high degree of specific business knowledge that a third party IT specialist can not be expected to possess.

(b) Can the system be relatively isolated? Functions that have only limited interfaces are most easily outsourced eg payroll.

(c) Do we know enough about the system to manage the outsourced service agreement? If an organisation knows very little about a technology it may be difficult to know what constitutes good service and value for money. It may be necessary to recruit additional expertise to manage the relationship with the other party.

(d) Are our requirements likely to change? Organisations should avoid tying themselves into a long-term outsourcing agreement if requirements are likely to change.

5.13 A key factor when choosing and negotiating with external vendors is the contract offered and subsequently negotiated with the supplier. The contract is sometimes referred to as the **Service Level Contract** (SLC) or **Service Level Agreement** (SLA).

5.14 The key elements of the contract are described in the following table.

Contract element	Comment
Timescale	When does the contract expire? Is the timescale suitable for the organisation's needs or should it be renegotiated?
Service level	The contract should clearly specify **minimum levels of service** to be provided. Penalties should be specified for failure to meet these standards. Relevant factors will vary depending on the nature of the services outsourced but could include: • Response time to requests for assistance/information • System 'uptime' percentage • Deadlines for performing relevant tasks
Exit route	Arrangements for an exit route, addressing how transfer to another supplier, or the move back in-house, would be conducted.
Software ownership	Relevant factors include: • Software licensing and security • If the arrangement includes the development of new software who owns the copyright?
Dependencies	If related services are outsourced the level of service quality agreed should group these services together.
Employment issues	If the arrangement includes provision for the organisation's IT staff to move to the third party, employer responsibilities must be specified clearly.

5.15 After a supplier has been selected, and the contact negotiated and signed, the contact provides the framework for the **relationship** between the organisation and the service provider.

5.16 The nature of the relationship between the organisation and the service provider will depend on the service that has been outsourced and the preferences and personalities of the people involved.

5.17 If full facilities management is involved, and almost all management responsibility for IT/IS lies with the entity providing the service, then a close relationship between the parties is necessary (a '**partnership**'). Factors such as organisation culture need to be considered when entering into such a close and critical relationship.

5.18   On the other hand, if a relatively simple function such as payroll were outsourced, such a close relationship with the supplier would not be necessary. A 'typical' supplier - customer relationship is all that is required. (Although issues such as confidentiality need to be considered with payroll data.)

5.19   Regardless of the type of relationship, a legally binding contract is the key element in establishing the obligations and responsibilities of all parties.

Question 1

Do any organisations with which you are familiar use outsourcing? What is the view of outsourcing in the organisation?

Answer

One view is given below.

The PA Consulting Group's annual survey of outsourcing found that 'on average the top five strategic outsourcers out-performed the FTSE by more than 100 per cent over three years; the bottom five under-performed by more than 66%'.

However the survey revealed that of those organisations who have opted to outsource IT functions, only five per cent are truly happy with the results. A spokesman for the consultants said that this is because most people fail to adopt a proper strategic approach, taking a view that is neither long-term nor broad enough, and taking outsourcing decisions that are piecemeal and unsatisfactory.

This lack of prescience is compounded by a failure to take a sufficiently rigorous approach to selection, specification, contract drafting and contract management.

The survey found that a constant complaint among many of those interviewed is the lack of ability of outsourcing organisations to work together.

Twenty-five per cent of those asked would bring the functions they had outsourced back in-house if it were possible.

Advantages of outsourcing arrangements

5.20   The **advantages** of outsourcing are as follows.

(a)   Outsourcing can remove uncertainty about **cost,** as there is often a long-term contract where services are specified in advance for a **fixed price.** If computing services are inefficient, the costs will be borne by the FM company. This is also an incentive to the third party to provide a high quality service.

(b)   Long-term contracts (maybe up to ten years) encourage **planning** for the future.

(c)   Outsourcing can bring the benefits of **economies of scale.** For example, a FM company may conduct research into new technologies that benefits a number of their clients.

(d)   A specialist organisation is able to retain **skills and knowledge.** Many organisations would not have a sufficiently well-developed IT department to offer IT staff opportunities for career development. Talented staff would leave to pursue their careers elsewhere.

(e)   New skills and knowledge become available. A specialist company can **share** staff with **specific expertise** between several clients. This allows the outsourcing company to take advantage of new developments without the need to recruit new people or re-train existing staff, and without the cost.

(f) **Flexibility** (contract permitting). Resources may be able to be scaled up or down depending upon demand. For instance, during a major changeover from one system to another the number of IT staff needed may be twice as large as it will be once the new system is working satisfactorily.

An outsourcing organisation is more able to arrange its work on a **project** basis, whereby some staff will expect to be moved periodically from one project to the next.

Disadvantages of outsourcing arrangements

5.21 Some possible **drawbacks** are outlined below.

(a) It is arguable that information and its provision is an **inherent part of the business** and of management. Unlike office cleaning, or catering, an organisation's IT services may be too important to be contracted out. Information is at the heart of management.

(b) A company may have highly **confidential information** and to let outsiders handle it could be seen as **risky** in commercial and/or legal terms.

(c) If a third party is handling IS/IT services there is no onus upon internal management to keep up with new developments or to suggest new ideas. Consequently, opportunities to gain **competitive advantage** may be missed. Any new technology or application devised by the third party is likely to be available to competitors.

(d) An organisation may find itself **locked in** to an unsatisfactory contract. The decision may be very difficult to reverse. If the service provider supplies unsatisfactory levels of service, the effort and expense the organisation would incur to rebuild its own computing function or to move to another provider could be substantial.

(e) The use of an outside organisation does not encourage awareness of the potential **costs** and benefits of IS/IT within the organisation. If managers cannot manage in-house IS/IT resources effectively, then it could be argued that they will not be able to manage an arrangement to outsource effectively either.

Insourcing

5.22 Outsourcing involves purchasing information technology expertise from outside the organisation. Several factors have led some to believe this is not the best solution in today's environment.

(a) Many organisations have found there is a shortage of qualified **candidates** with the skills they require.

(b) The **cost** of acquiring people with high-tech expertise and business skills, whether employing or outsourcing, fluctuates due to factors affecting supply and demand.

(c) Third, there is increasing recognition that to do a good job, IT professionals must understand the **business principles** behind the systems that they develop and manage.

5.23 Insourcing involves recruiting IS/IT staff internally, from other areas of the business, and teaching these business-savvy employees about technology. The logic behind the idea is that it is easier (and cheaper) to **teach technical skills to business people** than to teach business skills to technical people.

5.24   Supporters of insourcing believe it has the potential to:

(a)   Create a better quality workforce that combines both technical and business skills.
(b)   Reduce costs.
(c)   Improve relationships and communication between IT staff and other departments.
(d)   Increase staff retention - through providing an additional career path.

5.25   Possible disadvantages include:

(a)   The risk that non-technical employees will not pick up the IS/IT skills required.
(b)   Finding staff willing to make the change.
(c)   Replacing staff who do make the switch.

Case example

INSOURCING: IS DEPARTMENTS BECOMING MORE EFFICIENT AND IMAGINATIVE

IS managers find themselves caught between the proverbial rock and a hard place. While facing increasing pressure from management to launch development initiatives, they must somehow cope with backlogs of change requests to existing systems.

In the past, the solution might have been to throw more money at the problem, and hire more programmers. However, as companies tighten their belts to survive in a tremendously competitive marketplace, they are trying to meet these challenges by becoming more efficient and more imaginative.

How does an organisation reduce the number of programmers working on legacy applications and increase the number working on new development initiatives, while holding maintenance-level productivity at a constant, or even improved, level?

One option open to MIS is to bite the bullet and outsource maintenance tasks. But this is not an attractive solution to many IS managers. 'There's no way I'm going to turn over applications that are critical to the everyday running of the business,' said a director of a major company. 'Once you farm out these apps, they're gone. You've lost control of your own destiny.'

This loss of control over applications critical to the company's business is a major disadvantage of outsourcing. Once applications are maintained outside the IS department, the understanding of how to work on them is lost to the company; these systems gradually, but inevitably, become the possession of the outsourcer.

There is an alternative to outsourcing - 'insourcing'. Insourcing is based on the old maxim that it is far more effective to teach someone to fish than to fish for them. That is, rather than outsourcing maintenance, and then reengineering processes to free up resources, the company either uses existing staff with key skills to train other staff, or hires an outsider to facilitate the Insourcing process by improving the capabilities of existing staff.

For insourcing to work, staff must be capable and prepared to set aside the necessary time and resources, and management must be prepared to actively support and resource the process.

Case study link

The issues surrounding the possible outsourcing of an activity or function could be relevant to the Final Level Case Study paper.

BPP
PUBLISHING

Chapter roundup

- At the head of the information systems/information technology function will be either the IS/IT manager, or the **IS/IT director**. This person will be responsible for:
  - IS/IT strategy development
  - IS/IT risk management
  - Overseeing the steering committee
  - The IS/IT infrastructure

- The general purpose of an IS/IT **steering committee** would be to make decisions relating to the future use and development of IS/IT by the organisation.

- A key information systems role is that of **database administrator**. A database administrator is responsible for all data and information held within an organisation.

- An **Information Centre** (IC) is a small unit of staff with a good technical awareness of computer systems, whose task is to provide a support function to computer users within the organisation.

- A **centralised** IS/IT department involves all IS/IT staff and functions being based out at a single central location, such as head office.

- A **decentralised** IS/IT department involves IS/IT staff and functions being spread out throughout the organisation.

- Providing and maintaining information systems to deliver good quality information involves significant expenditure. There are three broad possibilities when **accounting for costs** related to information systems.
  - IS costs are treated as an administrative **overhead**
  - IS costs are **charged out at cost**
  - IS costs are **charged out at market rates**

- A **legacy system** is an old outdated system which continues to be used, but no-longer meets the information requirements of the organisation.

- **Outsourcing** is the contracting out of specified operations or services to an external vendor. There are various outsourcing options available, with different levels of control maintained 'in-house'. Outsourcing has **advantages** (eg use of highly skilled people) and **disadvantages** (eg lack of control).

- **Insourcing** involves recruiting IS/IT staff internally, from other areas of the business, and teaching these business-savvy employees about technology.

- Supporters of **insourcing** believe it is easier (and cheaper) to teach technical skills to business people than to teach business skills to technical people.

Quick quiz

1   'It is essential that an information systems director has exceptional 'hands-on' computer programming skills'.

   True   ☐

   False   ☑

2   List four possible responsibilities of an IS/IT steering committee.

   1   *COMPLIANCE WITH STRATEGY*

   2   *COMMIT RESOURCES*

   3   *MONITOR PROGRESS*

   4   *PROVIDE LEADERSHIP / GUIDANCE*

3   List three advantages of a decentralised IS/IT department.

   1   *Control remains with location u Self sufficient*

2 *NO need to rely on others/time scale/access*

3 *Accurate costing*

4 List three disadvantages of a decentralised IS/IT department.

1 *Self-sufficiency = lack of co-ordination*

2 *Risk of duplications*

3 *Control difficult – un co-ordinated*

5 What does the 'open systems' concept aim to achieve? *ENSURE COMPATIBILITY BETWEEN FIRMS*

6 Define 'legacy system'.

7 'Information systems that are strategically important should be outsourced to ensure those working with these systems have excellent technical knowledge'.

True ☐

False ☐

8 List four advantages of outsourcing the IS/IT function.

1 ....

2 ....

3 ....

4 ....

9 List four disadvantages of outsourcing the IS/IT function.

1 ....

2 ....

3 ....

4 ....

10 What would a SLA contain?

Answers to quick quiz

1 FALSE. An IS/IT director requires a wide range of skills including technical know-how, general management ability, a keen sense of business awareness and a good understanding of the organisations' operations. A knowledge of programming could be useful (as part of 'technical know-how), but exceptional hands-on skills would not be essential.

2 [Four of]

Ensuring IS/IT activities comply with IS/IT strategy

Ensuring IS/IT activities compliment the overall organisation strategy

Ensuring resources committed to IS/IT are used effectively

Monitoring IS/IT projects

Providing leadership and guidance on IS/IT

3 [Three of]

Each office can introduce an information system specially tailored for its individual needs.

Local offices are more self-sufficient.

Offices are likely to have quicker access to IS/IT support/advice.

A decentralised structure is more likely to facilitate accurate IS/IT cost/overhead allocations.

4   [Three of]

Control may be more difficult - different and uncoordinated information systems may be introduced.

Self-sufficiency may encourage a lack of co-ordination between departments.

Increased risk of data duplication, with different offices holding the same data on their own separate files.

Increased risk of errors and inconsistencies between systems.

5   Open systems aim to ensure compatibility between different systems. An open systems infrastructure supports organisation-wide functions and provide interoperability.

6   A legacy system is an old outdated system which continues to be used, but no-longer meets the information requirements of the organisation.

7   FALSE. Strategic IS are generally not suited to outsourcing as they require a high degree of specific business knowledge that a third party IT/IS specialist can not be expected to possess.

8   [Four of]

Cost control - services are specified in advance for a fixed price.

Certainty - long-term contracts allow greater certainty in planning for the future.

Economies of scale. Several organisations will employ the same company.

Skills and knowledge are retained within the specialist company who can offer staff career development.

New skills and knowledge become available. A specialist company can share staff with specific expertise between several clients.

Flexibility - resources employed can be scaled up or down depending upon demand.

9   [Four of]

An organisation's IS services may be too important to be contracted out. Information is at the heart of management.

Risky – confidential or commercially sensitive information could be leaked.

Opportunities may be missed to use IS/IT for competitive advantage - there is no onus upon internal management to keep up with new developments and have new ideas.

Locked in - an organisation may be locked into a contract with a poor service provider.

Hard to reverse - the effort and expense an organisation would have to incur to rebuild its own computing function and expertise would be enormous.

Outsourcing does not encourage an awareness of the potential costs and benefits of IT amongst managers.

10   The Service Level Agreement (SLA) or Service Level Contract (SLC) is a vital aspect of any outsourcing arrangement. It should specify minimum levels of service, arrangements for an exit route, transfer arrangements and dispute procedures.

Questions to try	Level	Marks	Time
3	Examination	25	45 mins
6	Examination	25	45 mins
12	Examination	25	45 mins

Part D
The social and organisational impact of IS/IT

THE HUMAN INFORMATION PROCESSOR (HIP)

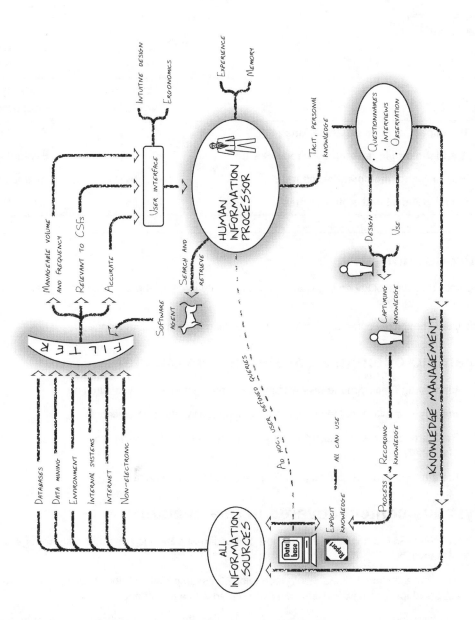

Chapter 8

SOCIAL AND ORGANISATIONAL FACTORS

Topic list	Syllabus reference	Ability required
1 The impact of IT on organisations	(iv)	Evaluation
2 IT and the employee/employer relationship	(iv)	Evaluation
3 Planning and implementing change	(iv)	Evaluation
4 Social, political and ethical issues	(iv)	Evaluation

Introduction

The impact of technology on organisations and society in general over the last ten years has been dramatic.

This chapter explores some of the wider issues arising from this rapid change.

Learning outcomes covered in this chapter

- **Identify** and **recommend** new working patterns to improve a given situation

- **Identify** and **evaluate** the impact of developments in telecommunications

- **Evaluate** and **recommend** strategies for managing change in an IT context *(Also see Chapter 7)*

- **Identify** and **evaluate** the cultural dimensions of IT acceptance

Syllabus content covered in this chapter

- The way IS/IT is changing the method of working and the increase in the knowledge content of many jobs

- The organisational impact of technology, its implications for structure and working relationships, and how individuals may be faced with a role change

- The growing awareness of remote working and the implication for the individual and the organisation

- The impact of IS/IT on the social aspect of the organisation and implications for organisational culture

- The management of change and potential staff reactions, particularly in respect of actual or perceived role changes

1 THE IMPACT OF IT ON ORGANISATIONS Pilot paper

Organisation structure

1.1 Information systems and information technology have played a significant role in the development of the modern business environment. For example, modern communications technology makes **decentralised** organisations possible, allowing decision making to be passed down to 'empowered' workers or outsourced to external companies.

1.2 There is a trend towards smaller, more agile companies. **Flexibility** and **speed** are increasingly seen as the key to competitive advantage. Advances in IT have allowed complex operating processes to be accelerated and made feedback information available almost immediately.

Span of control

1.3 Business automation and rationalisation, and improved management information systems, have often resulted in layers of middle management being removed in many organisations.

1.4 Managers or staff 'lower down' the hierarchy have been empowered to make decisions previously made by middle managers. Information technology has therefore had the effect of flattening organisation hierarchies and **widening spans of control**. (Span of control, or 'span of management', refers to the number of subordinates responsible to a superior. If a manager has five subordinates, the span of control is five.)

1.5 There is no universally 'correct' size for the span of control. The appropriate span of control will depend on:

 (a) **Ability of the manager**. A good organiser and communicator will be able to control a larger number. The manager's work-load is also relevant.

 (b) **Ability of the subordinates**. The more experienced, able, trustworthy and well-trained subordinates are, the easier it is to control larger numbers.

 (c) **Nature of the task**. It is easier for a supervisor to control a large number of people if they are all doing routine, repetitive or similar tasks.

 (d) The **geographical dispersal** of the subordinates, and the **communication system** of the organisation.

 (e) The availability of **good quality information** to assist in decision making.

Tall and flat organisations

1.6 The span of control has implications for the 'shape' of the organisation. An organisation with a narrow span of control will have more levels in its management hierarchy – the organisation will be narrow and **tall**. A tall organisation reflects tighter supervision and control, and lengthy chains of command and communication.

1.7 An organisation of the same size with a wide span of control will be will be wide and **flat**. The flat organisation reflects a greater degree of delegation - the more a manager delegates, the wider the span of control can be.

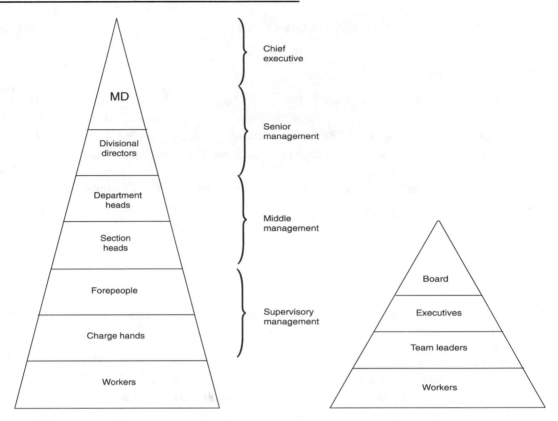

1.8 Some writers argue that tall organisation structures are too **inflexible** for the modern business environment. **Disadvantages** of **tall** structures are:

(a) The extra management levels increase costs eg salaries, office accommodation.

(b) They create a longer chain of communication. Management is more remote from operations - information may be distorted or blocked.

(c) Management responsibilities overlap and become confused as the size of the management structure gets larger.

(d) The same work passes through too many hands.

(e) Planning is more difficult because it must be organised at more levels.

(f) The rigid structure can stifle initiative and damage the motivation of subordinates.

(g) There are more 'rungs' available on the promotional ladder, but there are unlikely to be real increases in responsibility between levels.

1.9 The **advantages** of **flat** structures are the opposite of the statements above. The disadvantages of flat structures are the loss of management **control** and possible lack of organisation **coherency**. Tall structures may be better suited to situations where rigid supervision and control is required.

1.10 An **information system,** such as an intranet, can help provide organisation unity and coherency in flat, decentralised organisations.

1.11 The trend towards flatter structures is evidenced by talk of an 'e-lance economy', characterised by shifting **coalitions** of small firms collaborating on particular **projects**.

1.12 As we have emphasised elsewhere in this Text, information systems strategy and the way systems are structured, should support the **overall business strategy**.

Other effects of IT on organisations

Routine processing

1.13 The processing of data can be done in bigger volumes, at greater speed and with greater accuracy.

Digital information and record keeping

1.14 Information storage and transmission is now largely digital rather than paper-based. However, many people like 'hard copies' and print out information as required. Far from reducing the use of paper, computer systems seem to have encouraged greater use of paper.

1.15 The nature and quality of management information has also changed.

   (a) Managers have access to more information - for example from an EIS. Information is also likely to be more timely, accurate, reliable and up-to-date.

   (b) More detailed planning is possible through the use of models (eg spreadsheets).

   (c) Information for control should be more readily available.

   (d) Decision making should improve as a consequence of better quality information.

Employment issues

1.16 The infiltration of IT into almost every area of business means that the vast majority of employees are now expected to utilise information technology. IT skills are required and new ways of working have emerged. We look at the impact of IT on the employer/employee relationship in the next section of this chapter.

Technological change

1.17 A reliance on information technology commits an organisation to **continual change**. Systems are likely to be superseded after a few years.

Customer service

1.18 Information technology has enabled organisations to provide better customer service. Customer databases, Electronic Data Interchange, extranets, websites, and datamining can all be applied to improving service levels.

Interoperability and open systems

1.19 Interoperability means that any party can **share** and **exchange** information and facilities with other parties without having to use the same service provider or technology platform. Interoperability facilitates the formation of strategic alliances and encourages collaboration across organisation boundaries.

1.20 Open systems is a similar concept to interoperability, although it is usually (but not always) used in the context of different systems within the same organisation. As discussed in the previous chapter, an open systems infrastructure supports **organisation-wide functions** and allows for the transfer of information between networks and systems.

Information markets

1.21 The term '**information market**' reflects the growing view that information is a **commodity** which can be bought, sold or exchanged.

1.22 There has been a growing realisation that information is a resource and that it has many of the characteristics of any other resource. A key theme of this syllabus is the benefits which information, properly managed and used, can bring to an organisation.

Developments in communications

1.23 Communications technology is probably having a greater impact on organisational life than computers are at present. **E-mail** provides a quick and **efficient** means of communicating worldwide.

1.24 **Voice mail** systems allow **flexibility** in communication time and location. Computer Telephony Integration (CTI) systems can **route** incoming calls (they can be frustrating, particularly for callers with non-standard enquiries). CTI also enables information about callers to be gathered and stored allowing **personalised** communication.

1.25 Computer conferencing systems and organisation-wide **bulletin boards** encourage **communication** – both formal and **informal**.

1.26 **Video-conferencing** allows face-to-face contact between people who are spread widely across the world. If a video-conference is deemed sufficient, **travel costs** can be reduced.

2 IT AND THE EMPLOYEE/EMPLOYER RELATIONSHIP

2.1 The widespread use of information technology in the workplace has affected the relationship between employers and employees. Some of the effects are explained in the following table.

Effect of IT	Comment
Reduced need to follow the chain-of-command	Information technology allows quick and easy communication between staff at all levels. For example, an employee may be willing to e-mail the managing director, but would be unwilling or unable to telephone him or her.
	Efficient channels of communication that operate independently of the organisation hierarchy reduce the need to pass communications up the chain of command.
Information overload	Computing and communications developments have led to the capture, analysis and transmission of ever-increasing amounts of information. However, only relevant information is useful. An excess of irrelevant information is harmful - a person is more likely to miss or misinterpret vital information if they are swamped with irrelevant material. We cover approaches to avoiding information overload in the following chapter.
	Some would argue that information overload has caused significant employee **stress**.

Effect of IT	Comment
Nature of work	Technology has enabled the automation of many unskilled and semi-skilled tasks. This has resulted in the degrading of old skills and the requirement for employees to learn new skills.
	Some employees have found the change to well-established working patterns extremely stressful. Others have preferred to take redundancy or early retirement.
	Employers may need to provide training and re-training programs for staff.
	As technology becomes more user-friendly there could be opportunities for greater flexibility and job rotation.
Close business relationships regardless of geographical location	Information technology enables people located all over the world to enjoy close working relationships.
	Technology enables operations to be sited anywhere in the world. For example, many 'UK' call centres are based in India. To enable staff to make 'small talk' with UK-based clients, staff keep up-to-date with UK news, weather, sport and even soap operas via the Internet.
More flexible working arrangements	Advances in technology mean many tasks are able to be performed off-site. The need for flexibility in employee and employer attitudes has resulted in trends away from 'a job for life', towards shorter terms of service, freelance workers and contracting. Part-time positions are increasing.
	We look at homeworking later in this chapter.
Greater monitoring and control	Improved information systems should help managers to plan and control work more effectively.
	Technology also enables untrusting employers to monitor employee behaviour.
	• Closed-circuit cameras are now relatively cheap and easy to operate
	• Personal e-mail sent using the organisation's server can be monitored
	• Computer Telephony Integration (CTI) systems record phone numbers called and the call length
	Privacy laws regarding such activities differ from country to country. In many countries relevant law is still developing.

Teleworking or homeworking   **Pilot paper**

2.2   Some employers have encouraged **teleworking** or **homeworking**, sometimes in conjunction with a move towards a pool of freelance workers. Developments in information technology (eg e-mail, remote network access) allow these workers to be based off-site, often at home. The practise is sometimes referred to as **remote working** and **telecommuting**.

2.3   The **advantages to the employer** of homeworking include:

   • Cost savings on office accommodation
   • A larger potential pool of employees eg those with young children
   • Flexibility - if homeworkers are freelance who work only when required

2.4   The **advantages to the employee** include:

- No time is wasted commuting
- Work can be organised around other commitments
- In some situations there may be less distractions out of the office

2.5 The **disadvantages for employers** are chiefly problems of **control**. Managers who like to practise close supervision and who lack trust in their employees may view homeworking as an opportunity for laziness.

2.6 The problems of control depend to a large extent on the individual involved. Other issues for the organisation might be as follows.

- Co-ordination of the work of different homeworkers
- Training – where and when will training be performed?
- Culture – homeworkers are relatively isolated from organisation cultural influences

2.7 Problems for homeworkers include:

- Isolation
- Domestic intrusions
- Adequate space
- If contracting or freelance, fewer employment rights

Case example

Flexibility (and trust) is required for homeworking arrangements to succeed.

For example, BPP authors are able to work from home two days per week. The arrangement works well as the work performed by authors is relatively self-contained. However, when a book is nearing completion, final corrections pass fairly regularly between writers and the typesetting studio.

At this stage of the process homeworking is not practical as it would slow down production.

Sociotechnical design   5/01

2.8 The way in which information systems are designed can impact on the employer-employee relationship. While modern system building approaches attempt to ensure end-user input into system design this input tends to focus on operational aspects of the system.

2.9 Sociotechnical design looks at the wider picture. It recognises that an organisation is a **sociotechnical** system, consisting of three sub-systems.

(a) A formal **structure.**

(b) A **technological system** consisting of the work to be done, and the machines, tools and other facilities available to do it.

(c) A **social system** consisting of the people within the organisation, the ways they think and the ways they interact with each other.

KEY TERM

Sociotechnical design attempts to produce information systems that are technically efficient but also take into account organisational and staff needs.

2.10 Sociotechnical design gives users a say in the design of the information system and a say in the **role of information systems** in their workplace. A sociotechnical design plan would include human factors such as work group structures and job satisfaction. Technical and social factors are considered together and the alternative that best meets technical **and social** objectives is selected.

2.11 By ensuring organisational and social objectives are considered, employers are **reducing the risk** of a new system causing unforeseen disruption. In particular, employee acceptance of the system should be increased.

2.12 Before adopting a sociotechnical approach employers must be sure that they do wish to take employees' views into account. To solicit employee views, and then **ignore** them, is likely to cause **resentment** and increase the risk of employee rejection of the system.

2.13 'Human issues' which a sociotechnical approach could consider include:

- The skills required to operate the system and the skills of employees
- Task variety - ensuring monotonous tasks are spread around
- Autonomy - ensuring supervision and monitoring levels are not oppressive
- Ergonomics and employee health and safety issues (eg breaks from VDU work)
- User interface design

3 PLANNING AND IMPLEMENTING CHANGE

3.1 **Change**, in the context of organisation and management, can occur in many areas.

- The **environment**
- The **products** the organisation makes or the **services** it provides
- **How** products are made, or who makes them
- Management and **working relationships**
- Organisation **structure or size**

3.2 Change can affect individuals in a variety of ways.

(a) **Physiologically,** both as the natural product of ageing and as the result of external factors (eg a change in work patterns).

(b) **Circumstantial changes** such as living in a new house, establishing new relationships or working to new routines. This involves letting go of things and learning new ways of functioning.

(c) Change affects individuals **psychologically.**

(i) **Disorientation** before new circumstances have been assimilated.

(ii) **Uncertainty** may lead to **insecurity,** especially acute in changes involving work and/or fast acclimatisation (a steep learning curve may lead to feelings of incapacity).

(iii) New expectations, challenges and pressures may generate **role stress** in which an individual feels discomfort in the role he or she plays.

(iv) **Powerlessness.** Change can be particularly threatening if it is perceived as an outside force or agent against which the individual is powerless.

Resistance to change

3.3 Resisting change means attempting to preserve the existing state of affairs against pressure to alter it.

BPP PUBLISHING

3.4 General **sources of resistance** to change include:

(a) **Attitudes or beliefs,** perhaps arising from cultural, religious or social influences.

(b) **Loyalty** to a group and its norms.

(c) **Habit**.

(d) **Politics** - in the sense of resisting changes that might weaken the power base of the individual or group or strengthen a rival's position.

(e) The way in which any change is put forward and **implemented**.

(f) The **personalities** of those involved.

3.5 **Immediate causes** of resistance in any particular situation could include:

(a) **Self-interest** - if the status quo is perceived to be preferable.

(b) **Misunderstanding and distrust** - if the reasons for, or the nature and consequences of, the change have not been made clear.

(c) **Contradictory assessments** - disagreement over the likely costs and benefits of the change.

(d) **Low tolerance of change itself** - differences in tolerance of uncertainty.

3.6 Possible **reactions** to proposed change are outlined below:

(a) **Acceptance:** whether enthusiastic espousal, co-operation, grudging co-operation or resignation.

(b) **Indifference:** usually where the change does not directly affect the individual; evidence is apathy, lack of interest, inaction.

(c) **Passive resistance:** refusal to learn, working to rule; pleas of ignorance or defensiveness; procrastination.

(d) **Active resistance:** deliberate 'spoiling', go-slows, deliberate errors, sabotage, absenteeism or strikes.

Planning and implementing change

3.7 A systematic approach should be established, for planning and implementing changes.

Step	
1	Determine need or desire for change in a particular area.
2	Prepare a tentative plan. • Brainstorming sessions a good idea, since alternatives for change should be considered
3	Analyse probable reactions to the change
4	Make a final decision from the choice of alternative options • Decision taken either by group problem-solving (participative) or by manager alone (coercive)
5	Establish a timetable for change • 'Coerced' changes can probably be implemented faster, but may not be accepted. • The speed of implementation will depend on the likely reactions of the people affected. • Communication is key to minimising resistance to the change.

(continued on the next page)

> 6   Communicate the plan for change
>   • This is really a continuous process, beginning at Step 1 and going through to Step 7.
>
> 7,8 Implement the change - then after a period of operation review the change.
>   • Continuous evaluation and modification may be required.

The change process

3.8   In the words of *John Hunt (Managing People at Work)*: 'Learning also involves re-learning - not merely learning something new but trying to unlearn what is already known.' This is the thinking behind the three-stage approach to changing human behaviour, which may be depicted as follows.

UNFREEZE   ⟶   Attitudinal/   ⟶   REFREEZE

existing   behavioural   new

behaviour   change   behaviour

Step 1.   **Unfreeze** is the most difficult stage of the process, concerned mainly with 'selling' the change, with giving individuals or groups a **motive** for changing their attitudes, values, behaviour, systems or structures.

(a)   If the need for change is immediate, clear and necessary for the survival of the individual or group, the unfreeze stage will be greatly accelerated.

(b)   Routine changes may be harder to sell if they are perceived to be unimportant and not survival-based.

(c)   Unfreezing processes need four things

   •   A trigger (eg a crisis).
   •   Someone to challenge and expose the existing behaviour pattern.
   •   The involvement of outsiders.
   •   Alterations to power structure.

Step 2.   **Change** is mainly concerned with identifying what the new, desirable behaviour should be, communicating it and encouraging individuals and groups to adopt it. The new ideas must be shown to work.

Step 3.   **Refreeze** is the final stage, implying consolidation or reinforcement of the new behaviour. Positive reinforcement (praise, reward) or negative reinforcement (sanctions applied to those who deviate from the new behaviour) may be used.

Strategies for change management

3.9   Each of the causes of change identified below can be dealt with in a different way.

Cause	How to deal with it
Parochial self-interest	**Negotiation** (eg offer incentives to those resisting on grounds of self-interest).
Misunderstanding	This is best dealt with by **educating and reassuring** people. Trust has to be earned.
Different viewpoints of the situation	Change can be promoted through participation and by **involving potential resisters**.
Low tolerance of change	Force the change through and then **support** the new behaviours it requires. In short, people have to be encouraged (by carrot and stick methods) to adopt the new methods.

BPP PUBLISHING

Champion of change model: the role of the change agent

3.10   New information systems developments need management support. The **champion of change model** recognises the importance of change being led by a **change agent**, who may be an individual or occasionally a group.

Step 1.   **Senior management** decide in broad terms what is to be done.

Step 2.   They appoint a **change agent** to drive it through. Senior management has three roles.

- Supporting the change agent, if the change provokes conflict between the agent and interest groups in the organisation

- Reviewing and monitoring the progress of the change

- Endorsing and approving the changes, and ensuring that they are publicised

Step 3.   The change agent has to **win the support of functional and operational managers,** who have to introduce and enforce the changes in their own departments. The champion of change has to provide advice and information, as well as evidence that the old ways are no longer acceptable.

Step 4.   The change agent **galvanises managers into action** and gives them any necessary support. The managers ensure that the changes are implemented operationally, in the field. Where changes involve a new information system it is ultimately the users who are responsible for operating the new system.

Case example

Change Management, a pragmatic approach in Abbey National plc.

There have been many internal changes in Abbey National since becoming a plc.

- Change from 49 to 5 mortgage administration centres.
- Set up of 3 Teleservice Centres.
- Introduction of postal accounts.
- Reduction in the number of branches.
- Combine administrations of Scottish Mutual and Abbey National Life under same customer service structure and systems.

People do not resist change - they resist what they perceive that they will lose. Perception = reality.

Communication is critical and should be planned and managed by those who are communicating change. **The effects of good communication**:

- Reduces uncertainty
- Builds commitment
- Shapes assumptions
- Involve the people in the process

COMMUNICATE TO GAIN COMMITMENT - DON'T GET THE COMMUNICATION WRONG!

The communication process

Step 1.   Project team 'sell' concept to managers and supervisors

Step 2.   Supervisors present to their team with support from project team

Step 3.   Two day briefing/training for supervisors

Step 4.   On-ground support for supervisors throughout implementation

Step 5.   Remove support gradually

Step 6.   Continuous improvement course

Step 7.   Formal handover to managers

Change issues encountered at Abbey National plc

- Supervisor's confidence destroyed (security blanket removed)
- No PC experience to operate spreadsheets
- Task of planning day takes too long, no time to do other work
- This would not work in our area because we are different
- Frightened of raising issues
- Focus on backlogs - no time to do process management

Summary

- Involve the people who are impacted al all stages

- Caveat on initial stages or market-sensitive projects

- Communicate, communicate, communicate - tailored, early, often - if you have nothing to say people may believe you have a hidden agenda

- Consider the cultural differences

- Do not forget managers

What if you do not have the time to go through all the stages and give the level of support people require?

- Anticipate as many issues as possible
- Mobilise maximum power
- Expect/prepare for resistance

Source: CIMA articles database

---

4   SOCIAL, POLITICAL AND ETHICAL ISSUES   5/01

4.1   In this section we look at the social, political and ethical issues raised by the impact of information technology and information systems.

Social issues

4.2   The growing influence of information systems is part of a larger trend towards an accelerated **pace of change** in modern society.

4.3   To put this in perspective, consider the following.

The first wave

4.4   When the world changed from a **hunting and gathering culture** to an **agricultural age**, lifestyles changed and the speed of life accelerated. Old definitions and institutions collapsed and new ones took their place.

4.5   The agricultural age defined wealth as **land and property**. Little changed from generation to generation. You looked to the past as a guide to the future. The family farm was the focal point of everyday life. Values revolved around the church and the family.

The second wave

4.6   A **second wave** occurred when the world changed due to the **industrial revolution**. Again, the speed of life changed, human attitudes and patterns of interaction changed, and old power structures were replaced by the new.

4.7 **Wealth** in the industrial age was based on **capital goods made from raw materials**. Those who owned and manipulated the raw materials and their products gained power and affluence. The future was defined by the present. The influence of the extended family was reduced; the nuclear family becoming dominant.

4.8 The concept of the '**job**' was also invented by the industrial age. It pulled the children off the farms to the cities. A job required an employee to be at a certain place for a set amount of time, to do repetitive tasks, and to 'work' at producing things that were not immediately relevant to the individual's life, in exchange for wages.

4.9 The industrial age saw the creation of vacations, health insurance, and sick days. Some found this change traumatic and resisted. Respect for the wisdom of the elders of the society declined as their power was bypassed; they no longer controlled the source of wealth, and their knowledge was irrelevant to the new age.

The third wave

4.10 The **third wave** is the present change from the industrial age to the **communications** age or **information society**. As this shift occurs, we can expect life to speed up even more and we can anticipate new patterns of human interaction.

4.11 We can see evidence of the new age. The average life-cycle of a business is now only seven years. Technologies are being superseded before they have been fully implemented eg Wireless Application Protocol (WAP).

4.12 The communications age looks to the future to decide what needs to be done. The world is changing so fast that businesses must attempt to predict the future.

4.13 **Wealth** in the information society is linked to **knowledge**. Increasingly, successful people and organisations will be those able to create and distribute information and knowledge.

Social change

4.14 The increased pace of change requires visions of the future to be rapidly adaptable, that long-range plans be flexible, and that we build in mechanisms for adjusting to change. The society of the future will need people who are open-minded, tolerant and **flexible**.

4.15 People are becoming exposed to much greater volumes of information. It is estimated the amount of information in the world is doubling every seven years. It is no longer adequate to learn something once. Skills and knowledge must be **continually updated** to keep up with new developments.

4.16 New communication tools are destroying old power structures. As knowledge flows it empowers consumers. Consumers can scan the world for the best deals.

4.17 The Internet allows people to self-educate. The individual is **empowered**, particularly the individual who is flexible, self-motivated, and who has strong data-gathering and organisational skills.

4.18 Some commentators believe the information age will allow for greater individual choice, decentralisation of power (less centralised planning), a reduced urban population, a change from top-down leadership to lateral leadership, and a faster rate of adopting and dropping identities as jobs change frequently.

4.19 The following **social** phenomena are made possible by developments in information technology.

(a) **Reduced urban congestion**

People can obtain what they want without leaving their desk. This should make shops and roads less crowded. In the long-term it may affect where people choose to live.

(b) **Consumer choice**

A computer search for an item or service can be done in seconds, whereas it could take hours, days or weeks to find exactly what was wanted by more conventional means. Consumers are also not restricted to local providers: they can do business with any company in the world that has a website. On the one hand this increases choice for consumers, but on the other it may make the purchase decision more difficult, because there are more options.

(c) **The 'size' of society**

Following on from point (b), society itself becomes global. People do business in places and with organisations that they would never have considered or even known about before.

(d) **Time management and quality of life**

Rather than being restricted to business hours, people can obtain what they want 24 hours a day. This helps people to manage their time and do what they want to do at their own convenience.

(e) **Interaction**

Instead of dealing face-to-face or voice-to-voice with others, people interact with their computer. If human contact is valued, this makes the experience a poorer one. On the other hand it removes some possible sources of conflict.

(f) **Work opportunities**

There will be fewer opportunities for people who are not IT literate. Software tools may decrease the number of sales people required in roles that involve direct contact with others. There may be greater opportunities to work in call centres and distribution related roles.

Privacy

4.20 Within industry and commerce there are two important categories of privacy: consumer privacy and employee privacy.

4.21 **Consumer privacy** considers the information compiled by data collectors such as marketing firms, insurance companies and retailers, the use of credit information collected by credit agencies and the rights of the consumers to control information about themselves and their commercial transactions.

4.22 The extensive sharing of personal data is an erosion of privacy that reduces the capacity of individuals to retain control of factors which may affect their lives. Organisations involved in such activities have a responsibility to ensure privacy rights are upheld. The problems involved in the transfer of consumer data include:

- The potential for combining data to create detailed profiles of individuals
- The potential for data to be sold to unscrupulous vendors
- Problems correcting inaccurate information

4.23 **Employee privacy** deals primarily with the growing reliance on electronic monitoring and other mechanisms to analyse work habits and measure employee productivity. An important employee right is the right to control or limit access to personal information provided to an employer.

4.24 In the modern workplace there are increasing opportunities to monitor activity. Potential problem areas include:

- Programs that allow user files and directories to be monitored
- Systems that enable interception and scrutiny of communications
- Monitoring programs that track worker productivity and work habits
- Computer-controlled closed circuit television (CCTV) surveillance systems

Political issues

4.25 One of the main political issues of the information age is the extent to which governments should 'interfere' or legislate in the new environment. Some relevant political issues are outlined in the following table.

Issue	Comment
Privacy	Privacy is not just a social issue – it also has political consequences. The power of computer systems makes them a threat to the privacy of the individual. Increasingly, decisions are made about individuals on the basis of information held on computerised systems.
	As a result, most countries have introduced legislation designed to protect the individual. In the UK the current legislation is the Data Protection Act 1998.
	Key points of the UK Act are:
	• Data users must register with the Data Protection Registrar
	• Individuals (data subjects) are awarded rights, including the right to view data held that is relevant to them
	• Data holders must adhere to data protection principles contained in the act
Prosperity	For a modern economy to prosper, the information systems operating in that country need to be of good quality.
	Governments therefore have a vested interest in the standard of systems operating and being developed.
	It is not uncommon for governments to sponsor schemes encouraging higher standards in software development, and to encourage the adoption of best practices such as those recommended by the International Standards Organisation (ISO).

Issue	Comment
Property rights	Software, knowledge and other intellectual property is often reasonably easy to duplicate.
	Copyright (protection from copying a particular product) and patent (the right to develop an underlying idea) laws apply to software.
	There is difficulty enforcing laws to protect software. Copyright is usually asserted within the software licence agreement. However, 'Corporate Over-Use' - the installation of software packages on more machines than there are licences for - is common. The length of time it takes to patent an idea is too slow to be of use to software developers.
	The Internet means property stored in digital format can be transferred anywhere in the world in seconds. Any possible action against abusers of property rights is then complicated by differing international laws.
	Software suppliers are now trying to protect themselves and change attitudes towards software piracy. Organisations such as the Federation Against Software Theft (FAST) have encouraged the reporting of illegal software use within the business community. However, prosecutions are still reasonably rare compared to the extent of the problem. The software industry also believes penalties are inadequate.
Equality	To prosper in the information society people need access to information, knowledge and information technology.
	This phenomena has the potential to disenfranchise those who are unable or unwilling to learn how to use the new technologies. The potential of lower income groups being bypassed by technological developments has led to fears of the development of a permanent underclass.
	Government initiatives may be required to ensure all sectors of society are given the opportunity to develop the skills required in the information age.

4.26 The UK government's paper *Our Information Age* highlights the importance of capitalising on the opportunities of the information age to improve people's quality of life, their education and the UK's wider industrial competitiveness. It takes the view that information technology is central to these aims and undertakes that new developments in communications and computing will be reflected in proposals to help modernise government. The Government's approach is based around five central themes: transforming education, widening access, ensuring competition and competitiveness, fostering quality and modernising Government.

Case example

Technology Breeds (and Solves?) Uncertainty

Economists are struggling to cram the value of new technologies and services into the models they rely upon for forecasting. That the man responsible for monetary policy is fretting about the limits of his tools is worrisome at a moment when the US economy is on the threshold of recession.

Technology products have extremely short life-cycles and often are more valuable when they are combined to provide services (such as high-speed corporate networks) than they are as stand-alone products.

Economists used to be more confident in their forecasting skills. For a while in the 1960s we were increasingly mesmerised by the possibilities of econometric models as a crystal ball, However, we soon learned that the economic structure did not hold still long enough to capture its key relationships.

Ironically, technology can help dig economists out of the hole that technology has put them in. For example, technology might let economists gather data on transactions in near real time. Sampling electronic point-of-sale systems in stores could yield amazingly fast retail sales figures.

As the Nasdaq bubble has shown, people have been very confused by technology's impact. But now that we understand that we have been in a cloud, we can better harness technology to help us find a way out. When we emerge, what lies ahead could be an era of clarity where technology finally enhances our knowledge more than it promotes and then confounds our speculation.

Business 2 daily insight March 28 2001

Ethical issues

4.27 The ability that information systems have to change the way in which businesses and society operates mean that they are a powerful cause of change. The power and potential of information systems, and the general trend towards businesses being expected to act ethically, has led to discussion regarding the ethical use of information systems.

Ethical analysis

4.28 Ethics is concerned with judgements about whether human behaviour is morally right or wrong. The ethical factors relevant to a business situation or scenario depend on the particular circumstances involved. There are however four concepts relating to ethical questions:

Ethical concept	Comment
Accountability	Individuals and organisations are accountable for their actions (including their actions regarding the information they hold).
Responsibility	Individuals and organisations are accountable for their actions. Those who make a decision should consider and take responsibility for the consequences of that decision. The wider effects of the decision should be given due consideration.
Liability	Those who breach ethical norms should be liable to punishment, and those who have suffered as a result of a breach should be compensated.
Legal process	There should be a mechanism to ensure laws are applied and enforced fairly and correctly.

4.29 The concepts described above may be relevant to ethical situations in business (or in examinations). When faced with a scenario that has ethical implications, the following approach may help you identify and explore the relevant issues.

Step 1.	Separate facts from judgements.
Step 2.	Identify the ethical issues requiring judgement.
Step 3.	Identify the key stakeholders and their vested interests.
Step 4.	Identify the options available.
Step 5.	Evaluate these options and their consequences, including the wider, ethical consequences.
Step 6.	Is a compromise required/available?
Step 7.	Decide, communicate and implement the most appropriate course of action.

4.30 Ethical judgements will vary, depending on who is making the judgement. We will look at **three examples** relating to the use of information systems.

(a) Suppose a university's computer is used for sending an e-mail message to a friend or for conducting a full-blown private business (billing, payroll, inventory, etc.). An observer could say that both activities are unethical (while recognising a difference in the amount of wrong being done). Another might say that the latter activities were wrong because they tied up too much memory and slowed down the machine, but the e-mail message wasn't wrong because it had no significant effect on operations.

(b) A university lecturer uses her account to acquire the current grade average of a student from a class which she instructs. She obtained the password for this restricted information from someone in the Records Office who erroneously thought that she was the student. An observer could say that the instructor acted wrongly, since the only person who is entitled to this information is the student. Another may ask why the instructor wanted the information. If she replied that she wanted it to be sure that her grading of the student was consistent with the student's overall academic performance record, some may agree that such use was acceptable.

(c) At a particular university, if a professor wants an e-mail account, all she or he need do is request one but a student must obtain faculty sponsorship in order to receive an account. Some observers may think this policy perfectly acceptable. Someone else may, on the other hand, question what makes the two situations essentially different (e.g. are professors assumed to have more need for e-mail than students? Are students more likely to cause problems?

There are no right or wrong answers to such questions, as in 'grey areas' moral and ethical judgements depend on who is making them.

Question 1

Here are questions covering a variety of issues that may arise in connection with the use of IT.

Is personal e-mail private?

Is it necessary to encrypt e-mail files?

Is it appropriate to read someone else's computer files without permission?

Is it acceptable to copy computer programs or data files?

Is material on the Internet free?

BPP
PUBLISHING

Think about the relevant issues from the points of view of: the organisation that owns the system; the individual accessing the system or information; and (where applicable) the individual whose privacy could be invaded.

Chapter roundup

- Information systems and information technology have played a significant role in the development of the modern business environment including encouraging the **flattening** of **organisation hierarchies** and widening **spans of control**.

- Other **effects of IT on organisations** include:
    - Routine processing (bigger volumes, greater speed, greater accuracy)
    - Digital information and record keeping
    - New skills required and new ways of working
    - Reliance on IT
    - New methods of communication and of providing customer service
    - Interoperability (encourages collaboration across organisation boundaries) and open systems
    - The view of information as a valuable resource
    - The view of information as a commodity which can be bought, sold or exchanged ('information market')

- The widespread use of information technology in the workplace has affected the relationship between **employers and employees**:
    - Reduced need to follow the chain-of-command
    - Information overload
    - Enables the development of close business relationships regardless of geographical location
    - More flexible working arrangements
    - Greater monitoring and control

- **Sociotechnical design** attempts to produce information systems that are technically efficient but also take into account organisational and staff needs.

- **Privacy** has become a concern as the power and prevalence of computerised system has increased.

- The almost **constant change** prevalent in organisations and society as a whole is placing greater **demands on people**. A **systematic approach** should be established, for planning and implementing **changes.**

- **Ethics** is concerned with judgements about whether human behaviour is morally right or wrong.

- The power and potential of information systems, and the general tend towards businesses being expected to act ethically, has led to discussion regarding the **ethical use of information systems.**

Quick quiz

1   'The development of more powerful information systems has encouraged flatter organisation structures'.

    True   ☐

    False   ☐

2   Why is interoperability desirable?

3   List five ways in which IT has affected the employer/employee relationship.

    1   ....

    2   ....

    3   ....

    4   ....

    5   ....

4   What factors does the sociotechnical design aspect of systems development attempt to take into account?

5   List five general sources of resistance to change.

    1   ....

    2   ....

    3   ....

    4   ....

    5   ....

6   List four possible reactions to proposed change.

    1   ....

    2   ....

    3   ....

    4   ....

7   'When introducing change, it is wise to restrict the involvement of people likely to resist or resent the new arrangements.'

    True   ☐

    False   ☐

8   Distinguish between employee privacy and consumer privacy.

Answers to quick quiz

1   True.

2   Interoperability facilitates the sharing of information between separate organisations. This facilitates the formation of strategic alliances and encourages collaboration across organisation boundaries.

3   Possibilities include the following (you may have thought of others). Reduced need to follow the chain-of-command, increased chance of employees suffering from information overload, changes to the nature of work, closer working relationships with those who are geographically distant, more flexible working arrangements and the opportunity for greater monitoring and control.

4   Sociotechnical design attempts to produce information systems that are technically efficient but also take into account organisational and staff needs.

5   Attitudes or beliefs, loyalty to a group and its norms, habit, internal politics, protection of power or position, the way in which any change is put forward and implemented and the personalities of those involved. (*You may have thought of others.*)

6   Acceptance: whether enthusiastic espousal, co-operation, grudging co-operation or resignation. Indifference: usually where the change does not directly affect the individual; evidence is apathy, lack of interest, inaction. Passive resistance: refusal to learn, working to rule; pleas of ignorance or defensiveness; procrastination. Active resistance.

7   False.

8   Consumer privacy relates to the right of individuals (consumers) to control information about themselves and their commercial transactions. Employee privacy relates to employer/employee interaction, particularly the growing reliance on electronic monitoring and other mechanisms to analyse work habits and measure employee productivity.

Questions to try	Level	Marks	Time
1(b)	Examination	15	27 mins
4	Examination	25	45 mins
8	Examination	15	27 mins

Chapter 9

THE HUMAN INFORMATION PROCESSOR

Topic list	Syllabus reference	Ability required
1 The human information processor	(iv)	Analysis
2 The human computer interface	(iv)	Analysis
3 Managing individual information requirements	(iv)	Evaluation

Introduction

People are now exposed to more sources and types of information than ever before. As we have learnt, information and knowledge are key factors in organisation success. However, to be useful, information must be able to be processed effectively by people - by Human Information Processors.

Learning outcomes covered in this chapter

- **Explain** and interpret the concept of Human Information Processors

- **Evaluate** the use of 'intelligent agents' software

Syllabus content covered in this chapter

- The Human Information Processor and the implications of providing a user-friendly interface to gain maximum benefits whilst minimising the potential drawbacks, such as physical and emotional effects, providing the right volume of information, easy retrieval and storage facilities and merging sources of information reaching individuals so that they become a manageable number

- How intelligent agent software can be applied to monitor an individual's use of a system and learn what the user's information needs are

1 THE HUMAN INFORMATION PROCESSOR

5/01

> **KEY TERM**
>
> The term '**human information processor**' describes the process by which people receive, interpret and respond to their environment.

1.1 An understanding of the information processing capabilities of humans is useful for interface design.

Simple model

1.2   A simple model of the human information processor (HIP) is shown in the diagram below.

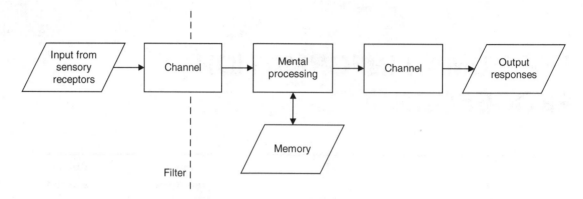

1.3   The sensory receptors include a person's **eyes and ears**. These pick up signals and transmit them to the processing unit (the brain), which includes a storage capability (memory). The results of processing are output in various forms including speech and writing.

1.4   As with all systems, the HIP has limited capacity. If this capacity is exceeded, information overload will occur, causing a deterioration in processing. To overcome this problem, the system goes through a process of **filtering**. This reduces the input to a manageable quantity. Filter types include the following.

(a)   Filters may be established by reference to the individual's **experience** and background. Over a period of time, humans establish patterns of data to support their understanding of a situation. This use of a **frame of reference** eliminates the need to develop a new processing routine each time a piece of input is received.

(b)   Decision procedures may be **standardised,** so that the making of a decision follows an established set of rules.

(c)   People automatically filter and prioritise information received by sensors. Efficient HIPs develop this filtering skill enabling them, even when under **stress,** to **focus** on the most important issues.

Newell-Simon model

1.5   The *Newell-Simon* model of the human information processing system is shown below.

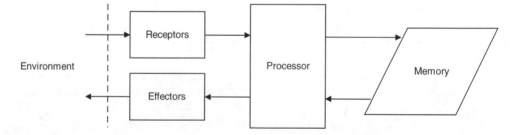

1.6   The system consists of sensory input, a processor and output (via effectors eg speech, document, e-mail etc) in the same way as the previous model. There are, however, three different components to memory.

(a)   **Long-term memory**, which has a vast capacity.

(b) **Short-term memory,** which is small (used for example to remember a telephone number for just long enough to dial it).

(c) **External memory,** which consists of external media such as a notepad or a computer.

Short-term memory

1.7 *Miller* identified a limitation in the human information processor's ability to use short-term memory. He coined the phrase 'the magical number seven, plus or minus two'. This describes the ability of humans to retain a certain number of symbols or characters in short term memory. The range is between 5 and 9 with a common limit of 7. As the number of symbols increases, so the error rate increases.

Feedback

1.8 The information received and processed may result in action which is fed back to the external environment. Human information processors have a psychological need for assurance that output has been received. This is why, for instance, computer software provides feedback as to what function the program is performing and how much longer the process should take.

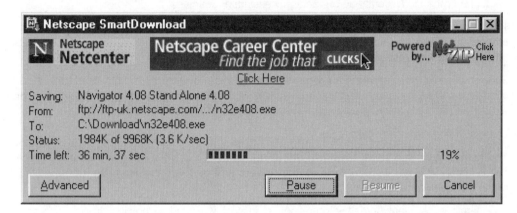

Human information processing strategies

1.9 Because of their processing limitations, humans adopt various strategies.

(a) **Concreteness.** This involves the use of information which is readily available and which does not need to be searched for or manipulated prior to use. For example, someone listening to a presentation may focus on the 'key idea' or 'the bottom line' to the exclusion of the rest of the message.

(b) **Anchoring and adjustment.** Humans tend to make judgements by establishing an anchor point and then making adjustments from this point, for example, in **budgeting**. Possible problems in this process are:

(i) An **inappropriate** anchor point might be chosen.
(ii) New evidence might be **undervalued** in making adjustments.

Case example

Human information processors

Each one of us is a very complex and sophisticated information processor. We are more powerful and have more capacity than the largest computers. That we use only a small percentage of this capacity, believed to be around 2-3%, is not important. What is important is that we process information in a particular way and, though similar, this varies for each of us.

The human information processor has five sensory mechanisms for picking up and inputting data. They are sight, hearing, touch, taste and smell. These sensory mechanisms are linked to the brain so that as data is 'sensed' it is interpreted by comparison with knowledge of past experiences and understanding of the world.

Human efficiency

The first key to efficiency in the human information processor is to have all **sensory mechanisms at work** and to be 'sensory aware' of what we are picking up. The second key is to have the knowledge, experience and understanding of our environment so that we can **assign appropriate meanings** to these signals and act accordingly.

When we are unable to assign meanings to the signals that we pick up we will endeavour to **discover meanings** through exploration, experiment and questioning. When we discover meanings we act upon them and monitor the result of the action. If we are satisfied we **store the meaning** as relevant interpretations of the signals and we have expanded our information base. This is the process we describe as **learning**.

We are largely unaware of these processes going on and we rely on our brains and senses to just get on with it. Some of us rely more heavily on the left hemisphere of our brain which is supposed to process data in an analytical and logical way. Others rely on the right hemisphere which is supposed to process data in an intuitive, visual way. This could be why some managers love columns of figures and others love graphics. However we do it, the outcome of this initial processing is either an assigned meaning or confusion. Sometimes rather than admitting the confusion people assign meanings that don't make sense, as if making a random choice of meaning. It is far **better to admit confusion and seek clarity** than to forge ahead on randomly assigned meanings.

The more we have learned and are open to learning the more effective we are as human information processors. If we desensitise ourselves by, for example, not listening, then we close down our efficiency and we cease to learn.

Even the most sophisticated management information system can only feed our senses with information. We have to constantly search for appropriate meanings to assign to this information before we act, and in doing so we grow and develop as human information processors, and as people.

Understanding and using information

The **assimilation and understanding of information** we receive is the first part of our process. The second part is the way we **disseminate our understanding to others** (communicate) and the way we **make choices** (decision making).

To operate as efficient human information processors we need to be able to organise and file the information, meanings, experience and understandings in our minds (knowledge) in such a way that we can assess it and enhance it (learn). Sometimes when information is provided by the system it isn't necessary for people to store it in their minds, and so they become 'system operators' rather than 'knowledge workers'.

The final stage is the output stage when people as human information processors provide information and advice to others, which is especially important when the 'others' are customers. The advantage of the human information processor over the system is that we can respond to questions and interact with the other person as a human information processor so that understanding can be enhanced.

However, unlike computers human beings lack the ability to store and access information with the same degree of accuracy and ease. Though the human brain has an almost unlimited capacity to handle information, people are **not very good at organising their memories** in a way which could be described as reliable.

Human inefficiency

In a similar way to use of memory our use of the brain's calculating ability is also underdeveloped. People increasingly rely on calculators and computers for even the simplest of calculating functions. Some of us, and often we are accountants, have developed an ability to use the brain's calculating capacity.

The human information processor is also notoriously poor at **outputting** information. Though the information may be in our minds some of us are unable to articulate it or write or type it in a form which is easily assimilated. These skills have to be developed and worked on. In the early days of computing, computers, because of the transfer of the human information processor's inability into the computer's programs, replicated this poor output of information. This is no longer the case and computers can offer a wide array of possible styles and formats, check spelling and grammar, convert data into attractive visuals, and so on.

Finally the human information processor is easily **distracted** and prone to make mistakes, especially in what might be seen as mundane data handling. This can still be apparent in data input but today the computer can check and reject many of these 'human' errors.

Human computer interfaces (HCI) attempt to bridge the gap between the limitations of the human information processor and the computer. Numerous approaches have been tried to make the process simpler, or as some say '**user friendly**'. This is only one aspect of a difficult problem. The other aspects concern the physical and mental demands of working effectively with computers.

Physical problems

The need to sit at a keyboard and to look at a screen is the starting point of the problem. Human beings are not built to spend long periods seated with their hands stretched out at ninety degrees to a keyboard and with their eyes on a screen. Even when the **ergonomics** are perfectly organised it is still an unnatural posture.

This leads to **fatigue and distractions arise**, errors are made and eventually - two hours is enough for most people - it is imperative for the human information processor to stop work and to stretch and relax.

Repetitive strain injury (RSI) is now recognised as a real and debilitating result of many hours at a keyboard, and most human information processors suffer from some degree of upper and/or lower back pain.

Headaches and migraine can arise for some people due to the subliminal flickering of the computer screen. This can also seriously affect our ability to concentrate on what we are doing.

Mental problems

For most human information processors the ability to concentrate for long periods of time is limited. Again research has shown that two hours is about as much as most people can tolerate without a break.

Mental problems can best be defined as affecting our ability to take in information from the screen, to respond appropriately and/or quickly enough to what we see and to understand what we are doing.

It's important for everyone working with computers to recognise the problems that can occur in maintaining the highest levels of concentration and awareness of the work they are doing and how they are feeling as they are working. It is lack of this level of awareness that leads to the many errors that human information processors are capable of.

Working with computers is not natural. It calls for a combination of physical and mental attributes that many people don't find easy. Developing the necessary skills is easier when people start at an early age, when the ability to adapt is greatest. For many older people who have not had this advantage, computer literacy, as it is sometimes called, is difficult to attain and many never even make the attempt.

Human information processors have to be able to handle data in order to survive and we become very good at doing this in the way we can co-ordinate our movements and link information provided by all our senses. Even the best computer robots find it difficult to simulate eating a meal or crossing the road. In these respects the human information processor beats the computer hands down. But in the more systematic storage, handling and retrieving of information the computer is the undoubted champion.

Source: Trevor Bentley, *Management Accounting,* May 1999

---

2   **THE HUMAN COMPUTER INTERFACE**   5/01

> **KEY TERM**
>
> The **Human-Computer Interface** is the set of commands or menus through which a user communicates with a program.

BPP
PUBLISHING

2.1 A command-driven interface is one in which you enter commands. A menu-driven interface is one in which you select command choices from various menus displayed on the screen.

2.2 A well-designed human-computer interface is one that takes account of the following factors.

(a) **Efficiency.** The system should be designed with the user in mind, so that menus and program groupings are arranged to match actual usage.

(b) **User-friendliness.** This covers on-line tutorials, on-screen help, clear menus/icons and suitable dialogue boxes such as OK or Cancel.

(c) **Alternative options.** Although icons are user-friendly, they can hamper speed of operation. An experienced keyboard user will find it quicker, for example, to select 'Ctrl P' or similar than to click on a 'printer' icon then on a 'yes' button.

(d) **Ease of learning.** Common features across the HCIs of different packages should reduce training costs. A well-designed system with a good HCI should be easy to learn.

Input design

2.3 People usually collect and input the data that the computer system will use, and in input design the **requirements of the system** must be balanced with the personal **capabilities of its users**. Input design is closely bound up with data collection and data capture.

2.4 There are a number of considerations for input design.

(a) There should be no **unnecessary re-input** of data - for example, if standing file data includes a customer's name, address and code (account) number, it should only be necessary to input the unique **customer code.**

(b) What **volumes** of input are expected? **Large volumes** of input are more likely to require automated input procedures.

(c) What will be the **frequency** of input? Infrequent transaction data might suggest a random access system from keyboard terminals. With batched input, however, the frequency of input must be considered.

(d) In what **sequence** should batched data be input? For example, outstanding file maintenance ought to be input before transaction data, to ensure that the standing data is up-to-date before the transaction data is processed.

(e) **Where** will data be collected or captured for input? Where will it be converted into machine-sensible form?

(f) What should be the **input medium**?

(g) The **need for accuracy.** How extensive should built-in data validation checks be?

Screen layout

2.5 The screen should display the information in a way that enables users to easily see and understand it.

2.6 The screen provides 'feedback' for the user, allowing the system to be flexible, interactive and conversational.

2.7 This **dialogue** between the program and the user should be concise, clear and helpful. A balance needs to be struck between dialogue that provides new users with all the information they require, without significantly slowing down proficient users who already 'know the system'.

Form filling

2.8　Form filling is a common way of laying out data input screens. Relevant data fields may be set up within an on-screen **skeleton** form. The input fields are arranged to facilitate ease of data entry.

2.9　**Screen formatting** for this purpose usually includes several features.

- **Different colours** for different screen areas
- **Flashing** items
- **Larger characters** for titles
- Paging or **scrolling** depending on the volume of information

2.10　Default values may be entered **automatically** in some fields to speed up data entry. Entries are made by **moving the cursor** from one field to the next and typing in the data.

Graphical user interfaces (GUI)

2.11　Graphical user interfaces (GUIs) were designed to make computers more '**user-friendly**'. Dialogue is conducted through selecting images, rather than typed text (which was required with older Character User Interfaces such as MS-DOS).

2.12　A GUI involves the use of two design ideas and two operating methods which can be remembered by the abbreviation **WIMP**. This stands for 'Windows, Icons, Mouse, Pull-down menu'.

Windows (the generic term rather than the operating system)

2.13　Graphical user interfaces allow the screen to be divided into sections or 'windows', which can be opened and closed. This enables two or more applications to be open at the same time.

Icons

2.14　An icon is an image of an object used to represent a program, function or a file in an **obvious** way. For instance, Windows-based packages use a picture of a printer which is simply clicked to start the printing process.

Mouse

2.15　As the mouse moves around on the desktop a *pointer* (cursor) on the screen mimics its movements. A mouse can be used to pick out and activate an icon or button, to highlight a block of text for deletion/insertion, or to drag data from one place on the screen to another. It also has buttons to execute commands.

Pull-down menu

2.16　A '**menu-bar**' will be shown across the top of the window. Using the mouse to move the pointer to the required item in the menu, the pointer '**pulls down**' a subsidiary menu, which may lead to more menus.

User-friendliness

2.17　The easier a package is to use, the more efficient it (and the user) will be. The following features all improve the user-friendliness of a system.

Ease of data entry

2.18 It must be easy for the user to input data into the system. This has several aspects.

(a) The **data entry screen** should be designed in a **logical order.** If an **input form** (source document) is used, the on-screen and off-screen order should be the same.

(b) The data entry screen should be **clearly designed,** so that, for example, input fields are highlighted, perhaps by **colour.** The position of the cursor should be clear.

Titles of fields should be **easy to read** and should **match** the titles used on **source** documents.

(c) **Default entries** should be provided for items such as the date (usually today's date) or the standard VAT rate.

The defaults will remain unless the user wishes to change them. This can speed up data entry considerably.

Intuitiveness

2.19 It should be possible for users to make reasonable guesses about what they need to do. Clear icons and menus help this process.

Consistent design

2.20 Most users will utilise many software packages, such as a spreadsheet and a word processing package.

2.21 This means that the more systems can 'look and feel' the same the easier it will be for users to switch between packages.

2.22 One of the advantages of the Windows environment is that packages written for Windows are generally similar in design. This reduces training time and costs and makes skills transferable.

Question 1

Examine the menus and features of at least two software packages written for Microsoft Windows. You should notice many similarities.

Answer

Amongst the similarities are:

Common menu design eg drop-down menus, the File and Edit menus, Common function keys (F1 is 'help'). Common features eg Cut and Paste, use of toolbars, viewing options such as magnification, scroll bars etc.

On-screen help

2.23 It is increasingly common to find software pre-loaded onto computers without manuals being provided or to find that, when manuals *are* provided, they are rarely referred to. This is because packages invariably include **on-screen help**.

2.24 If a user requires help, he or she requests it at the touch of a **single key** (eg **F1**) or by clicking on '**Help**' on a **pull-down menu.** The help screen is usually **context specific,** so that, for example, if a particular dialogue box in a package is open, the system will offer help related to relevant functions and options. Problems can be resolved more quickly and productivity improved.

2.25 Help files are often written in **hypertext,** which provides **links** between topics. The user can click on words that are underlined and move directly to another topic.

Use of dialogue boxes and on-screen prompts

2.26 The more critical the potential effect of a command issued by the user, the more important it is that the user is not allowed simply to **start a process by mistake**.

2.27 Thus where commands such as **delete** a file, **format** a disk or **update** a ledger are being made, user-friendly software should issue a **warning** that such an operation is about to be carried out, *after* the initial command is entered.

2.28 This gives the user a **second chance** to confirm that the command was intended and that the computer is indeed required to carry out the specified process.

2.29 In turn this means that users will spend less time attempting to reverse the effects of **unintentionally-used commands**.

Escapability

2.30 Programs should always provide users with the ability to 'back-track', allowing them to reverse their most recent action(s).

2.31 Most modern programs provide this functionality by way of a **'Cancel'** button displayed in a dialogue box to check the user wishes to proceed with a command. A related option found in many programs is the **'Undo'** function.

Convenience

2.32 Many users find that they perform the **same series of actions** so frequently that it becomes tedious to click their way through menus and dialogue boxes. User-friendly software will recognise this and offer **fast alternatives**.

   (a) **'Shortcut keys'** (typically pressing the Ctrl key together with one or more other keys) can be assigned to standard actions so that they are performed literally at the touch of a button.

   (b) A series of actions can be 'recorded' as they are done in the form of **'macros'**, which can then be activated using a shortcut key or user-defined button.

Exam focus point
Issues relating to the HIP and HCI could have been used in a May 2001 question relating to viewing websites using mobile telephones.

The working environment

2.33 The ability of people to process information will also be influenced by their environment. Research has shown that while a good working environment is not a motivating factor to enhanced performance, **a** poor environment will hinder information processing and become a source of general dissatisfaction.

2.34 The **physical environment** can influence people through:

(a) The **health and safety** of workers. A hazardous or unhygienic environment will distract, and may cause sickness or injury.

(b) **Enabling performance**. Good planning and layout of workstations and work areas can contribute to the efficiency of work flow and of people employed in that environment.

(c) **Organisational culture**. The physical environment is an expression of the organisation's self-images. It can alter the way people feel about their work and their organisation. It can also affect the amount of social contact and interaction available to workers: consider the difference between cubicles and open plan offices, for example, in encouraging informal communication.

Layout and facilities

2.35 A working area layout requires **flexibility** - to cope with the needs of different individuals and activities and the constraints of the shapes and sizes of available rooms. There are some basic features which should be considered when planning working areas.

(a) Efficient use of space, with flexibility and room for expansion.

(b) How layout can **complement the work-flow**.

(c) **Convenient access** to shared equipment and facilities.

(d) Arrangement for **ease of communication** and supervision.

(e) Provision for **security** where necessary.

(f) The **health and safety** of people.

(g) The '**image**' portrayed.

(h) Heating, lighting and ventilation.

(i) **Noise** levels. Constant loud noise, or intermittent noise at any volume, is distracting.

(j) **Decor**. A well-planned colour scheme can influence the mood of people. Brown, yellow and magnolia are considered good for work areas as they are warm colours. White and cream are light colours which can give an impression of space in small rooms.

(k) **Ergonomics** includes the design of office equipment so that, for example, chairs and desks are designed to be comfortable and supportive.

Ergonomics

2.36 Ergonomics is the study of the relationship between **people** and their **working environment**. The aim is to establish working conditions which are best-suited to the capacities and requirements of people.

2.37 Ergonomics has been applied to a wide range of environments – from factories to offices. We will look at ergonomics in the context of a computer workstation.

2.38 A comfortable user should **process** information more **efficiently** than one distracted by factors such as a poorly designed chair. The following factors should be considered.

(a) Computer **monitors** should be free from glare, and be able to swivel and tilt. 'Glare guards' should be fitted to reduce eye strain

(b) **Keyboards** must be **adjustable** (eg tilt), and the workspace in front of them must be 'sufficient' for the operators to rest their forearms.

(c) **Desks** must allow 'flexible' arrangement of equipment and documents.

(d) **Chairs** must be adjustable in height, and the back in height and angle. Footrests should be made available if required.

(e) **Lighting** - there must be 'appropriate contrast' between the screen and its background. Windows should have effective curtains or blinds.

(f) Heat and humidity levels must be **comfortable**.

(g) **Breaks** - Screen-based work should be periodically interrupted by breaks or changes in activity. This has a physical and mental benefit, reducing boredom which can lead to errors. Task rotation can also be used in this context.

(h) **Training** in the use of equipment should be provided.

(i) Wherever possible the workstation should be tailored to the requirements of the **individual user**.

3 MANAGING INDIVIDUAL INFORMATION REQUIREMENTS

Pilot paper, 11/01, 5/02

Critical success factors

> **KEY TERM**
>
> **Critical success factors** are a small number of key operational goals vital to the success of an organisation.

3.1 We discussed critical success factors (CSFs) in Chapter 3 in the context of determining the information requirements of an organisation. We will now look at how CSFs can be used to establish the information needs of individual managers.

3.2 The organisational CSFs that an individual manager is responsible for should be the driving force behind the manager's information needs. The process is summarised as follows.

Step 1. Interview managers to obtain their Critical Success Factors.

Step 2. Aggregate individual CSFs to establish organisational CSFs.

Step 3. Determine the performance indicators used to monitor each CSF.

Step 4. Determine what information is required to track each performance indicator.

Step 5. Review information and information systems to establish if this information is available.

Step 6. Take action to provide any missing information (eg system amendments, new systems).

Step 7. Provide each individual manager with a summary of the information that will be provided to support the CSFs they are responsible for.

Information overload and intelligent agents

3.3 Many managers complain that they receive too much irrelevant information. There are two main approaches to avoiding information overload. Firstly, the **characteristics of the**

information need to be considered (remember the ACCURATE mnemonic from Chapter 1). Secondly the **number of information sources** feeding an individual can be managed.

Limiting the number of information sources

3.4 The approach taken to limiting the sources of information will depend on the situation. In some instances it may be sufficient to implement temporary measures to **delay** non-urgent information reaching a person at a particularly busy time. Other situations may require a **permanent change** to information flows. Some examples are shown in the following table.

3.5

Limiting tool	Comment
Delegate to colleagues	Communications regarding certain issues may be dealt with by others within the organisation. For example, routine client contact could be delegated to junior staff, and only strategic issues referred 'up the chain'.
Review reports received for duplicated information	Regular reviews of information received should be made. If information is duplicated one source should be deleted. The review should also consider what information would best be received together to aid interpretation.
Re-route incoming telephone calls	A secretary could be allocated to take telephone messages, putting through only calls of significance that require immediate attention. To be effective, the instructions concerning calls that should be put through, and how messages should be relayed must be specific.
Voice-mail	While voice-mail can be frustrating when trying to reach someone, it may be useful to temporarily divert calls to voice-mail when work pressures require no interruptions - and no other staff are available to divert calls to.
Filter incoming e-mail	E-mail programs have the ability to review and re-direct messages based on the message content, priority, sender and/or intended recipients. Non-selected messages may be copied to a selected person, or redirected to a non-urgent inbox to be dealt with later.
Use an Internet news-clipping service	A person may face a constant stream of industry-related journals. These should be reviewed for relevant information - a time-consuming process. However, a news-clipping service could review relevant journals and newspapers on the Internet, and forward via e-mail copies of articles that meet user-defined criteria.
Use intelligent agents	These are discussed on the following page.

KEY TERM

Intelligent agents are programs that perform tasks such as retrieving and delivering information and automating repetitive tasks.

3.6 **Intelligent agent** software can be applied to monitor an individual's use of a computerised system, 'learning' about the users work patterns.

3.7 Although the theory behind agents has been around for some time, agents have become more prominent with the growth of the Internet. Many companies now sell software that enables you to configure an agent to **monitor** and **search** the **Internet**.

3.8 The term **intelligent agent** is used to denote a computer system that has the following properties.

(a) **Autonomy**: agents operate without direct intervention.

(b) **Social ability**: agents interact with other agents and people.

(c) **Reactivity**: agents perceive their environment and respond to changes that occur in it.

(d) **Pro-activeness**: agents do not only act in response to their environment, they are able to exhibit goal-directed behaviour by taking the **initiative**.

3.9 **Interface agents** are computer programs that employ artificial intelligence techniques in order to provide assistance to a user dealing with a particular application. A fairly crude (some might say annoying) example is the Office Assistant within Microsoft Office.

3.10 An **information agent** is able to collate and manipulate information obtained from various sources to meet parameters set by users and other agents. The information sources may include traditional databases or Internet searches.

Case example

Intelligent software agents – an attempt at classification

The following are examples of developed, ready-to-run, agent software that may be used on a company intranet to enhance information retrieval and knowledge management. Agents may be categorised as:

Interface agents

Interface agents are used to decrease the complexity of the increasingly sophisticated and overloaded information systems available. They may add speech and natural language understanding to otherwise dumb interfaces, or add presentation ability to systems.

System agents

System agents run as integrated parts of operating systems or network protocol devices. They help managing complex distributed computing environments by doing hardware inventory, interpreting network events, managing backup and storage devices, and performing virus detection. These agents do not primarily work with end-user information.

Advisory agents

Advisory agents are used in (complex) help or diagnostics systems.

Filtering agents

Filtering agents are used to reduce information overload by removing unwanted data, ie data that does not match the user's profile, from the input stream. Simple versions are built-in to many e-mail clients and Agentware and InfoMagnet provide a more general kind of server-based filtering capabilities.

Retrieval agents

Retrieval agents search and retrieve information and serves as information brokers or documents managers. Many products claim to be retrieval agents, including the client-based AT1, BullsEye, Go-Get-It, Got-It, Surfbot, and WebCompass, and the server-based Agentware and InfoMagnet.

Navigation agents

Navigation agents are used to navigate through external and internal networks, remembering short-cuts, pre-load caching information, automatically bookmarking interesting sites. IBM's Web Browser Intelligence (WBI - pronounced Webby) is an example.

Monitoring agents

Monitoring agents provide the user with information when particular events occur, such as information being updated, moved, or erased. Enterprise Minder does this but is no agent. WBI from IBM has this as a feature, as do BullsEye and SmartBookmarks.

Recommender agents

Recommender agents are usually collaborative; they need many profiles to be available before an accurate recommendation can be made. Examples are Agentware, Firefly, and GroupLens, which are all server-based. Learn Sesame is an exception that is user-oriented and bases its conclusion on the user's previous behaviour.

Profiling agents

Profiling agents are used to build dynamic sites with information and recommendations tailored to match each visitor's individual taste and need. The main purpose is to build customer loyalty and profitable one-to-one relationships. Available examples are Agentware, Firefly, and GroupLens on the server side. Learn Sesame and IBM's Knowledge Utility also do this but on a user-oriented level.

3.11 Agents are an example of '**push**' technology. Instead of the user searching for information, selected information is 'pushed' to the user. Newsclipping services, that search selected publications for articles that meet user-defined criteria, work on similar principles.

Chapter roundup

- The term **Human Information Processor** describes the process by which people receive, interpret and respond to their environment.

- In computerised systems the link between the human information processor and the computer is the **Human Computer Interface**.

- **Graphical user interfaces** were designed to make computers more user-friendly.

- **Ergonomics** is the study of how people interact with their working environment.

- The organisational **CSFs** that an individual manager is responsible for should be the driving force behind the manager's **information needs**.

- The dramatic increase in the volume of information available to people has in some situations led to **information overload**.

- Steps may need to be taken to **limit** the **volume** and **number** of sources of information reaching an individual. Examples include:
  - Delegate to colleagues
  - Review reports received for duplicated information
  - Re-route incoming telephone calls
  - Voice-mail
  - Filter incoming e-mail
  - Use an Internet news-clipping service
  - Use **intelligent agents**

Quick quiz

1   List four factors Human Computer Interface design should take into account.

    1   ....

    2   ....

    3   ....

    4   ....

2   What does HIP stand for?

    H............................. I............................. P.............................

3   What is the main advantage of Graphical User Interfaces over Character User Interfaces?

4   List five features of a user-friendly software package.

    1   ....

    2   ....

    3   ....

    4   ....

    5   ....

5   'A data input clerk who is allowed regular breaks should process data more efficiently than one that works constantly.'

    True   ☐

    False   ☐

6   What is 'ergonomics'?

7   List five possible responses to information overload.

    1   ....

    2   ....

    3   ....

    4   ....

    5   ....

BPP PUBLISHING

Answers to quick quiz

1   Efficiency. The system should be designed with the user in mind, so that menus and program groupings are arranged to match actual usage.

   User-friendliness. This covers on-line tutorials, on-screen help, clear menus/icons and suitable dialogue boxes such as OK or Cancel.

   Alternative options. Although icons are user-friendly, they can hamper speed of operation. An experienced keyboard user will find it quicker, for example, to select 'Ctrl P' or similar than to click on a 'printer' icon then on a 'yes' button.

   Ease of learning. Common features across the HCIs of different packages should reduce training costs. A well-designed system with a good HCI should be easy to learn

2   Human Information Processor.

3   Graphical User Interfaces are considered more user-friendly.

4   Possibilities include the following. Ease of data entry, intuitiveness, consistent design, on-screen help, use of dialogue boxes and on-screen prompts, escapability and convenience. Further details are provided within section 2 of this chapter.

5   True - although data input operators may have trouble convincing their employer that this is the case!

6   Ergonomics is the study of the relationship between people and their working environment. The aim is to establish working conditions which are best suited to the capacities and requirements of people.

7   Possibilities include: Delegate to colleagues, review reports received for duplicated information, re-route incoming telephone calls, use voice-mail, filter incoming e-mail, use an Internet news-clipping service and use intelligent agents.

Question to try	Level	Marks	Time
17(a)	Examination	17	30 mins

Exam question bank

Questions 7 – 13 and Question 17 of this Exam question bank are from the **Pilot Paper**. Question 17 includes **detailed guidance** within the question and answer.

Detailed guidance is also provided with the question and answer for Question 16.

1   JH LTD: IS/IT STRATEGY   *45 mins*

The board of JH Ltd has become aware that there is no IS/IT strategy in place within the company. A decision has therefore been made to establish a working group to produce an outline IS/IT strategy. The group members are as follows.

Senior manager	Does not have much knowledge of IT or IS. Has avoided IT in general as he sees it as not relevant to his job. He is actually quite fearful of IT. He is very task-orientated and dislikes wasting time on non-essential work. He is very good at producing overall policy directives.
IS/IT professional	She has an excellent knowledge of mainframe computers and enjoys being in charge of a large department. Her knowledge has arisen from 20 years in computing. She has tended to ignore the recent shift towards end-user computing, believing that 'IT is best handled by specialists'. Has some limited knowledge of PCs and client-server systems. She has very little contact with the users of the information that the IS/IT department produces. She believes that users should accept the information given and not make difficult demands on the department.
IT user: trainee accountant	He is a CIMA Final Level student, who has been working in various roles within the accounts function: this is his first major assignment. His agenda is to try and ensure that IT is used effectively and that all staff within the company can therefore use PC applications to support their work. He is already well read on IT matters and is now looking to advance rapidly in the company by being the IT 'champion'.

Required

(a)   Comment on the disadvantages that could arise for JH Ltd by not having an overall IS/IT strategy in place.   **10 Marks**

(b)   Explain how the background of each individual in the working group may present barriers to the production of an IS/IT strategy as required by the board.

Suggest how these barriers may be overcome.   **15 Marks**

Total Marks Q1 = 25

2   IT STRATEGY   *45 mins*

Explain *five* reasons why it is essential for a modern organisation to have an IT strategy.

Illustrate your answer with examples of these reasons drawn from your own knowledge and experience.   **25 Marks**

3   JH PLC: INFORMATION CENTRE   *45 mins*

JH plc trades in an overseas country, arranging freight forwarding contracts for up to 2,000 corporate clients. The company's mission is to be the most profitable freight forwarder in that country. The company is very profitable, partly due to its high investment in modern IT systems, and its narrow focus on its corporate mission.

The company's IT systems are supported by its Information Centre, which has a staff of 20. Although large, the centre is always well utilised.

In a recent corporate review, the Board of JH plc noted that the Information Centre was costing the company £4,000,000 per annum with no discernible income. The Board is therefore considering whether to close the Information Centre to improve the company's profitability.

The most recent addition to the computer system is a network that links all departments. It is anticipated that an increasing number of clients will send their requirements direct to the company via the company's gateway to the Internet.

Required

(a)   Write a memo to the Board to justify the continuance of the Information Centre on non-financial grounds.   **16 Marks**

(b)   Explain how JH plc's Information Centre can provide an enhanced service to the staff of JH plc using the recently installed computer network within the company.   **9 Marks**

Total Marks Q3 = 25

4   CP LTD: HOMEWORKING   *45 mins*

CP Ltd is a small but successful company which specialises in selling car and home insurance to individuals. All sales are made over the telephone, and there are no personal callers to the company's offices. The company employs 25 staff, 22 in the telephone sales department and the remaining three running all the accounts and administration functions. As a consequence of its recent success in the market, CP Ltd is planning to expand its operations.

The company has been evaluating its cost structure and has discovered that the cost of providing office space for each worker is £3,500 per annum. New workers would require office space with a cost per worker of £4,000 per annum. This amounts to a significant cost in the company's operating budget. The Management Accountant has calculated that 90% of office costs can be avoided if the telephone sales staff worked from their homes. This idea has, so far, been discussed only at board level.

At present, employees appear to enjoy working in the office, where they spend most of their time using the telephone and computer system to sell insurance. Coffee and lunch breaks are normally spent in the rest area where staff also compare some notes and queries concerning their jobs. All the data that they need to perform their job is otherwise available on the computer system. This data includes:

- Records on each customer.

- Access to a value added network (VAN) providing costs of insurance from competitors.

- Word-processing and other systems for producing letters and insurance quotes to customers.

The proposal to work from home was put to staff last week and this has met with some initial resistance although the Management Accountant stressed that this proposal was only a possibility.

Required

Write a report to the Managing Director explaining:

(a)   From the viewpoint of the staff, the potential *benefits* that will be gained by homeworking. Explain the *concerns* that staff may have over homeworking and whether the IT infrastructure can help alleviate these concerns.   **16 Marks**

(b)   What can be done to encourage staff to accept the proposed change.   **9 Marks**

Total Marks Q4 = 25

5   CC PLC: INTRANET AND INFORMATION SHARING   *45 mins*

CC plc is a company employing 2,560 staff in 20 different offices within one country. The company offers a wide range of specialist consultancy advice to the building and construction industry. This includes advice on materials to be used, relevant legislation (including planning applications) and appropriate sources of finance.

The information to meet client requirements is held within each office of the company. Although most clients are serviced by a single office, a lot of the information used is duplicated between the different offices. This is surprising given that legislation and other standard information such as details of materials used are the same for the whole country. In the past there has been no attempt to share data because of the cost of transferring information and the lack of trust on the part of staff in other offices. Some senior managers tend to keep part of client data confidential to themselves.

The company has recently provided all employees with e-mail for communication within CC plc and to clients. Software providing Internet access is also available so that staff can obtain undated planning information from appropriate websites. The hardware in the company is quite old and only just meets the minimum specification for these purposes.

The Marketing Director has suggested that an intranet should be established in the company so that common information can be shared rather than each office maintaining its own data. This suggestion is meeting with some resistance from all grades of staff.

Required

(a)   Explain the objectives of an intranet and show how the provision of an intranet within CC plc should result in better provision of information.   **10 Marks**

(b)   Comment on the organisational and human reasons why information may not become more widely available in CC plc, and suggest methods for overcoming these problems.   **15 marks**

Total Marks Q5 = 25

6 FACILITIES MANAGEMENT

45 mins

The directors of DS are not satisfied with the GDC Ltd facilities management company which was contracted two years ago to run the IT system of the company. At that time, the existing in-house IT development and support department was disbanded and all control of IT systems handed over to GDC Ltd. The appointment of GDC Ltd was relatively rushed and although an outline contract was agreed, no detailed Service Level Agreement was produced.

Over the last few weeks the number of complaints received from staff regarding the service has been increasing and the provision of essential management reports has not been particularly timely.

A recent exchange of correspondence with GDC Ltd failed to resolve the matter. Staff at GDC Ltd recognised the fall in standards of service, but insisted that it has met its contractual obligations. DS's lawyers have confirmed that GDC Ltd is correct.

Key features of DS's contract with the GDC Ltd facilities management company:

> The contract can be terminated by either party with three months' notice
>
> GDC Ltd will provide IT services for DS, the services to include:
>
> - Purchase of all hardware and software
> - Repair and maintenance of all IT equipment
> - Help desk and other support services for users
> - Writing and maintenance of in-house software
> - Provision of management information
>
> Price charged to be renegotiated each year but any increase must not exceed inflation, plus 10%.

Required

(a) Explain, from the point of view of DS, why it might have received poor service from GDC Ltd, even though GDC Ltd has met the requirements of the contract. **12 Marks**

(b) Explain the courses of action now available to DS relating to the provision of IT services. Comment on the problems involved in each course of action. **13 Marks**

Total Marks Q6 = 25

QUESTIONS 7 - 10 ARE BASED ON THE FOLLOWING SCENARIO (Pilot paper)

90 mins

Q.NET

Q.NET sells books on the Internet. It has a turnover of £50 million with gross profits of £5 million. Operating costs are relatively low because most transactions are carried out electronically by the computer system with little or no manual intervention. Q NET's main expense is interest on bank loans which were used to purchase initial hardware and software and provide some working capital for new business. Over £20 million was invested in computer hardware, software, stocks of books and warehousing space when the organisation commenced business last year. Interest repayments alone mean the Q.NET is unlikely to see any profit being made in the next three years.

Business strategy and vision

The overall vision of Q.NET is to obtain 10 per cent of the retail book market within three years with a positive net profit. The underlying business strategy of Q.NET supports this vision by providing:

- Appropriate information to, and ordering facilities for, customers
- Basic financial information for management
- Suppliers with appropriate information on book sales

Information systems - ordering and sales

Expenditure on hardware and software for transaction processing included mainframes linked to the Internet to receive orders from customers, maintenance of a large database of books in print and sophisticated encryption technology to ensure that payments on the Internet are secure. Some sections of the hardware configuration were below the recommended specification when they were implemented.

Q.NET, along with the other major bookshops on the Internet, offers information on up to four million books in print. Books are ordered over the Internet using a secure landline and credit card facility. Despatch of popular titles is normally within 48 hours; rarer books in four to five weeks. All Internet booksellers offer a similar lead-

255

time for orders. Payment is made with the customer's authorisation for a credit card transaction on despatch of the order. Payments are made to suppliers within the standard credit period of 30 days.

Customers purchase books after identifying their book requirements by author or book title from the database of books maintained by Q.NET. Information provided about each book includes price and shipping time; popular books also have a scanned image of the cover. Additional information on each book is available on Q.NET's database, although the lack of bandwidth from the database to the Internet server means that this information cannot be displayed to the customer.

Details of customer orders are maintained on the system for six weeks, or until the order is fulfilled. This information is then removed from the hard disk to save space.

Information system for sales and support staff

Sales and support staff work from their homes using Virtual Private Network (VPN) to access the main computer systems at Q.NET's head office. Sales and support staff are required to:

- Answer customer queries via e-mail

- Check stock movements and order additional copies of popular books, which would normally be in excess of normal forecast sales

- Review new books from publishers so that Q.NET's website can be updated with details of each book prior to publication

- Write amendments to the website to add new books and remove discontinued books

Each member of staff focuses on one of the main activities outlined above. Staff work from home, partly as a result of the security of the VPN, but mainly to minimise the use of expensive office space. Q.NET provided all the hardware and software required and had no difficulty in recruiting the 25 staff required. However, six months after initial recruitment, more than half of the staff have resigned and Q.NET is facing increasing charges from having to reallocate computer hardware to new support staff as well as, in some situations, providing appropriate ISDN telephone connections to the VPN.

Future activities

The board of Q.NET is concerned that the organisation is not using technology effectively to gain any competitive advantage over its rivals. One proposition is to have additional EDI links to major book publishers to order books that Q.NET currently does not have in stock. However, the publishers are unwilling to be locked into this type of agreement in case they are seen to be favouring one bookshop over another.

---

7   Q.NET: IT STRATEGY AND COMPETITIVE ADVANTAGE   *36 mins*

Required:

Evaluate how Q.NET can use IT to gain competitive advantage using Porter's Five Forces model as a framework for your answer.   **20 Marks**

8   Q.NET: STAFF RETENTION   *27 mins*

Required:

Discuss the reasons why sales and support staff turnover is so high. Explain methods for improving the retention of these staff.   **15 Marks**

9   Q.NET: INFORMATION STRATEGY   *9 mins*

Required:

Evaluate the purpose of an information strategy in a commercial organisation.   **5 Marks**

10   Q.NET: IT AND BUSINESS STRATEGY   *18 mins*

Required:

Evaluate how effective the IT system at Q.NET is in supporting the business strategy.   **10 Marks**

Total Marks Q.Net scenario = 50

11   **HB LTD: IT AND PROFITABILITY; COMPETITIVE ADVANTAGE (Pilot paper)**   *45 mins*

HB Ltd manufactures cement from a range of raw materials. The basic product is used in many different applications from building sites to road construction. Competition within the cement market has been increasing in recent years, with a significant number of new manufacturers commencing production in the last year. There are few barriers to entry; the main factor limiting competition is the availability of mining sites from which the raw materials are obtained to make the product.

Like most manufacturers, the production system at HB Ltd uses very few computers and relies extensively on the skill and judgement of the production staff to make an acceptable product. For example, raw materials can only be weighted to the nearest 100kg because of a lack of accurate weighing equipment. There is very little quality control, with the skill of the production supervisor being the main check on the acceptability of the cement being despatched to customer.

There is a growing market for some specialist cements to be used for a wide range of purposes, including earthquake-proofing of buildings and use in sculptures, as well as coloured cements for identifying special bicycle-only lanes on roads. HB Ltd is attempting to capture a significant share of this market because the margins that can be obtained are higher than for the normal cement applications. However, success has been limited because of poor quality control and delivery times.

In an attempt to improve the company's performance in terms of increasing market share and improving profitability, the board of HB Ltd hired a consultant with a brief to show how the company could meet these objectives. The consultant's report included a graph (Figure A) which was used to explain how HB Ltd could meet its objectives. Two main areas of improvement were noted:

- Increasing the contribution from each unit of cement sold
- Decreasing the fixed costs of the company

Fixed costs in HB Ltd include staff in all departments, factory overheads and selling and marketing activities.

Figure A HB Ltd: Shift in breakeven point arising from changes in contribution and fixed costs.

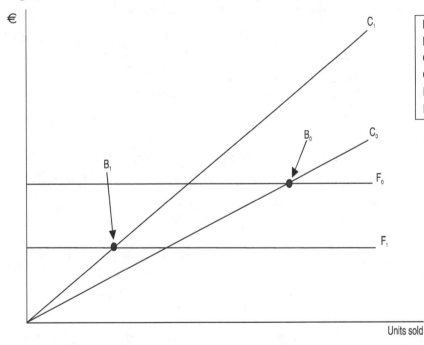

B_0	Old breakeven point
B_1	New breakeven point
C_0	Old contribution line
C_1	New contribution line
F_0	Old fixed costs
F_1	New fixed costs

The main recommendation from the report was that investment was needed in a new computer system to monitor the whole production process from purchase of raw material to monitoring of customers' orders and delivery schedules. The board of HB Ltd welcomed the suggestion, although some further work on qualifying the benefits of the investment is still required.

BPP PUBLISHING

Required

As the management accountant of HB Ltd, produce a report to:

(a) Explain how the proposed investment in a new IT system could help to produce the shifts in the contribution and fixed costs lines shown in the consultant's graph. **18 Marks**

(b) Discuss any other ways in which the new IT system will help HB Ltd to gain competitive advantage over other cement manufactures in sales and marketing activities. **7 Marks**

Your answer should make appropriate references to the computerised production system.

Total Marks Q11 = 25

Note: You should assume that there are no significant changes to the size of the company in the short term, although existing resources could be diverted into specialist cement manufacture.

12 **SN PLC: INFORMATION SYSTEMS INFRASTRUCTURE (Pilot paper)** *45 mins*

SN plc provides a large range of insurance services and advice to clients ranging from private individuals to large corporate organisations. The sales staff are supported by a wide range of information systems, which are designed to be user-friendly. The systems are regularly reviewed to ensure that the information requirements of the professional staff are being met by those systems.

The information systems are maintained and upgraded by a team of trainers; sales personnel are not involved in the design of systems because this would result in a loss of chargeable time. The actual process of maintaining the information system is outlined in *Figure B* (see the following page).

Other relevant information

- Costs of training and IT department are allocated to the different user departments in accordance with staff numbers in those departments. The costs of the IT department include software development and all costs relating to the SLA managers.

- The IT staff work in the main development centre, which is located on a university campus for reasons of cost and accessibility to a supply of trained programmers.

- The IT department has a reputation within the company for not meeting user requirements in a timely manner.

Required

As the management accountant of SN plc, write to a report to the board which:

- Explains the weaknesses in SN plc's infrastructure for maintaining the information systems for sales staff, and

- Produces specific recommendations to alleviate those weaknesses.

Total Marks Q12 = 25

Marks are allocated evenly across the two requirements.

Figure B Maintaining SN plc's information systems

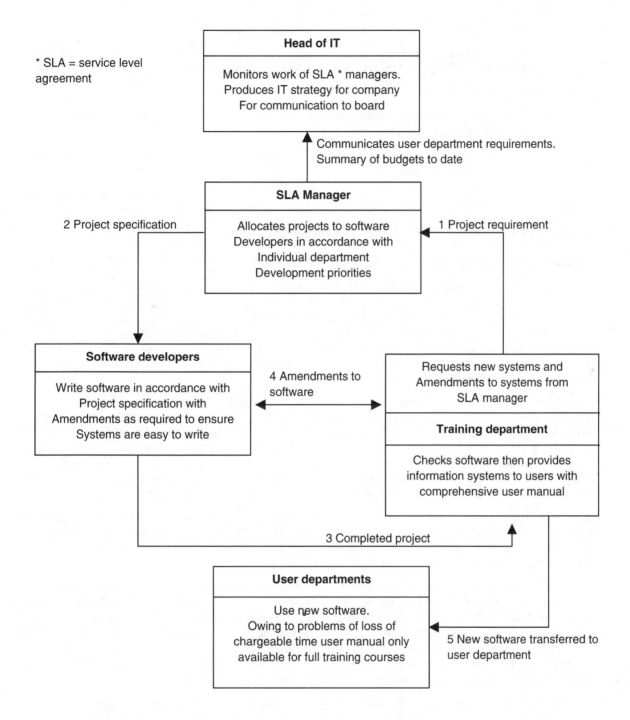

* SLA = service level agreement

Head of IT

Monitors work of SLA * managers.
Produces IT strategy for company
For communication to board

Communicates user department requirements.
Summary of budgets to date

SLA Manager

Allocates projects to software
Developers in accordance with
Individual department
Development priorities

2 Project specification

1 Project requirement

Software developers

Write software in accordance with
Project specification with
Amendments as required to ensure
Systems are easy to write

4 Amendments to software

Requests new systems and
Amendments to systems from
SLA manager

Training department

Checks software then provides
information systems to users with
comprehensive user manual

3 Completed project

User departments

Use new software.
Owing to problems of loss of
chargeable time user manual only
available for full training courses

5 New software transferred to
user department

13   **E-COMMERCE (Pilot paper)**   *45 mins*

Required

Compare and contrast the organisations specified below in terms of:

(a)   Whether e-commerce should be adopted as part of the business strategy.   **20 Marks**
(b)   Showing which organisation will benefit more from the use of e-commerce.   **5 Marks**

The two types of organisation to be considered in this question are:

*   A local independent supplier of garden plants, fences, sheds and other garden accessories selling within 20 kilometres of its main site; and

*   An international consultancy supplying financial advice to private individuals and large multinational organisations.

Total Marks Q13 = 25

QUESTIONS 14 - 16 ARE BASED ON THE FOLLOWING SCENARIO

Pattersons Electrical Suppliers

Pattersons Electrical Suppliers own a chain of retail outlets throughout the city and surrounding area. In recent years they have expanded these outlets from their one original store to the current seven stores. The head office is based on the original site. The business originated as a cash and carry company supplying the public with all types of electrical appliances, varying from light bulbs to fridge freezers. Electrical goods supply is a very competitive business; Pattersons have to compete with all the national suppliers that tend to dominate the market. In order to compete successfully they have adopted a business strategy of fast turnover and low profit margins coupled with a high customer service level.

Each store holds approximately nine thousand item lines; the majority of the smaller items are on display in the sales area, a selection of the larger appliances are also on display, this is complemented by a variety of brochures that carry information about the whole range of products. Experienced sales personnel are available to assist customers in their selection of appropriate goods. Following selection and payment of goods, customers tend to 'carry' the smaller items from the store; larger items are delivered within forty-eight hours. Each store has its own warehouse that is replenished when necessary from the company's main storage depot; the main storage depot's inventory control system is managed by head office.

Every store has its own computer system to control the day-to-day business; all of these are linked to the head office system. Information technology and information systems (IT/IS) development strategy has gone hand in hand with the business strategy that has enabled the dramatic expansion of the business. The IT centre is based in the head office and offers support to all of the satellite stores.

The Chairman and the Board of Directors recently employed the services of a business management consultant; the major aim of the exercise was to aid the development of a business strategy for the medium-to-long term. At a recent meeting of the board, the directors discussed the consultant's report. One of the recommendations stated 'Pattersons have previously been successful in automation and rationalisation of its business processes, maybe it's time for the business to consider reengineering in its future long-term business strategy'. This statement resulted in a heated discussion and disagreement, so much so that it was eventually decided to commission an internal study that would report back to the board at a later date.

A further recommendation involved the development of an integrated inventory distribution system. Currently when goods reach their re-order level in the individual stores, and the main storage depot cannot supply the goods, they are purchased from suppliers - even though other stores have more than adequate levels of the goods. It was decided to conduct a feasibility study, including a cost-benefit analysis before the proposed project would be given support.

Overall the consultant's report was encouraging, generally indicating a healthy business position from a management perspective. One point of concern was the recent implementation of a company-wide computerised shift scheduling system, for the shop workers, warehouse personnel and support staff. This system basically involves the scheduling of shift patterns and hours worked by the individuals. Previously individuals negotiated their working shifts with middle management within the bounds of certain parameters, number of shifts per week, maximum number of hours etc. There is resistance to the imposition of the system, thus the system is not fully utilised. To work successfully the system requires a great deal of manual intervention and updating. Generally the system is viewed as a failure by both middle management and the staff affected.

14   **PATTERSONS ELECTRICAL SUPPLIES: INFORMATION SYSTEM FAILURE**   *27 mins*

In the scenario it was stated that the implementation of the computerised shift scheduling system had 'failed'. Recent research suggests that IT investment has emerged as a high-risk, hidden-cost process. At least 20% of such spend is wasted, and between 30-40% of IS projects realise no benefits whatsoever, however measured, failures and rejections are commonplace.

Required:

Discuss the reasons for the apparent high levels of failure in the implementation of information systems. Make reference to the computerised shift scheduling system recently installed into Pattersons.   **15 Marks**

15   **PATTERSONS ELECTRICAL SUPPLIES: IT/IS STRATEGY AND BUSINESS STRATEGY**   *36 mins*

A statement in the scenario 'Information technology and information systems (IT/IS) development strategy, has gone hand in hand with the business strategy this has enabled the dramatic expansion of the business.'

Required:

(a)   Discuss the implications and importance of this statement in respect of Pattersons and possibly the majority of all businesses, if they wish to survive and succeed in the twenty-first century market place.   **10 Marks**

Mr Smith the business consultant claimed, 'Pattersons have previously been successful in automation and rationalisation of its business processes, maybe it's time for the business to consider re-engineering in its future long term business strategy'.

Required:

(b)   Explain in terms of business processes what he meant by the terms: automation, rationalisation and re-engineering. (Give examples where appropriate in relation to the case study.)   **10 Marks**

Total Marks Q15 = 20

16   **QUESTION 19 ALSO REFERS TO PATTERSONS, AND INCLUDES DETAILED GUIDANCE - SEE THE FOLLOWING PAGE.**

Total Marks Pattersons scenario = 50

16 PATTERSONS ELECTRICAL SUPPLIES: INTERNET, EXTRANET, INTRANET *45 mins*

Currently Pattersons computer based systems applications portfolio predominantly consists of in-house business systems. They are considering expanding this portfolio to include the 'new' web-based technologies and systems.

'There is one major change in information technology on whose importance business executives, academics and technologists all agree. It is the explosive growth of the Internet and related technologies and applications and their impact on business, society and information technology. The Internet is changing the way businesses are operated and people work and how information technology supports business operation and end-user work activities.'

O'Brien (1999)

Required:

Describe and discuss the impact of the above quote with reference to the case study where appropriate in terms of:

(a) Business-to-Consumer commerce (Internet).

Include in your answer customer requirements. **10 Marks**

(b) Business-to-Business applications (extranet).

Include in your answer how major business functions can be supported by electronic commerce. **8 Marks**

(c) Internal business processes (Intranet). **7 marks**

Total Marks Q16 = 25

Approaching the answer

You should read through the requirement, and then re-read and annotate the question, highlighting points to include in your answer. An example is shown below.

> Use website to extend reach?

Pattersons Electrical Suppliers own a chain of retail outlets throughout the city and surrounding area. In recent years they have expanded these outlets from their one original store to the current seven stores. The head office is based on the original site. The business originated as a cash and carry company supplying the public with all types of electrical appliances, varying from light bulbs to fridge freezers. Electrical goods supply is a very competitive business Pattersons have to compete with all the national suppliers that tend to dominate the market. In order to compete successfully they have adopted a business strategy of fast turnover and low profit margins coupled with a high customer service level.

> Website must match this level

> Competitors web-based activities

> Efficient internal processes essential

> Easy access to large number of product details

Each store holds approximately nine thousand item lines; the majority of the smaller items are on display in the sales area, a selection of the larger appliances are also on display, this is complemented by a variety of brochures that carry information about the whole range of products. Experienced sales personnel are available to assist customers in their selection of appropriate goods. Following selection and payment of goods, customers tend to 'carry the

> Could this assistance be automated?

smaller items from the store; larger items are delivered within forty-eight hours. Each store has its own warehouse that is replenished when necessary from the company's main storage depot; the main storage depot's inventory control system is managed by head office.

> Consider delivery and back-office procedures

> Intranet could improve co-ordination

Every store has its own computer system to control the day-to-day business; all of these are linked to the head office system. Information technology and information systems (IT/IS) development strategy has gone hand in hand with the business strategy that has enabled the dramatic expansion of the business. The IT centre is based in the head office and offers support to all of the satellite stores.

> Strategies must remain aligned

> Do staff have the skills required for web/intranet/extranet?

The Chairman and the Board of Directors recently employed the services of a business management consultant; the major aim of the exercise was to aid the development of a business strategy for the medium-to-long term. At a recent meeting of the board, the directors discussed the consultant's report. One of the recommendations stated 'Pattersons have previously been successful in automation and rationalisation of its business processes, maybe it's time for the business to consider reengineering in its future long-term business strategy'. This statement resulted in a heated discussion and disagreement, so much so that it was eventually decided to commission an internal study that would report back to the board at a later date.

> IT/IS considered?

> Role of new technologies

> Integrate with intranet/extranet/ Internet

A further recommendation involved the development of an integrated inventory distribution system. Currently when goods reach their re-order level in the individual stores, and the main storage depot cannot supply the goods, they are purchased from suppliers - even though other stores have more than adequate levels of the goods. It was decided to conduct a feasibility study, including a cost-benefit analysis before the proposed project would be given support.

> An improved stock system is essential

Overall the consultant's report was encouraging, generally indicating a healthy business position from a management perspective. One point of concern was the recent implementation of a company-wide computerised shift scheduling system, for the shop workers, warehouse personnel and support staff. This system basically involves the scheduling of shift patterns and hours worked by the individuals. Previously, individuals negotiated their working shifts with middle management within the bounds of certain parameters; number of shifts per week, maximum number of hours etc. There is resistance to the imposition of the system, thus the system is not fully utilised. To work successfully the system requires a great deal of manual intervention and updating. Generally the system is viewed as a failure by both middle management and the staff affected.

> Could be available to all on the intranet

> System not working correctly, avoid these mistakes in future implementations

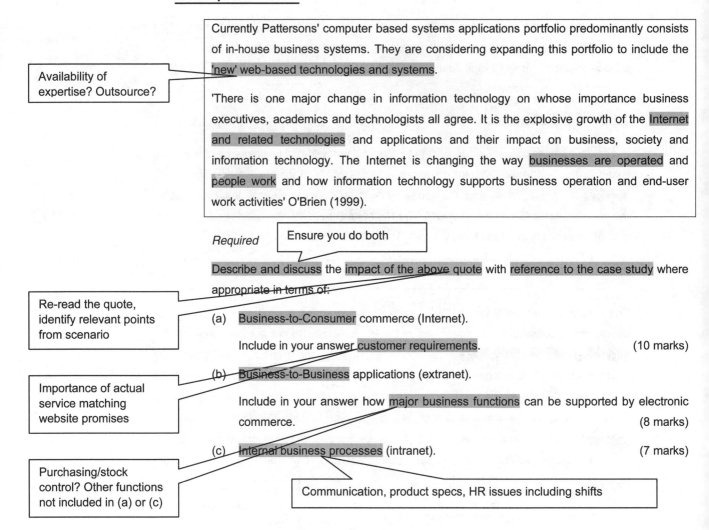

Availability of expertise? Outsource?

Currently Pattersons' computer based systems applications portfolio predominantly consists of in-house business systems. They are considering expanding this portfolio to include the 'new' web-based technologies and systems.

'There is one major change in information technology on whose importance business executives, academics and technologists all agree. It is the explosive growth of the Internet and related technologies and applications and their impact on business, society and information technology. The Internet is changing the way businesses are operated and people work and how information technology supports business operation and end-user work activities' O'Brien (1999).

Required

Ensure you do both

Describe and discuss the impact of the above quote with reference to the case study where appropriate in terms of:

Re-read the quote, identify relevant points from scenario

(a) Business-to-Consumer commerce (Internet).

Include in your answer customer requirements. (10 marks)

(b) Business-to-Business applications (extranet).

Importance of actual service matching website promises

Include in your answer how major business functions can be supported by electronic commerce. (8 marks)

(c) Internal business processes (intranet). (7 marks)

Purchasing/stock control? Other functions not included in (a) or (c)

Communication, product specs, HR issues including shifts

Answer plan

Then organise the things you have noticed and your points arising into a coherent answer plan. Not all the points you have noticed will have to go into your answer – you should spend a few minutes thinking them through and prioritising them.

(a) **B2C (Internet)**

Intro

- Access to all consumers with Internet access - expanding market
- Competitors in electrical goods offering on-line option

User requirements

- Website must provide product info
- User-friendly, easy to use
- Returns/support policy and procedures
- How products delivered?
- On-line transaction processing?

Customer retention/website promotions

- Loyalty schemes?
- How can website attract NEW customers

Other points

- Use of information collected from website visitors/customers
- Cross-selling

(b) **B2B (extranet)**

Intro

- Define and explain extranet

Stock

- Automated re-ordering via links to supplier
- Order history available to suppliers - indication future requirements?

Suppliers

- Improved communication links
- Access to marketing info that could influence future stock requirements
- Use extranet to facilitate EDI?
- Closer relationship

Payments

- Supplier payment via EFT?
- Automated discounting for prompt payment

Other points

- Links to banking organisations - financial management

(c) **Internal (intranet)**

Intro

- Define and explain intranet

E-mail, bulletin boards

- General use of e-mail
- Bulletin-board style discussions
- Product query database

General info sharing

- Information held in one location available to all
- Should reduce stock-outs
- Detailed product specs available
- Info more easily maintained and updated
- General competitive info can be shared with all staff

You should flesh out the points contained in your plan and link them to form a coherent answer. Structured answers, with short paragraphs, should help ensure your answer remains focussed.

BPP PUBLISHING

17   **HK CONSULTANCY: INFORMATION OVERLOAD; INFORMATION QUALITY (based on a Pilot paper question)**   *45 mins*

The HK Consultancy Company specialises in helping organisations to benefit from the implementation of IT systems. On a typical client project, staff from HK Consultancy will review the use of IT within an organisation, identify how staff should be using the IT systems, obtain information about the proposed IT systems and then ensure that the revised IT system meet the requirements of the users.

As the newly-appointed, experienced management accountant, your responsibilities include ensuring that the information systems of the company support its strategic direction, and advising the board of any changes that could be made to the overall company strategy. Prior to your appointment, the board recognised that growth in its existing market was limited, and required some diversification to meet the consultancy's objectives of sales and profit growth.

An intranet has been established utilising a package which provides databases for technical information, bulletin boards, electronic mail and customer contact information. The intranet is used by the management accountant frequently throughout the day, mainly to answer e-mails, but also to check information on the technical databases and bulletin boards. You also receive information from:

- Professional staff who visit client organisations, in the form of verbal queries and written reports

- Various journals specialising in IT systems

- Administration staff who produce client proposals for review prior to sending out consultants to potential clients

- Telephone queries directly from clients regarding the status of different projects

- The Internet, where different client and competitor websites are reviewed on a daily basis by the management accountant

Your first project is to provide a report to the board summarising the company's current strategic situation compared to its major competitors and suggesting alternative strategies for diversification.

Required

(a) As the management accountant, it is important that you are able to focus on this project. Briefly explain the concept of information overload, then explain how you would refine or amend the information system in the HK Consultancy to limit the amount of information being delivered to you.   **17 Marks**

(b) Evaluate the characteristics that should apply to the information being given to the management accountant to ensure that the information is quickly and accurately understood.   **8 Marks**

Total Marks Q17 = 25

Approaching the answer

You should read through the requirement, and then re-read and annotate the question, highlighting points to include in your answer. An example is shown below.

HK has much in-house expertise relating to IS

The HK Consultancy Company specialises in helping organisations to benefit from the implementation of IT systems. On a typical client project, staff from HK Consultancy will review the use of IT within an organisation, identify how staff should be using the IT systems, obtain information about the proposed IT systems and then ensure that the revised IT system meet the requirements of the users.

As the newly-appointed, experienced management accountant, your responsibilities include ensuring that the information systems of the company support its strategic direction, and advising the board of any changes that could be made to the overall company strategy. Prior to your appointment, the board recognised that growth in its existing market was limited, and required some diversification to meet the consultancy's objectives of sales and profit growth.

> Information required to support high level decisions

> Information systems strategy will require adjusting if overall company strategy changes

An intranet has been established, utilising a package which provides databases for technical information, bulletin boards, electronic mail and customer contact information. The intranet is used by the management accountant frequently throughout the day, mainly to answer e-mails, but also to check information on the technical databases and bulletin boards. You also receive information from:

> Could be expanded - extranet?

- Professional staff who visit client organisations, in the form of verbal queries and written reports

> Could be e-mailed or posted on intranet?

> Potential for frequent interruptions

- Various journals specialising in IT systems

- Administration staff, who produce client proposals for review prior to sending out consultants to potential clients

> Delegate? Use extranet?

- Telephone queries directly from clients regarding the status of different projects

- The Internet, where different client and competitor websites are reviewed on a daily basis by the management accountant

> Intelligent agents? IT journal review too?

Your first project is to provide a report to the board summarising the company's current strategic situation compared to its major competitors and suggesting alternative strategies for diversification.

> External info required

> 'Forward looking' info required

> High-level, comprehensive

Required

(a) As the management accountant, it is important you that you are able to focus on this project. Briefly explain the concept of 'information overload', then explain how you would refine or amend the information system in the HK Consultancy to limit the amount of information being delivered to you. (17 marks)

> Use broad definition, not just 'computers'

> Procedures, IT screening tools, delegation

(b) Evaluate the characteristics that should apply to the information being given to the management accountant to ensure that the information is quickly and accurately understood. (8 marks)

> Consider 'ACCURATE' mnemonic

> Remember that scenario tells us the accountant is focussing on strategic issues

BPP PUBLISHING

Answer plan

Then organise the things you have noticed and your points arising into a coherent answer plan. Not all the points you have noticed will have to go into your answer – you should spend a few minutes thinking them through and prioritising them.

(a) **Information overload and information system amendments**

Intro

- Explain information overload
- Include role of advances in IT/IS in increasing amount of info available

Steps to limit information reaching management accountant

- Telephone queries to go through secretary
- Delegation of some tasks
- Use Internet newsclipping service to send targeted information
- Intelligent agents to monitor websites

(b) **Information characteristics**

Intro

- Accountant's current tasks require info to support strategic decisions

Information characteristics (use ACCURATE mnemonic to jog memory)

- Needs to see big picture - summarised
- Presentation should aid understanding
- Complete
- Timely
- Relevant
- Some outward-looking info

You should flesh out the points contained in your plan and link them to form a coherent answer. Structured answers, with short paragraphs, should help ensure your answer remains focussed.

Exam answer bank

1   JH LTD: IT STRATEGY

> **Tutorial note**. As with most questions set at Final Level, you could have included a wide range of possible points to answer both parts of this question.
>
> If you struggled with part (a), refer back to Chapter 3 of this Text. The answer you provide can be fairly general in nature, but you should refer to JH Ltd occasionally as the question asked for ' disadvantages that could arise for JH Ltd'.
>
> Part (b) requires more thought and application of knowledge, rather than simply reproducing 'book knowledge'. Ensure your answer covers both parts of the requirement - firstly explaining the barriers then suggesting how the barriers could be overcome.
>
> Our answer deals with each individual's possible barriers, and then makes suggestions relating to that individual, before moving on to the next person. You may have preferred to deal with all barriers first and then make suggestions in the second part of your answer.

(a)   **Disadvantages of not having an overall IT strategy**

JH Ltd's IS/IT strategy should compliment its **business strategy** by providing the information and communication tools necessary to achieve the overall aims of the organisation. An important element of this is that the **information needs** are clearly identified and defined before information systems are decided upon. Disadvantages of JH Ltd not having an IS/IT strategy include:

(i)   JH Ltd may **spend large sums of money** on IS/IT projects, but the resulting systems may not meet the organisation's key information requirements.

(ii)   Without a strategy, there is greater risk of investing in **incompatible** systems that increase the cost and complexity of working. This in part relates to the technical issues to be dealt with, and also the need to ensure that systems introduced allow some **flexibility** for future changes.

(iii)   Many companies are able to use IT to gain a competitive advantage, either by exploiting IT in their operations or by managing their information better. It therefore follows that not having a strategy can lead to the company **losing advantage to its competitors** and falling behind in terms of technology used.

(iv)   Not only do organisations rely on IS and IT far more than they used to but **IT is changing the way many industries work**. For example the availability of information over the Internet is changing the way information is gathered and managed in many industries that are information-driven. Companies need to **build this into their future plans** and therefore plan IT to help them cope with the changes and remain competitive in the industry.

For example, retailing is becoming much more information-driven and many aspects of service industries such as travel agencies can do business over computer networks. The absence of an IS/IT strategy will mean that the organisation is **not matching its future information needs** and **retaining its ability to compete** in a changing environment.

(v)   IT is changing the **way** information is **collected**, the **amount** of information **collected** and **what is done with information** once it has been collected. For example, in retailing, EPOS systems and loyalty card schemes are allowing supermarket chains to build up vast databases of individual consumer preferences. Companies that do not take advantage of this are liable to **fall behind the competition** and find it impossible to **reap the benefits** of using information as a strategic resource.

(vi)   **Exchange of information** between various **stakeholders** is facilitated via IS/IT and is also having an impact upon the **structure** of organisations making them more flexible, or softening the organisational boundaries. Where an organisation does not plan for this, it will **limit its ability to react quickly to changes**.

(vii) It is important for organisations to ensure they provide their **employees** with the resources (including IS/IT) they need to do their jobs well and to keep morale high. Employees may see other organisations utilising the latest technology and become **demotivated**: the older technology will limit their own effectiveness and harm their career prospects.

(b) **Barriers and suggestions relating to each of the three individuals**

    (i)   **The senior manager**

The senior manager has **little knowledge** of IS/IT and is also **fearful** of it. Underlying his dismissive attitude may be a fear of losing face in front of his more IT-literate colleagues. He will therefore have little appreciation of the potential business benefits of IT.

He may also **fail to see the relevance of IT** to the industry in a wider sense, which could result in **missing a strategic advantage**. The fact that he is good at producing overall policy may mean that he produces a general policy that skims the surface of the issues. His being task-orientated may also mean that insufficient time is taken to consider the issues fully. He is more likely to try and **push through his ideas** as fast as possible.

To overcome these barriers, firstly it is necessary to increase the manager's **general awareness** of IS and IT and its capabilities. This should enable him then to explore the benefits of IS/IT for LT Ltd. Providing him with copies of **relevant, well-written articles** from non-technical journals (for example the FT's regular IT articles and supplements) should open his eyes to what his company may be missing.

Provided he is not totally resistant, the senior manager could be provided with a **desktop PC** and be shown how to use some **simple but useful applications** that will save him time from day to day. This process could include training in an Executive Information System (EIS) that provides easy access to information relevant to the senior manager's role. This should raise his confidence, kindle some enthusiasm and help to overcome his fear of IT.

    (ii)   **The IS/IT professional**

The IS/IT professional believes that IT is best left to specialists, yet her knowledge is **not as up to date** as one would expect a specialist's knowledge to be. Her knowledge seems to be focussed on the existing systems used within JH Ltd.

This lack of awareness of alternative architectures (such as client-server) may cause her to be biased against strategies that would require different types of systems to be introduced. She may not be in a position to judge what type of system and strategy would best meet **user needs**. Many of the users may be familiar with PCs but she is unlikely to recommend devolving computing power into the hands of the user as she neither **understands** their needs nor **believes** they should be involved.

Her natural tendency will be to suggest an IT strategy that **preserves her empire** and revolves around the technical **IT department** rather than the **business needs**. There is also the danger that she will suggest continued use of technology within her own current knowledge, **ignoring current trends and developments**. Given that the Senior Manager may wish to rely on her knowledge to produce a quick solution, this could result in an inappropriate strategy.

These barriers may be overcome in a variety of ways.

(1) She needs to **update her knowledge** by reading computer journals and business press.

(2) She will probably need **further training** (probably a course run by a specialist training provider) in areas such as client-server systems.

(3) She must be given top-level encouragement to look at the benefits of IS/IT from the **business needs** viewpoint, rather than seeing IT as an end in itself.

(4) She must spend time with **users**, establishing a clear picture of user needs that is used to drive the development of the IS/IT strategy.

(5) Visits to **other organisations** that utilise relevant technology should assist in overcoming her resistance to more recent systems.

    (iii)   The trainee accountant may bring a lot of enthusiasm to the project, wishing to **prove himself** and bring all his knowledge to bear, but his desire to be the **IT champion** may well mean that he has a **private agenda** which may not be beneficial.

His focus on IS/IT may only be **short-term,** and may recede after he has completed his studies.

His **limited experience** and position in the organisation may limit his ability to see the **wider picture** effectively. However, being a user of IS/IT, he will bring a valuable perspective to the project if his enthusiasm can be contained.

His input could also be resented by the IT manager who may try to blind him with science, especially as he is pushing for more end-user computing and less reliance upon her department. This could be a significant source of **conflict** within the group.

It will be important to **overcome any conflict** between the group arising from personal differences and background. Each person participating in the strategy development process should be spoken to by a board member, ensuring that they all know why they have been included, and what their respective **roles** will be. It should be emphasised that they all have different skills, and all have a **valuable contribution** to make. Each member of the group must be made aware of the overall **objectives** of the group.

2   IT STRATEGY

> **Tutorial note**. This question refers to an 'IT strategy' rather than an 'IS/IT strategy'. This should not have prevented you from including material relating to information systems that utilise IT in your answer.
>
> In a question such as this ensure you structure your answer clearly - dealing with each of the five reasons you provide separately and providing sufficient information, including an example, to earn five marks for each reason.

Reasons for having an IT strategy

In this answer we identify five reasons for developing an IT strategy, using the example of a typical small firm offering domestic services such as plumbing and electrical work. For convenience we shall refer to this firm as **EG Ltd**.

(1)   **Rationalising the existing investment in IT**

Because of the benefits it offers (speed, accuracy, and so on) IT has become a **key component of most aspects of modern businesses**. Most organisations have reached the stage in their IT maturity whereby IT has been used to automate tasks previously performed manually or by obsolete technology. Most organisations could **not now conceivably disinvest in IT**, and return to traditional methods of getting work done.

However, it is common in organisations, from small to large, for IT to have been **introduced piecemeal** to address specific requirements without due regard having been paid to the way that the individual systems **work together and communicate**.

Adoption of a strategy is therefore necessary to guide the direction and scope of the **whole** IT development of a firm allowing it to match the **resources available** to the changing **environment** and enable the firm to meet its **primary business objectives**. All of these matters - overall use of resources, environmental issues and overall objectives – are key issues in the formulation of business strategies.

The next stage of IT development is to **exploit the utmost that IT has to offer** by **re-engineering the processes** with the aid of IT rather than just automating current processes.

Example

EG Ltd originally invested in stand-alone PCs for basic administrative tasks such as writing letters to customers and keeping accounts. None of its systems were fully integrated, and much work still involves inefficiencies such as re-inputting of data, or manual searches for information that is held in computerised form but is not accessible by a computer search.

An **organisation-wide strategy** needs to be formulated if the **various systems are to be brought together**, enabling further gains, for instance, automatic generation of letters to debtors, proper accessible databases of customers, suppliers, materials, staff resources.

(2)   **Beating competitors and enhancing relationships**

The **traditional** view of IT's role in competitive strategy is largely **reactive** - that is, a response to existing competitive strategy and business process, but not a critical factor in **shaping** that strategy and process.

A more sensible approach is to position IT in a **pro-active** role where the competitive strategy is not viewed as given, but rather as something that should be challenged, extended and perhaps modified, in light of **emerging technologies and applications**.

The perspective of IT strictly as a **support** function in competitive strategy is increasingly outdated. Firms are now seeking ways to exploit IT to transform their basic businesses, **enhance their relationships** with suppliers and customers, and **create new market opportunities**.

Today, successful competitive strategy and corporate results are likely to focus on a small number of performance attributes including **speed, flexibility, quality** and **scale**. All four areas are **profoundly affected** by an organisation's **effective use of IT** to facilitate, enhance and accelerate strategic execution.

Example

EG Ltd's original investment in IT was made partly **because their competitors and suppliers** were clearly investing in such systems too, and EG's manually-produced communications with the outside world made the entire firm **look old-fashioned and inefficient**.

Greater use of technologies now available, or becoming available, could enable EG Ltd to **surpass** many competitors and **deal much more effectively** with suppliers and customers. For instance, **computerised scheduling and booking systems** could enable EG to respond more quickly to urgent call-outs and **make and honour promises** to customers about when work will be done and how long it will take (something at which the industry in general is notoriously bad). **EDI links** to suppliers could greatly simplify ordering and administration for both parties. A good **website** could generate a great deal of new business.

(3) **Getting the systems that are really needed**

In the past many organisations have found that information systems have **failed to deliver expected benefits** for reasons such as the following.

(i) There is no **commitment by the top management** of an organisation. IT strategy invariably involves some degree of **change**, and, unless top management is behind the strategy, its implementation can prove to be impossible.

(ii) The **users and providers of IT** in the organisation have not been fully enough involved. If new systems are simply imposed on such people and they are given no chance to explain their **real needs** there is a strong chance that the system will not reflect their needs.

The process of going through the planning stage in itself is extremely valuable as it provides a mechanism not only for determining what needs to be done but, if properly handled, it also ensures that the result is **achieved by consensus of all interested parties**. This means that the plan is far more likely to be put into effect satisfactorily. The formulation of an **IT strategy** should then result in a clear and **generally understood and agreed** document which sets out the relative priorities of each approved project together with the identification and allocation of the appropriate **resources**, **approval and delivery** dates, arrangements for **testing and training**, **and** so on.

Example

EG Ltd originally acquired computers in cases where the manager of a function wanted one and had sufficient influence in the organisation to obtain funding. Other managers were either not interested or did not have the influence. Users, therefore, either had computers imposed on them or were deprived of them.

A **culture change** is needed: those who are opposed to computerisation or simply lack enthusiasm need to be persuaded of the benefits.

(4) **Continually improving the management of the organisation**

IT brings **ongoing** revolution in the way information is created, used and presented to management. After the strategy has been developed, it must be regarded as a living entity that the organisation needs to review on a regular and systematic basis as circumstances change.

Any strategic view of IT must take technical developments into account. For instance the **Internet** and **Intranet** popularity has forced many managers to rethink the direction of applications and infrastructure investments. The most popular applications use web publishing for existing documents, web forms for transaction entry or web-to-database links to access corporate data.

Example

EG Ltd could benefit from introducing an Intranet in ways such as the following.

(i) An organisation-wide phone directory that is always up-to-date, containing internal numbers and frequently used external numbers.

(ii) Sales information including price lists for jobs, staff availability for urgent call-outs, and supplier and competitor information, including links to suppliers' and competitors' web sites

(iii) A technical database for staff such as plumbers and electricians showing how various jobs are done, how the latest tools and materials should be used, legal and safety requirements and so on.

(5) **Obtaining synergies and economies of scale**

If IT is not integrated to corporate strategy a business is almost certain to be **spending too much,** if only because a sizeable percentage will be **spent on the wrong things**. If this goes unchecked there is very little chance that the company will realise the economies of scale and informational synergies that the business needs.

A company's IT architecture comprises **five different component architectures**: applications, technology, data, methods and management practices, and **spending needs to keep these architectures in balance**. For instance, if a large amount is spent on new technologies, but **nothing on training and data conversion** then at best there will be a lag before the new facilities are exploited to the full. The benefits of the IT expenditure might be delayed until the skills of users are available to produce them.

Example

EG Ltd is typical in that it has only computerised its administration so far: it has not considered benefits that could arise from using technology in **other areas of its business,** such as mobile phones and portable PCs for staff such as plumbers and electricians to use on site.

3   JH PLC: INFORMATION CENTRE

> **Tutorial note**. The central theme to part (a) is one that often crops up in examination questions - requiring justification for significant expenditure on IS/IT. Organisations are becoming increasingly reliant on information technology for day-to-day operations - it is essential that a support infrastructure is in place to ensure business critical systems run smoothly and to ensure full value is obtained from funds spent on IS/IT.
>
> There are a wide range of points that could have been made in part (b). Ensure you relate the points you make to the situation at JH plc, rather than explaining the general advantages that networks may bring.

(a) **MEMO**

To	The Board, JH plc
From	Management Accountant
Date	24 November 200X
Subject	Proposal to close the Information Centre

This memo sets out a justification for the continuance of the company's Information Centre on **non-financial** grounds.

JH plc, IT and the Information Centre

One of the main factors in the success of JH plc is considered to be its high investment in modern IT systems. The scale and complexity of the company's operations is such that it could not function without effective information management: this alone justifies the level of IT investment.

The Information Centre plays a key role in ensuring that this investment continues to be used to maximum advantage. This is essential if the company is to achieve its mission of being the most profitable freight forwarder in the country.

The contribution of the Information Centre

The IC performs its role in a wide variety of ways.

(i) The IC's **Help Desk** ensures that staff time is spent on **customer service** rather than on IT problems.

BPP
PUBLISHING

(1) It has sufficient **staff and technical expertise** to respond quickly to problems with hardware or software. It maintains **good contacts** and relationships with **suppliers** to ensure that they fulfil their maintenance obligations and that their maintenance staff are quickly on site when needed.

(2) It maintains a **record of problems** and identifies those that occur most often. If the problem is that users do not know how to use the system, **training** is provided. If the problem is with the system itself, a solution is found, either by **modifying the system** or by investment in appropriate **hardware or software.**

(3) It considers the viability of **suggestions for improvements** to the system and brings these into effect, where possible, for all users who stand to benefit.

(ii) The IC sets, and encourages users to conform to, common **standards**.

(1) **Hardware standards** ensure that all of the equipment used in the organisation is **compatible** and can be put into use in different departments as needed. The recent upgrade of the marketing department's old Apple Mac computers to IBM-compatible Pentium PCs is an example of this.

(2) **Software standards** ensure that **information** generated by one department can easily be **shared** with and worked upon by other departments. The recent introduction of Windows 98 and Office 2000 throughout the organisation is an example.

(3) **Programming standards** ensure that applications developed by individuals to help them perform their jobs (for example word-processing macros or spreadsheets for data analysis) follow **best practice**, are **easy to modify**, and are **replicated to others** in the organisation where this is of benefit.

(4) **Data processing standards** ensure that certain conventions such as the format of **file names** are followed throughout the organisation. This facilitates **sharing** and **storage and retrieval** of information by as many users as possible.

(iii) The IC helps to preserve the **security** of data.

(1) It has developed a **utility program** and recommended **procedures** for company-wide use, to ensure that **back-ups** are made at regular intervals. Second copies of back-up files are stored off site and this system of archiving is operated and maintained by the Information Centre.

(2) The IC helps to preserve the company's systems from attack by computer **viruses**. The latest versions of anti-virus software are available to all users. Users are regularly reminded about the dangers of viruses and IC staff give training in the use of anti-virus software.

Conclusion

The IC is well utilised by staff. It fulfils a need that would still exist if the centre were closed. Staff will feel that they have been left to sink or swim, and they may very well **sink** if they have nowhere to go to obtain the support they are used to.

The idea that the IC has no discernible **income** does **not mean** that it has no positive impact on **profitability**. The annual **saving** of £4m from closing the centre needs to be weighed against the **costs** to the organisation if support is not provided (such as wasted time, ill-advised investment and sales lost because customers perceive inefficiencies in the system and receive an increasingly unreliable service). The cost **of buying in support** when it is needed, as experience shows it undoubtedly will be, should also be considered.

The **costs of the centre could be re-allocated** on a fair basis to the departments that actually give rise to those costs - **the users of its services**. At the same time the centre itself could be subject to **performance standards** to ensure that it is giving the best value for money. Performance standards may be established by means of a **benchmarking** exercise with similar services in other companies.

(b) **How the network can enhance IC services**

The newly installed network provides opportunities for the IC to improve its services in a number of ways, including the following.

(i) **Training software** can be developed or purchased and made available over the network from a central server. Training applications often contain analysis software, drawing attention to **trainee progress** and **common problems** (the **Mavis Beacon** typing tutor is a well-known example), and the availability of such information will enable the IC to identify and address specific training needs more closely.

(ii) **Help** can be made available directly through users' computers, using an **e-mail** system for queries and responses. Common problems and their solutions can be posted on a bulletin board for all to read (problems with using the Internet are an obvious candidate for such treatment). The network will speed up the process of sorting out problems and sharing knowledge.

(iii) **Remote diagnostic software** is available which will enable staff in the IC to 'take control' of a computer whose user is having problems and sort out the problem for them without leaving their desk, in the same way that they would if they paid the user a visit. Again this will speed up the problem-solving process.

(iv) The IC can take responsibility for **protecting** the system against possible abuses now that it is linked to the **Internet**. Anti-virus measures will become even more important in this environment, but network software should make it easier for the IC to **control the problem centrally**.

(v) The Internet link will also make **control over access** an important issue. The Information Centre can set up and operate '**firewalls**', which disable part of the communications technology that normally allows two-way communication.

This means that **internal** users can go out to the Internet to search for and retrieve information, but **external** parties are denied access to sensitive parts of the company's systems. (Clients will be able to visit JH plc's website and send in their requirements, perhaps choosing options from menus and filling in forms on screen, but they will not be able to interfere with the **processing** of their requirements.)

(vi) A location on the network could be set-aside for solutions to **common problems** or frequently asked questions - enabling users to find solutions to some questions without the direct intervention of IC staff.

4   CP LTD: HOMEWORKING

> **Tutorial note**. Homeworking may sometimes be referred to as 'teleworking'. As homeworking is becoming increasingly common, and often involves setting up appropriate information systems, it is a highly examinable topic.
>
> Part (a) has three separate requirements; potential benefits for staff, concerns staff may have and how the IT infrastructure could help. Ensure your report addresses all three areas.
>
> Your answer to part (b) should have included reference to the importance of keeping staff informed, and ensuring sufficient training was provided. Steps that could be taken to include homeworkers in the culture of the organisation are also relevant.

REPORT

To: Managing Director
From: Management Accountant
Date: 22nd May 200X
Subject: Homeworking

1   Introduction

1.1   This report sets out the potential **benefits** to the staff that will be gained by homeworking and the **concerns** they may have together with an assessment of the help that can be provided via the IT infrastructure to alleviate these.

2   Potential benefits

2.1   **Savings in travel time and cost**

The staff will not have to travel to work, which could be a significant advantage to those who have long or difficult journeys. They will also save the cost of travel to and from work.

2.2   **Flexibility**

Staff can be more flexible about the hours they work (eg 7 to 3, 8 to 4, 9 to 5, or whatever suits them) and about the timing of breaks. This may allow CP Ltd to actually **increase** the total hours available for customer contact, allowing staff to provide a **better service** and increasing their potential **sales bonuses** (this is, of course, a benefit to the company too).

2.3 Work environment

There are many **disruptions** at work, which can hinder or distract employees: examples are constantly ringing telephones, printer noise, and loud conversations. These would not be present at home, and although there may be **other distractions** these are less likely to be stressful ones.

2.4 Quality of life

More generally, homeworking should provide a better quality of life for the individual working at home. The home is likely to be **better lit**, **heated** to suit individual taste, more **comfortable**, and have **more facilities**. It will not be necessary to cram domestic chores such as shopping, cleaning, washing into evenings and weekends. It may be possible to adapt working hours to accommodate **family commitments**, such as taking and collecting children from school.

3 Staff concerns

3.1 Employment relationship and legal implications

Staff may be concerned about their **employment rights** if they work from home and whether there are any implications in terms of **health and safety** regulations, **insurance and tax**, mortgage and council tax.

A further concern in this area is whether they will have enough **space** to work effectively at home.

I suggest we clarify these matters and then **brief the staff** about any potential implications on an individual basis if necessary.

3.2 Isolation

Staff currently have a great deal of interaction in the office, so a concern of staff could be that they become **cut off from their colleagues** and will miss the social contact. This could engender a feeling of uncertainty in staff, which could affect their ability to provide an efficient service. They may also fear that being out of sight and out of mind will damage any **prospects of being considered for advancement** within the organisation.

3.3 Exchange of information

Staff help each other by **exchanging information** about work-related matters and **sharing the problems** they have experienced. There may be fears that they will lose this mutual support if working at home.

4 IT infrastructure

4.1 Much of the information that is required for the staff to carry out their jobs is on the computer system. It should be fairly straightforward to provide a connection to the office computer system from the homes of employees, and provide them with the necessary hardware.

There will obviously be an associated **cost** to this which we will need to quantify to ensure that it is not prohibitive.

The link could be a permanent link or a dial up facility. The **dial-up facility** may be more appropriate if it is possible to download the files staff need to access onto a local PC. This could then be updated at intervals avoiding the need to be permanently connected.

4.2 The same link could also be used to provide **e-mail** and **bulletin board** facilities to enable the staff to keep in contact and exchange information.

4.3 Access to the **VAN** would also be possible using the same link, but again the **cost implications** would need to be investigated in more detail.

4.4 Local copies of **software** such as word-processing packages and spreadsheets can be provided to produce the necessary documents and letters.

4.5 IT is only part of the answer, however: telecommunications links are a poor substitute for the actual **direct social contact** currently enjoyed. A carelessly worded e-mail, for instance, can easily be misunderstood.

5 **Overcoming the concerns of staff**

5.1 It will be important for us to ensure that the staff are **kept informed** of developments and that we consult with them to **identify any worries** they may have. This will enable us to prepare them for the change and to alleviate their key concerns. The key **benefits** to them and the organisation should be **stressed**. It is important that they realise that the individual and not just the organisation will benefit. This will hopefully enable them to **own** the change and buy into it.

5.2 Consideration could be given to **piloting** the method of working with a few individuals who are already pro-homeworking. They will **champion the change** later if we decide to implement it throughout the sales staff. Asking for volunteers and for suggestions on implementation will ensure that staff feel that they have been properly consulted.

5.3 Consideration could also be given to setting up a **demonstration** to impress upon them that they will still be able to perform their jobs and keep in touch with each other. A visit to (home and office) sites of an organisation that already uses this method of working may also help staff to realise its benefits and its operability as well as its ease of use. It will also help us to assess the **level of training** necessary, which must be given to support the staff.

5.4 **Social contact** could be retained to a limited extent by providing **regular meetings** at a convenient place. This could be used to update staff collectively of developments, organisational matters and reinforce the commitment and cultural aspects of the organisation whilst providing the opportunity for social contact.

5.5 The company will **save** a considerable amount of money (90% of £3,500 to £4,000 per employee per annum). Part of this could be **offered to staff** as an incentive to work at home.

5 **CC PLC: INTRANET AND INFORMATION SHARING**

> **Tutorial note**. The material explaining the objectives of an intranet can be general in nature - a rare opportunity to earn marks for reproducing book knowledge. However, the second part of your answer to part (a) must refer to the situation at CC plc.
>
> Part (b) consists of four requirements. Your answer could have been structured using four headings: Organisational reasons, Human reasons, Overcoming organisational reasons, and Overcoming human reasons. This should ensure that you cover all areas of the question - and makes it easier for markers to give marks.

(a) An **intranet** uses software and other technology originally developed for the Internet on internal company networks. An intranet comprises an **organisation-wide web** of internal documents that is familiar, easy to use and comparatively inexpensive. Each employee has a **browser** enabling him or her to view information held on a server computer and may offer access to the Internet.

The main objective of an intranet is to **provide easy access to information** that helps people perform their jobs more efficiently. Many roles require increased access to knowledge and information. An intranet is a way of making this knowledge readily available.

Other objectives are outlined below.

To encourage the use of reference documents. Documents on-line are more likely to be used than those stored on shelves, especially if the document is bulky (for instance procedure manuals).

To create a sense of organisational unity. An intranet 'pulls together' in a co-ordinated fashion information from disparate parts of an organisation. It may be the only visible way some parts of a large organisation are linked.

The provision of an Intranet within CC plc should result in **better provision of information** by:

Ensuring consistency in information held and provided to clients. The intranet will enable one set of data to be held and accessed by all 20 offices.

Providing easy access to a larger pool of data. Information that managers previously 'kept to themselves' will be available to others.

An intranet at CC plc would enable information that is common to all offices to be **held centrally**, on the intranet, and accessed from local offices. This should improve communication and remove the problem of data inconsistencies between offices.

The intranet-Internet link will ensure the most **up-to-date planning information** is available. It would be useful to develop an intranet page complied from appropriate websites, that would **save staff time**, reducing the amount of time spent searching for information. (This page must be kept up-to-date.)

(b)   Even after an intranet and e-mail have been implemented at CC plc, organisational and human reasons will hinder the process of making information more widely available. Steps need to be taken to overcome these barriers to information sharing.

Human reasons that will need to be overcome include the following.

Information is only available if people know how to find it. The people at CC plc who could use the information held on the intranet must be told that the information is available, and trained so that they are confident enough to access it.

Efficient **communication** (including a company-wide e-mail explaining the intranet) and staff **training programmes** demonstrating intranet use will help overcome this problem.

Some staff will not choose to share information or knowledge. People may protect the information they have to boost their own performance relative to their colleagues. A culture change within CC plc is required before staff will be willing to share knowledge and information so that the organisation as a whole can benefit.

To tackle this problem techniques and processes to **encourage the sharing of information** could be included as part of a communication and knowledge management programme. Bonus schemes could include a company-wide element so that all staff would benefit from colleagues performing well.

Organisational reasons that will need to be overcome include the following.

The **hardware** used by CC plc is too old to support the new communication tools. This is likely to lead to user frustration with slow response times and problems gaining access to various systems. Unless the systems provided are efficient, users will abandon them.

To overcome this problem CC plc will need to make a **significant investment** in new hardware.

Work practices that do not involve or encourage the sharing of information have become established. A significant number of CC plc staff are likely to have a building and construction background, and may not be enthusiastic towards computing developments. These staff may see these new communication tools as an unnecessary waste of resources by IT staff who do not have a feel for the business.

This problem could be minimised by **involving staff** in the design of systems from the outset. Staff should be asked what information would make them more efficient. A tool that helps them do their job better will be welcomed by even the most sceptical.

Staff training programmes and a **user-friendly human-computer interface** should also reduce staff resistance.

6   FACILITIES MANAGEMENT

> **Tutorial note**. The various forms of outsourcing are likely examination topics - particularly the advantages and disadvantages of the outsourcing approach.
>
> 'Alarm bells' should have sounded loudly when reading this scenario, particularly the statement 'The appointment of GDC Ltd was relatively rushed and although an outline contract was agreed, no detailed Service Level Agreement was produced'. Because of this, GDC Ltd is able to provide relatively poor levels of service, yet still meet the terms of the contract.

(a)   GDC Ltd appears to have met its legal obligations even though the level of service it has provided to DS has been poor. There are a number of reasons for this.

DS rushed the appointment of GDC and did not insist on a **detailed Service Level Agreement (SLA)**. The contract does not specify the level of service that GDC will provide.

For example, GDC is obligated to provide 'management information', but there is no detailed definition of what this information will entail, and no deadline for the provision of the information. (eg '...within 5 working days of month-end').

DS handed **complete control** of its IT systems to GDC Ltd. The absence of IT expertise within DS puts it at a **disadvantage** when arguing its case with GDC Ltd.

For example, GDC could spend significant amounts of DS money on sub-standard hardware and software. DC Ltd would **not have the expertise to question** or challenge this purchase, resulting in poor use of DS funds and a poor level of service. However, even when purchasing sub-standard hardware GDC would not have breached the requirement of the contract to 'purchase all hardware and software'.

GDC Ltd is also responsible for the writing and maintenance of in-house software. **Unless GDC has a detailed understanding of DS the software written may not be suitable**. As GDC receives a set annual fee, it may be tempted to produce software as quickly and cheaply as possible. As the contract has no mention of software standards, GDC would be meeting its legal obligations.

Another reason that could be contributing DS receiving poor service is that **the agreement is now two years old**. Changes could have taken place inside DS within the past two years that an outside organisation such as GDC does not understand. The nature of management information required now may be different to that required two years ago.

Service levels could also be suffering because **GDC has no financial incentive to provide a good standard of service**. GDC Ltd has the right under the contract to increase the annual fee, above the rate of inflation, without any consultation and with no reference to the satisfaction of DS.

(b) The courses of action now available to DS relating to the provision of IT services, and the problems involved in each, are outlined below.

    (i) **DS could carry on under the existing agreement**, protecting the knowledge that GDC has built up on the provision of IT services to DS, **but applying 'moral' pressure** (in the form of complaints and meetings with GDC management) to obtain a better level of service.

        The main problem with this course of action is that the level of service may not improve at all.

    (ii) DS could terminate the existing contract by giving three months' notice, and **negotiate a new contract with GDC with a well-defined SLA**.

        Possible problems include the fact that GDC may not wish to negotiate a new SLA leaving DS with no IT services, or GDC may agree a new SLA but still provide the old shoddy service.

    (iii) DS could terminate the existing contract by giving three months' notice and **look for a new supplier** of all its IT services.

        However, this would mean 'starting from scratch'. Even an efficient provider would take time to develop a feel for the requirements at DS, and build up their expertise. There is no guarantee the new service provider would be better than GDC, although a more detailed SLA would help.

    (iv) **DS could establish its own in-house IT team**, probably using a combination of contractors and 'permanent' employees.

        The main problems with this option are the time and cost of finding setting up the team and that the team would be 'starting from scratch' and may only receive limited help from GDC during the hand-over.

    (v) Another option would be to include staff with a good understanding of DS's operations, but little IS/IT expertise, in a new in-house team (**insourcing**). If these people can be taught IT skills, they should then be able to utilise their business knowledge to ensure relevant IT services are provided.

        Problems with this option include finding staff that are suitable and willing to make this dramatic career switch, and replacing any staff who do move to the IT team.

BPP PUBLISHING

7   **Q.NET: IT STRATEGY AND COMPETITIVE ADVANTAGE**

> **Tutorial note**. The requirement instructs you to use Porter's Five Forces model as a framework for your answer – ensure that you do this by using each force as a separate heading.
>
> However, don't fall into the trap of simply explaining Porter's Five Forces. You must relate each force to the situation described, and most importantly, focus on how Q.NET could use IT for competitive advantage.
>
> Ensure your answer is reasonably balanced across each of the Five Forces, although if you feel one area to be more relevant than the others do make the points you believe are relevant.
>
> Try to be concise; there are a wide range of issues to include within the 36 minutes available.

How Q.NET could use each of Porter's Five Forces to gain a competitive advantage is explained below.

Rivalry between competitors

Q.NETs competitors are all organisations that sell books. Ways in which Q.NET could achieve an increase in sales compared to competitors include:

Improved customer service.

Additional investment in the IT infrastructure, and closer links with book suppliers, will facilitate more efficient operations in ordering, stock and dispatch. The end result will be a reduction in the time between a customer placing an order and delivery of that order.

Improved marketing.

Book, customer and transaction data will be able to be stored in a database, and used for competitive purposes. For example, tailored information can be presented to a customer whenever they access Q.NET's website. The type of marketing information presented would be influenced by past purchases, and the customer profile. This will encourage the development of a long-term relationship with the customer, and will further differentiate Q.NET from traditional booksellers.

Threat of substitutes. The publishing industry is undergoing rapid change with the growth of the Internet. Books (paper based products in general) are under threat from the new digital communication forms.

Alternatives to books include buying the material on CD-ROM, to be viewed on screen and a hard copy printed off if required. Alternately, printed material could be accessed and read on a website, or downloaded from a website. A hybrid product, combining a paper book, a CD or DVD and website links is likely to become the norm in some areas of publishing.

Q.NET should monitor developments in this area and consider moving into the 'e-books' industry.

Threat of new entrants. New book re-sellers entering the market could attract customers away from Q.NET. The high capital costs required to set up as an Internet based re-seller form some protection against this (ie entry-barrier), although this barrier is unlikely to be effective against a large organisation. The establishment of a strong Q.NET brand and reputation, combined with competitive pricing policies will form the most effective long-term barrier.

The establishment of a close relationship with suppliers, cemented through the use of mutually beneficial systems (eg EDI links) should discourage new entrants. To compete effectively any new entrant would need a similar relationship.

The power of buyers. A customer can buy the same book from a number of sources. As the product is identical, the deciding factor for the customer will be a combination of price and service. Books are a relatively low value, non-essential product. Collective action by buyers is therefore unlikely.

The main power of buyers in this market is the ease by which they can change supplier. Buyers can switch to other websites within seconds to compare book prices and delivery times. Search engines are also available which will check the various Internet suppliers and provide a summary of prices on those sites. A person may also pass a number bookshops several times a day without making a special trip (eg on the way home from work).

So, as well as price and service, further incentives such as 'book miles' or 'loyalty discounts' for repeat purchasers may be justified.

The power of suppliers. An individual title is usually only produced by one publisher. The supplier therefore holds a monopoly position for that individual book. Q.NET cannot therefore threaten to switch suppliers to obtain a better price. On the surface it would appear the supplier is in a very powerful position. However, the price of books is consistent within the market. Consumers know that a paper-back novel costs £X and a hard-back reference book costs £Y. The supplier would realise that any price increase would result in a higher retail price and meet consumer resistance.

By establishing closer IT links with a supplier Q.NET may be able to facilitate the operation of Just in Time systems – reducing supplier stock-holding costs. This partnership approach should benefit the competitive position of both Q.NET and the supplier.

8   Q.NET: STAFF RETENTION

> **Tutorial note**. After reading the requirement, quickly re-read the case study searching for points that could be relevant to staff retention. Wider issues such as organisational culture may be relevant, as well as factors more directly related to working conditions.
>
> The second part of your answer should suggest ways the problems you have identified could be addressed – although you could also bring in other points relevant to sales and support staff retention.

Sales and support staff turnover could be high for any of the following reasons.

There is no sense of belonging.

For most employees Q.NET is simply the organisation that pays their wages. There is little employee consultation regarding the direction of the company, resulting in low levels of employee commitment.

Lack of job variety.

Using a computer for most of the day to either answer e-mails or make changes to the website book database would become monotonous. Concentration levels and motivation would be hard to maintain. Employees are likely to become bored and may seek other jobs that appear more interesting. A related issue is that constant computer use can cause eye strain and Repetitive Strain Injury – anyone developing these problems is likely to leave.

No 'in-person' customer contact.

Employees will receive e-mail messages concerning problems customers have encountered using Q.NET, and will be subject to the 'stress' complaint brings, but will not experience the satisfaction of hearing a satisfied customer say 'thank-you'. This lack of personal contact is likely to be demotivating. Demotivated employees are likely to leave either of their own accord or because their performance is not deemed acceptable.

Homeworking issues.

Many employees may find homeworking difficult. The **distractions** caused by working at home, such as family members and neighbourhood noise, can make concentration difficult. Employees working at home may also miss the **social interaction** of colleagues.

Methods that Q.NET could use to improve staff retention are outlined in the following paragraphs.

Encouraging interaction with other employees.

This interaction could take the form of organised meetings, on maybe a bi-monthly basis. The geographic spread and cost of the meetings would have to be considered. Providing e-mail and telephone connections now so that employees can share problems and simply talk socially may provide a partial solution to the problem.

Introducing work rotation.

Periodically changing the tasks performed by staff may help to alleviate boredom. Employees could answer e-mails and provide input to the web pages on alternate days.

Re-structure the sales and support team.

This would be a more radical approach. Constant re-recruitment costs will eliminate any savings homeworking has brought. Q.NET may wish to look into the feasibility of locating all staff in an expanded office.

283

9   Q.NET: INFORMATION STRATEGY

The purpose of an information strategy in a commercial organisation is to ensure information is best used to support operations, support the business strategy and facilitate customer service.

Supporting operations.

Operational level information will be required by individual user departments. The information should enable the department or unit to meet its responsibilities under the business strategy. For example, if the business strategy includes limiting the time between customer orders and delivery, accurate order-status and stock information must be available.

Supporting the overall business strategy.

The overall aims of an organisation should be reflected in the stated overall business strategy, which will outline what that organisation wants to do and how it will be achieved. The information strategy should support the business strategy by providing appropriate information to those who require it. The information provided should be geared towards specific goals and strategies of the organisation.

Facilitating customer service.

In the 'consumer age' customers are increasingly requesting information about a product or service, so they can make an informed purchase. The amount of information required will vary depending on the nature of the product or service. For example customers may only want to check the ingredients of a food item, but would require extensive information if purchasing a new car. Part of the organisation's information system should therefore be externally focused to ensure that appropriate information is available for customers. The information may be made available to customers on websites, included in targeted brochure mail-outs or provided as part of an advertising campaign.

10   Q.NET: IT AND BUSINESS STRATEGY

The effectiveness of the IT system at Q.NET can be evaluated in terms of how well it provides the information to meet the objectives of the information strategy.

Supporting operations.

The system does not provide supplies with customer purchase information. If this information was available, suppliers could calculate more accurately the ongoing demand for books. Book production and delivery could then be modified to meet Q.NET's specific sales requirements. This would ultimately support the core function of getting books to customers as quickly as possible.

Supporting the overall business strategy.

The information system can only provide detailed customer history for six weeks. This is a major limitation preventing the best use of information. The non-availability of this information will hand a competitive advantage to booksellers able to build detailed purchase histories and target customers appropriately. Seasonal patterns in purchasing will not be apparent, meaning incorrect buying decisions may be made.

Facilitating customer service.

All of the information on an individual title is not available to customers. This is a weakness, as people are more likely to purchase a product that they can not physically touch if they have sufficient information to reassure them.

11   HB LTD: IT AND PROFITABILITY; COMPETITIVE ADVANTAGE

> **Tutorial note**. This question may appear daunting on first reading. However, when analysing the question requirement you should realise that, for part (a), you can include any benefit an improved system may bring that could result in increased turnover or reduced costs. There are a wide range of possible benefits you could include. Although many of the benefits of information systems are difficult to quantify, better quality information should lead to better decision making, improved customer service and greater efficiency. The ultimate effect of these factors should be improved profitability.
>
> The examiner stated that other formats of solution, for example using the value chain, would have been acceptable.
>
> For part (b), think about what type of data and information will be held on the computerised system, and how this could be utilised for sales and marketing purposes. Remember that to gain a competitive advantage the activities must be superior to those undertaken by competitors.

REPORT

To: Board of HB Ltd
From: Management accountant
Subject: Investment in IT system
Date: May 200X

(a)   This report will attempt to explain some of the benefits of implementing a new computer-based production monitoring system. I will firstly clarify how the movements in contribution and fixed costs (indicated in the report issued by our consultant) can be achieved, and then will discuss other ways in which the system will help us gain a competitive advantage.

Increase in contribution per unit

Increased contribution per unit will require the lowering of the variable costs of production, and/or an increase in the selling price. HB Ltd's variable costs comprise raw materials, machine usage and labour. (The variable element of our labour cost is due to overtime levels of existing staff. If production levels change to such an extent that more or less staff are required, labour becomes a stepped cost.)

Concentrate on more profitable lines

The system will provide more accurate costing information enabling HB ltd to accurately monitor the contribution obtained from each type of cement. Less profitable lines may require an adjustment in price – or if this is not sustainable HB Ltd may consider ceasing production of those cement types. Production could then be focused on lines that make higher contributions.

Improved product

The use of IT to monitor the input mix and production process of cement itself will enable the company to increase the quality of the cement being produced. Higher quality cement should allow HB Ltd to charge a higher price – although some education of customers as to the improved quality and hence better overall value would be required.

Reduced waste

Computer-aided measurement of raw materials will cut down raw material usage. This will reduce the cost per unit, and increase contribution per unit.

Reduced overtime cost

The increased automation and accuracy of the production process should reduce the number of hours production staff need to produce the same volume of cement. This saving will lower cost per unit.

Reduced machine downtime and repair costs

Machines will be monitored by the computer system, which will build up a profile of the history of each machine. Maintenance schedules can be more accurately monitored reducing breakdowns. Any problems should be seen before they develop into costly repairs. Minimising machine downtime and repair costs will decrease the cost per unit.

Fixed costs

Fixed costs do not change with changes in the level of production. HB's fixed costs include administration staff, rent, rates, office power etc.

Production overheads

In the long-term fewer machines may be required as the efficiency of each machine increases - meaning more machine hours can be obtained from a smaller number of machines. This would reduce the amount of factory space required, reducing the associated fixed costs of rent and rates assuming the freed-up space can be sold, or income obtained for its alternate use.

Staff

Additional staff will be required to look after the computer system, raising costs. This increase will be more than offset by the reduction in production staff costs referred to earlier.

Distribution costs

The inclusion of customer and distribution details in the system will allow for better co-ordination of deliveries. The overall number of delivery vehicles and drivers may fall, reducing fixed costs.

(b) **Other ways of obtaining competitive advantage.**

The improved IT system will also allow HB Ltd to obtain competitive advantage through:

Providing better information to customers

Customers will have access to information showing the progress and expected delivery time of each order. Being able to supply customers with definite delivery dates they can plan around should win new customers, and help retain existing ones.

Providing improved quality of products and customer service

The industry has a reputation for poor quality control and for not meeting agreed delivery times - particularly for specialist cements. The new system should improve product quality and customer service by allowing closer monitoring of production and order tracking.

Building up customer histories/profiles

Using a computerised system will facilitate the establishment of a database containing the order history of all customers. Database interrogation techniques and data mining can be used to search for trends that will help production planning and marketing. This will provide a significant competitive advantage over competitors using manual or less advanced computerised systems.

Signed: Management accountant

12 SN PLC: INFORMATION SYSTEMS INFRASTRUCTURE

> **Tutorial note**. This question could be answered by making a wide-range of points - the answer provided here is one example of how this question could be approached.
>
> You could have split the report into two main sections, Problems and Recommendations, or adopted the approach shown below - with each problem followed by a corresponding recommendation.
>
> It is best to structure your answer in one of the two ways suggested above, rather than simply writing a general narrative. A structured answer should help ensure you cover all areas of the question, and help markers allocate marks!

REPORT

To: Board of SN plc
From: Management accountant
Subject: Information system maintenance
Date: May 200X

I have reviewed the systems for providing information to the company's professional sales staff. This report will outline the specific weaknesses identified, and recommend how the weaknesses can be alleviated.

No strategy review

The head of IT produces the overall IT strategy for SN plc, but there does not appear to be a process to ensure that any new information system fits with this strategy. IT is an expensive investment that requires co-ordination and management to ensure the best value is obtained.

Recommendation

A process should be introduced whereby the head of IT must review all proposed projects to ensure they are consistent with, and complementary to, the IT strategy.

Lack of user training

The provision of a user manual does not constitute user training! It is unlikely staff will have the time, motivation or necessary information to work through the manual. The likely outcome is that the system will be used incorrectly, resulting in incorrect or inaccurate data being held.

Recommendation

A training plan must be drawn up and implemented as a matter of urgency.

IT department is physically isolated from users

Having the IT department in a separate location has allowed programmers to focus on their primary task - programming. However, the systems programmers build must meet user requirements. Being isolated from users means they have limited contact with users and trainers. The separate location also means it is difficult to monitor and test completed modules with user input. Co-ordination is not helped, and a 'them and us' mentality seems to have developed.

Recommendation

Moving the IT department to the main site would make user-programmer liaison easier, and provide physical evidence that this is a joint effort requiring input and co-operation from all concerned. Directing queries from users regarding software to a specific Help Desk should ensure the programmers do not become bogged down in operational queries.

No ownership of data

As stated earlier, the users of information systems at SN plc are not involved in the development process. This reduces the incentive for users to take ownership of the system, or the data held on it. The consequences of decisions being taken on incorrect or incomplete information could be costly.

Recommendation

A data dictionary should be complied by systems personnel in consultation with users. The data dictionary could then be used to establish responsibility for all data and information held within the information systems of SN plc.

User requirements not being met

The lack of user input into the design of systems at SN plc has led to the development of systems that do not meet user requirements. There appears to be no design committee, and no overall control of the design and maintenance of information systems

Recommendation

An information systems steering committee should be established to oversee the development of information systems within SN plc. User representatives must be included in this committee. The committee must ensure that clear and comprehensive user requirements are established before system development progresses.

Conclusion

User input at all stages of system development is essential to ensure a new system does what users need it to do. In SN plc, user input is not obtained until a new system is ready for implementation. This is far too late. The system should be built to meet user requirements, not built and then presented to users!

At SN plc there is a very good chance the new system will be rejected by users because it does not fully meet their requirements. Even if a reasonable system is offered, the chance of user-acceptance is small as users generally do not enjoy having systems imposed on them – without having been involved in its development.

Implementing the recommendations contained in this report should help ensure future developments are more successful.

13   E-COMMERCE

Tutorial note. The format of this question is slightly unusual, requirement first then details of the organisations relevant to the requirement. Ensure in the exam you read the question carefully, and then do exactly what you have been asked to do.

As with many Final Level questions a wide range of answers could have scored well. To prevent 'rambling' in part (a), use sub-headings to show each area of business strategy you are dealing with. You could also have dealt with each organisation under separate headings. Part (a) is worth 20 marks, so a fairly substantial answer is required - as substantial as you can manage in the 36 minutes available.

In part (b) it is important that you provide sufficient justification for your choice to earn the five marks on offer.

(a)   The two organisations should consider the following areas when deciding whether to adopt e-commerce as part of their business strategy.

Overall business strategy

To undertake any activity an organisation should first ensure the activity is consistent with the overall business strategy. We will contrast and compare a few areas of business strategy that the two organisations should consider when deciding if e-commerce will support the strategy of the organisation.

Market segment

Both organisations know what goods they want to sell and who they wish to sell them to – they have a clearly defined market segment. However, the selling of financial advice may be more applicable to e-commerce because more profit is made per sale than for garden products. This means that fewer Internet transactions would be required to recover the outlay of establishing and maintaining the website.

Product range

The product ranges of both organisations are likely to be wide (eg many types of financial advice, many types of garden products). A website would therefore be a useful tool in the dissemination of product information. The next step, that is the carrying out of transactions on the web, would require further consideration.

Competitor and customer characteristics

The garden centre's competitors are other local outlets. Their customers will probably have the choice of a number of centres they could visit fairly easily. So, the 'task' of gathering knowledge about garden products using traditional means is not too difficult. In fact, many see this as a leisure activity that fills their weekends. For these reasons, and also the fact that a high proportion of garden centre customers may not be computer literate, establishing an Internet site with e-commerce may not be beneficial.

Customers looking for financial advice would require full and detailed information. Customers would also expect a multinational financial organisation to provide an informative website. This assumption would be based on the size and reputation of the organisation, and the fact that similar organisations would invariably have such a site. The selling of financial products online may also be expected. There is no physical product, so the transaction could be completed electronically (although a signature on documentation will probably be required to finalise the transaction).

Objectives of the organisation

The business objectives of the organisation will be more specific. The actual objectives may include profit maximisation, growth, employee satisfaction, and organisational citizenship.

For the international financial organisation, profit maximisation is likely to be the main objective. Therefore, if e-commerce can be shown to increase sales and profit, it should be adopted.

The objectives of employee satisfaction and organisational citizenship will have limited influence on the decision regarding the use of e-commerce. If e-commerce is chosen then there will be a requirement to ensure proper employee welfare (eg in the UK – The Health and Safety at Work Act). Good organisational citizenship could be claimed as the digital medium could reduce paper use. Some financial organisations gain the reputation as 'sharks' out to fleece a gullible public. A friendly image should therefore be portrayed by the website – in line with the organisation's other marketing material.

The garden centre will also require sufficient profit to justify the capital tied up in the business. Growth may be less important, depending on the long-term strategic aims. Employee satisfaction may be of greater concern than with the multi-national organisation as closer relationships often develop in small locally-focussed retail outlets. Organisational citizenship should not be too much of an issue – garden centres have a relatively green and friendly image which should be fostered.

The local garden centre has goals and customer characteristics which e-commerce would most likely not contribute to enough to justify the expenditure required. The large multi-national financial organisation would be able to utilise e-commerce to achieve greater profitability and growth.

Competitors

The competitors of the international financial organisation will almost certainly have a website, and are likely to use e-commerce. Establishing a website is necessary to match the service offered by competitors, and reinforce the organisation's standing. The intangible nature of financial advice is suited to e-commerce, but the importance of the product to a customer may mean that a high proportion of people want some direct contact with a representative before making a purchase. The customer's hand-written signature will also be required on various documents - requiring either some face-to-face contact, or the posting of documents for signature.

The garden products supplier is selling a more generic product where specialist selling skills and customer contact are likely to be less important to the customer. There are likely to be competitors in the surrounding area. Additional sales potential is limited due to the small area they can sell into. There is no need to establish a site simply to remain competitive and the costs of setting up e-commerce may outweigh the benefits. Given the cost of setting up a website (consultant's time, ISP hosting fees etc) and the limited benefits it appears unlikely that a garden centre would find e-commerce profitable.

Customers

Whether customers are likely to use the Internet for purchasing will affect the decision as to whether e-commerce is adopted by an organisation. If the product or service has an established Internet presence and an organisation wishes to be considered a 'credible player', a website is vital.

Customers who want to purchase financial services are likely to be in higher income brackets and therefore are more likely to have Internet access at home or work. They also require detailed information on the organisation and products that can be easily provided on a website. Use of e-commerce therefore would complement the service provided by a provider of financial advice, and should be adopted.

Purchasers of garden products are likely to be drawn from a wide range of socio-economic groups, with perhaps a slight bias towards middle-aged to older people. This group are not strongly represented among current Internet users. Garden products are tangible products, and in many cases (eg fencing style) are subject to individual taste. People are therefore likely to want to physically see and feel what is being purchased. Only a picture or video could be provided on a website. A website may be useful in providing overviews of product availability and illustrations with the purpose of encouraging customers to visit the garden centre.

Legal issues

If e-commerce is adopted various legal issues must be considered. Selling financial products in different countries means the differing laws and regulations of each market must be met. This may mean some product customisation is required in some markets. The adaptation of the website to prevent the sale of certain products to people in 'ineligible' countries may also be required.

Expertise available

To be able to implement and maintain that strategy an organisation must have access to the required expertise.

A large organisation is more likely to be able to afford to set up a website and to start using e-commerce. The cost of setting up and maintaining the site can be offset against a larger sales value. If the expertise is not available internally, the fee charged by an external organisation could be afforded and justified.

A smaller organisation will find the expense of setting up and maintaining a website a bigger drain on its resources. Internal staff are unlikely to posses the necessary expertise, and the costs of an external consultancy would probably not be justified in light of the limited benefits the site would bring.

(b) The supplier of financial services is more likely to benefit from e-commerce because:

    (i)   It has a wider potential market and an intangible product that can be explained efficiently on a website.

    (ii)   It is targeting customers who are more likely to have Internet access.

    (iii)   Its business strategy requires increased sales.

    (iv)   Competitors are utilising e-commerce.

The garden centre has some persuasive reasons for not making a significant investment in e-commerce at this stage.

    (i)   Insufficient financial resources.
    (ii)   Lack of skilled staff.
    (iii)   Their business strategy can be achieved without the adoption of e-commerce.
    (iv)   Customers may not require it.

14 PATTERSONS ELECTRICAL SUPPLIES: INFORMATION SYSTEM FAILURE

> **Tutorial note**. The requirement allows you to discuss all reasons that contribute to the failure of information systems. These reasons should be reasonably well known to you from your studies. Use these general reasons as headings – then explain how this reason contributes to the failure of implementation systems in general. Then, for each reason, comment on the situation at Pattersons.

There are four main reasons for systems failure during implementation.

(i) **Lack of user involvement**

One of the key success criteria for system implementation is to have user input with effective communication between the users and designers of the system. User involvement means that

    (1)   Users have opportunities to ensure that the new system meets their requirements.

    (2)   Users are more likely to feel that they own the finished product, and so are more likely to use the final system.

    (3)   It will be more difficult to reject the final system.

In Pattersons, it is unclear how much involvement users have actually had in system development or implementation. The fact that users see the system as a failure indicates that user involvement was severely limited. Any lack of involvement, or breakdown of communication will increase the risk of system failure.

(ii) **Level of management support**

Management support is normally essential to ensure the success of any project. Managers will normally be involved with a project to:

    (1)   Show commitment to that project

(2)   Understand the issues and problems involved so these can be addressed quickly

(3)   Ensure all other interested parties are also involved with the project.

The fact that management also views the shift system as a failure indicates lack of management support for the project. The change in work practices also appears to be cumbersome, which may be one of the reasons for lack of support and potential rejection of the project now. If management were not involved, then this is another reason why users will also not been involved with implementation.

(iii) **Level of complexity and risk**

There are three factors, which affect the level of complexity and risk in a project.

Firstly, a large project is more likely to fail at implementation than a small project. Size can be stated in terms of expenditure, duration of the project, number of staff involved and number of business units affected.

In Pattersons, the shift project appeared to affect the whole organisation; this gave a high risk because many business units were affected and many staff. The duration and expenditure are unclear, but given the size of the project, it is likely to have been expensive and lasted a reasonable amount of time. The risk of failure based simply on project size, is high.

Secondly, the type of project structure also affects the risk of failure. Well structured projects are less likely to fail at implementation than poorly structured projects. Structure provides a framework for the project, decreasing the risk of failure.

In Pattersons, it is not clear how structured the project actually was. However, the high level of user intervention now indicates that the initial analysis was not carried out very effectively. Similarly, the resistance to the system indicates lack of involvement and appropriate user sign-off of the different project stages. It is therefore likely that the project suffered from poor planning and structure and this has increased the risk of failure.

Thirdly, the experience available in respect of the technology being used. The user of newer technology and relative inexperience of IT staff will also increase the risk of failure. Newer technology may not be fully understood, while lack of experience will increase risks, as staff may not understand how the software works.

In Pattersons, it is not clear why the IT system requires manual amendments. This situation may have arisen because the technology is new and it has not been implemented correctly, so this has increased the risk of failure.

(iv) **Management of the implementation process**

Poor management of the implementation process in terms of

- Poor estimation of the time to complete the project
- Not allocating sufficient resources to the project, and
- Poor communication between members of the project team

will all increase the risk of project failure.

In the case of Pattersons, it is not clear how far these factors actually affected the project. However, not meeting user requirements does indicate some poor management, possibly in terms of communication, and this may have attributed to the failure of the project.

15   **PATTERSONS ELECTRICAL SUPPLIES: IT/IS STRATEGY AND BUSINESS STRATEGY**

Tutorial note. For part (a), think about the integration of IT/IS and business strategy, and how one supports the other, then important areas such as information provision and the benefits of IT may start to become apparent. You could use the different levels of information required by an organisation to provide structure to your answer – but remember to answer the question, not simply describe different types of information and strategy.

In part (b), structure your answer around the three terms mentioned in the question. The requirements of this part are specific – so do exactly what is expected. Start by explaining automation in general terms, then relate this definition to the situation at Pattersons. Do this for each of the three terms, and you will score well.

(a) Business strategy and IS/IT strategy are normally developed together in an organisation, because the IS/IT provides essential support to the overall business strategy. For example, information systems will be required to provide appropriate information for each level of management to enable the business to be run efficiently.

The information that can be provided by the IS/IT systems is outlined below.

(i) **Strategic level information**. This is for the use of senior managers and will relate to long term planning. For example, in Pattersons, information may be provided to assist in decisions regarding the location of new stores.

(ii) **Management level information**. Information to support the activities of monitoring, controlling and decision making carried out by middle managers. In the case of Pattersons, information may be provided on total sales by product line and current stock levels to help in planning promotions or special offers within certain stores.

(iii) **Knowledge level information**. This is information to support the knowledge workers in an organisation. Pattersons may provide customer databases for workers to try and identify trends in customer data in order to improve advertising and overall sales.

(iv) **Operational level information**. Within Pattersons, as in any retail organisation, this will relate to current stock levels, re-order details, information about individual sales invoices etc. The information will be summarised and input to the MIS for additional analysis.

Almost any organisation can provide these information systems for their managers and workers. To remain competitive, Pattersons will need to ensure that the appropriate systems are in place to provide the necessary management information.

If the business and IS/IT strategies are not congruent with each other, then there is a danger that either appropriate information will not be provided, or that the IT infrastructure will be built up without reference to the information requirements of the organisation. Careful planning is therefore needed, with control from the Board level, to ensure that these errors do not occur.

Appropriate IS/IT strategy planning will be facilitated by the appointment of a Chief Information Officer to the Board of directors. This individual will be responsible for:

(i) Developing the information systems in-house to meet business needs. For example, there may be the opportunity to re-structure the whole ordering and sales processes within Pattersons by using Internet related technology. However, any change must be carried out in accordance with the business aims of Pattersons.

(ii) Looking for opportunities to use IT to create business advantage. Within Pattersons, this will involve the use of the proposed Internet site.

(iii) Ensuring that the IT systems support the overall business strategy. The proposed Internet site must fit in with the overall strategy at Pattersons. Establishing the site without appropriate planning may cause significant problems, such as rejection of the site by store managers because they feel that their store income is threatened.

(iv) Ensuring that sufficient IT resources are available to maintain and develop systems. For example, the directors may require additional information about actions of competitors including Internet links to their sites and information services such as Reuters. The CIO will need to ensure that appropriate IT infrastructure is available to support this business requirement.

The important point is to ensure that the IT / IS strategy is congruent with the business strategy. Pattersons appears to have achieved this, although changes in the future will need to be planned and monitored closely to ensure that this remains the case.

(b) **Automation** refers to the computerisation of existing tasks and procedures. IT is used to make those existing tasks more efficient and effective, rather than to amend or change the tasks to provide additional benefits.

This use of IT is a fairly low risk strategy, as the business processes are essentially unchanged. Within Pattersons, automation will have occurred in the sales systems, probably by installing electronic point of sale equipment and in stock control and monitoring by maintaining the stock balances on a database. However, the underlying process of the customer paying for goods at a checkout, and stock balances being available from some form of stock recording system, are essentially unchanged.

Rationalisation involves some changes to the business, normally to make existing processes more effective or efficient in some way by linking them together.

The need for rationalisation can occur from two main areas:

(i)   Business reviews indicate that existing IT systems would be more efficient if they were linked. For example, stock control information is available on a computer system, and details of stock items sold are also recorded electronically. However, the stock database is only updated with sales information at the end of each working day. Linking these two systems on-line provides the benefit of sales being recorded immediately in the stock system. Real-time stock information is now available rather than the balances being up to one day out of date.

(ii) The process of automation may start to cause inefficiencies in other areas. For example, when a sale is made, customer details are entered into a computer system. However, those details are printed out to provide a list of goods to obtain from a warehouse, with the list being sent in the post to arrive at the warehouse next day for delivery in say, one week. Previously, when customer details were recorded manually, there was no expectation that goods would be available within say 48 hours, but now that information is captured electronically, a seven day delivery seems a very long time. Automation is also needed to link the sales systems with warehouse stocks to provide quicker response times.

The Pattersons business appears to have rationalised the IT systems already as an integrated accounting system and 48 hour delivery of goods from a warehouse are already available.

Re-engineering involves the re-design of business processes to try and maximise the benefits from IT. Savings are normally obtained in terms of reduced cost, elimination of duplicated activities, or improved speed of response from the processes.

The process of re-engineering will involve a review of the entire business processes, with the expectation that IT will provide different, and significantly more efficient work methods. Change in this respect will be much more significant than either automation or rationalisation. Because change is significant, re-engineering is a high-risk strategy for any organisation.

Before re-engineering can take place, the organisation will need to consider what the objective of each business process is, and how IT can best support that process. This means re-designing the process, rather than simply making it more efficient by automation. In the context of Pattersons, setting up the Internet site is a form of re-engineering because this is a different method of carrying out business compared to cash and carry; the latter could not be adopted to provide Internet trading so new processes are required.

~~18~~ 16 PATTERSONS ELECTRICAL SUPPLIES: INTERNET, EXTRANET, INTRANET

Tutorial note. If you have used the Internet to buy something, think what attracted you to a specific organisation's website. Remember also that some contact may best be conducted using other means – such as the telephone – but that the website could facilitate this through features such as 'call back requests'. It is vital the back-office procedures are in place to meet any requests made via the website.

In part (b) our answer, explains methods of sharing information electronically. The extranet could be used as the platform that facilitates a whole range of data and information exchange.

For part (c), think of the intranet as an internal Internet that facilitates the sharing of information with internal customers.

Start with a brief explanation of the Internet	(a) The Internet provides businesses with access to a rapidly expanding market of customers as the number of people with access to the Internet increases. Most businesses have established their own website in an attempt to take advantage of this growth. A business that does not provide some form of web purchasing option, or at least viewing of products on-line, risks losing customers to competitors who do provide these options.

(i) **User requirements**

Potential customers require information when visiting a store or a website. Key data that must be available includes product, price, availability, features of the product and any additional charges such as delivery or insurance contracts to guard against product failure. The website must provide this information in an easy-to-use format.

Vital that web-based operations are integrated with back-office systems	Pattersons could establish a website providing this information (the site can be linked to the integrated stock system). However, the concept of cash-and-carry would be lost as all purchases would have to be delivered to the customer, unless a 'pick up from store' option was made available. Also, Pattersons would not be able to offer the services of their trained sales representatives, as the Internet simply displays text and pictures, and not interactive customer service. An alternative would be to provide a telephone call back system (similar to Dell computers) where customers can click on a web-link and receive a call from a Patterson sales representative to discuss their purchase.

(ii) **Retaining the customer**

Could mention 'cookies', but don't become bogged down with technical aspects	Customers are likely to visit a number of websites to compare prices and product details. Providing some form of personalisation of the website for repeat visits, such as welcoming the customer by name or displaying a list of products already reviewed, would help make the site more customer friendly. Software is available to provide this type of service on the Internet.

Again Pattersons could establish a website to provide these features. Any other features that will add value to the site, such as offering a list of related products or spare parts for the product being purchased could also help to make the site more attractive to customers.

(iii) **Incentives to use the web site**

Want new customers rather than cannibalising existing sales	Using the Internet for purchasing does provide a risk that sales will fall in the individual shops maintained by Pattersons. However, new customers may also be reached, especially those who are not located within travelling distance of a Pattersons store, or who do not like shopping for large electrical items. In this situation, providing some incentive to use the web site such as coupons or a loyalty points scheme may help to attract additional purchasers.

(iv) **Other value added activities**

Databases, datawarehousing, datamining and CRM could all be relevant	When a purchase is made on a website, customer information will be stored by the supplier's computer system. This information can be used to help provide repeat business for the organisation.

For example, if a vacuum cleaner is purchased from Pattersons, then an e-mail can be sent to that customer in a few weeks with information about replacement bags for that cleaner. Similarly, data can be mined to identify relationships in purchases, for example, Pattersons may find that customers purchasing a washing machine often purchase a tumble dryer a few months later. Offers can be sent via e-mail direct to the customer including coupons for tumble dryer purchase.

(b) An extranet is an extension of an internal intranet. The intranet provides information about an organisation such as stock levels, customer details, product information etc. to employees within that organisation. An extranet means making this information available to specific third parties. For example, the Dell database of technical information about computers is made available to some customers to help diagnose faults with those computers.

> Start with a brief explanation of an extranet

Pattersons may be able to use direct electronic links with customers and suppliers to provide business benefits, particularly in managing the supply chain.

Stock levels. Suppliers can be given access to stock levels at Pattersons. Where stocks fall below a re-order level, either at head office or a store, the supplier will automatically send replacement stocks. This will benefit Pattersons because less employee time is spent reviewing stock levels and replacement stocks will be sent immediately they are required.

> Focus on business processes

Supplier communications. E-mail can be used to inform suppliers about new stock requirements or changes to trading conditions. This communication method provides significant time and cost savings over other forms of communication. For example, Pattersons can inform suppliers about upcoming promotions on specific products so that more of those items can be produced ready for re-sale.

> The extranet could facilitate the sharing and exchanging of information with other businesses

Stock purchasing. Information concerning stock deliveries and receipts can be sent by Electronic Data Interchange. This will again provide time and cost savings in terms of staff as well as providing up-to-date information on stock movements. Pattersons already has an integrated order system, so linking this to an external EDI system is possible.

Payment. Payments can be made electronically using Electronic Funds Transfer. This will speed up the payment process, if Pattersons want to do this. Similarly, payments can be made automatically based on the receipt of goods. For example, Pattersons may want to reward quicker delivery of goods by paying those suppliers in a few days rather than a few weeks.

Other applications, such as financial management of funds are available, although these may have limited use for Pattersons at the moment.

(c) An intranet is an internal Internet-like network for use within an organisation. The intranet uses the same technology as the Internet, namely a web-browser to view web pages. However, those pages are only available to employees in the organisation and so they will normally contain information specific for use by those employees.

> Start with a brief explanation of an intranet

An intranet may be able to assist staff at Pattersons in various ways.

(i) **Provision of internal e-mail and discussion forums**

E-mail can be used as a basic communication tool within the company. However, discussion forums can be set up to provide a forum on various matters such as product queries. A sales representative in one store may not know the answer to a question concerning a product. This query can be placed on a discussion database, and a representative in a different store may be able to provide the answer. This system will help to improve the knowledge of different products being sold.

> Choose internal processes related to Pattersons' situation

(ii) **Remote sharing of information**

Intranets allow information on central databases to be viewed from any location. In this situation, stock levels at head office and all stores could be viewed enabling sales representatives to confirm stock availability across all stores, and hopefully increase overall sales. This system will provide a significant advantage over the current system of centralising information at head office only.

> Use the information contained in the scenario

(iii) **Sharing of reference material**

Any reference material, such as detailed information about products or even the organisation's telephone list, can be placed on the intranet. As well as making it more accessible to all members of staff, this also allows for efficient and timely update. The information can be updated frequently in one location rather than having out-of-date paper-based copies of the information in each store. Having better information on products will also help provide enhanced customer service.

Other information such as competitor prices and promotional activities can also be shared via the intranet, making all staff more aware of the competitive environment.

20 17 HK CONSULTANCY: INFORMATION OVERLOAD; INFORMATION QUALITY

> **Tutorial note.** The requirement states that you should 'briefly' explain the concept of information overload – this implies that the majority of the marks for this question will be awarded for the other parts of the requirement.
>
> When discussing amendments to the HK consulting information system, think of 'information system' in its broadest sense. Any process, procedure or tool used to collect, process, store, analyse or communicate information could be brought into your answer.

(a) Developments in information technology and information systems have enabled organisations to collect, store and analyse large quantities of information. This should lead to better decision making. However, as the quantity of information available has increased, it has become more important to ensure that individuals only receive the information that they require to do their job. Otherwise, the danger is that an individual will be swamped by so much information that they will overlook the information that is most important.

Action that could be taken to limit information being received include:

Route incoming telephone calls via a secretary.

The accountant should not face regular telephone interruptions. A secretary should be allocated to take telephone messages, putting through only calls of significance that require immediate attention. To be effective, the instructions concerning calls that should be put through, and how messages should be relayed must be specific.

Using intelligent agents.

Agents could be set up to obtain information from the Internet or an internal intranet. The criteria set down as to what should be retrieved should be specific to reduce the likelihood of irrelevant information being selected. The use of agents would reduce the amount of time the accountant would need to spend reviewing websites.

Delegate some client contact.

Some decisions the accountant is taking may not require the consideration of such a senior person. Ongoing routine contact with clients could be delegated to one of the more junior managers. This should considerably limit the information received by the accountant.

Subscribing to a newsclipping service.

The reviewing of journals for relevant information is time-consuming. A news clipping service could review relevant journals and newspapers and forward via e-mail copies of those articles that meet specific criteria.

Filtering e-mail.

Up-to-date e-mail programs have the ability to review and re-direct messages based on the message content, priority, sender and/or intended recipients. The accountant may decide only to review messages that are sent as urgent or which contain specific text, such as a client name. The non-selected messages could be copied to a selected person, or just redirected to a non-urgent inbox for review later.

Margin notes (left column):

Start with a brief explanation of information overload

Don't ignore 'obvious' or simple solutions if they are relevant

Provide enough explanation to show you understand what you are saying

People are an important part of information systems

Ensure you apply 'book knowledge' to the scenario

(b) The accountant has a strategic decision-making role within the organisation. Strategic decision-making requires information with the following characteristics:

The information should be **summarised**. An overview of how a given situation could affect the organisation as a whole will be of more use to the accountant than the detail. Detail may be available in the form of appendices should this be required.

Information should be **presented appropriately**. The method of presentation should help understanding. It may be appropriate to present information in an electronic document, which can be amended quickly, rather than in a paper-based report. If information is presented in the form of a lengthy report, a table of contents and summary of the report's findings should be provided at the beginning. The report should also have appropriate paragraphs and headings and use clear language. If appropriate, the information may be posted on the company's intranet (if the contents are not confidential and the intranet is used efficiently by those who need to view the information).

The information needs to be **complete**. All the information that can affect a decision should be received and reviewed. Strategic decisions based on incomplete information could result in an inappropriate strategy being followed.

The information must be **timely**. In many situations, circumstances may change quickly, meaning information goes out of date rapidly. Strategic decisions often depend on 'first mover' advantage.

The information should be **relevant**. Information should be filtered to remove material not relevant to the recipient. Irrelevant information contributes to information overload.

Information for strategic decision-making should also include **external** information – such as competitor and industry related information.

> The type of information required depends on what it will be used for.

> Again, don't be afraid to 'state the obvious' if it is relevant.

> You may have chosen other characteristics. At this level there are usually a range of answers that would score well

298

Index

Note: **Key Terms** and their references are given in **bold**.

REVIEW FORM & FREE PRIZE DRAW

All original review forms from the entire BPP range, completed with genuine comments, will be entered into one of two draws on 31 January 2003 and 31 July 2003. The names on the first four forms picked out on each occasion will be sent a cheque for £50.

Name: _____   Address: _____

_____

How have you used this Text?
(Tick one box only)

☐ Self study (book only)

☐ On a course: college (please state)_____

_____

☐ With 'correspondence' package

☐ Other _____

Why did you decide to purchase this Text?
(Tick one box only)

☐ Have used BPP Texts in the past

☐ Recommendation by friend/colleague

☐ Recommendation by a lecturer at college

☐ Saw advertising

☐ Other _____

During the past six months do you recall seeing/receiving any of the following?
(Tick as many boxes as are relevant)

☐ Our advertisement in CIMA *Insider*

☐ Our advertisement in *Financial Management*

☐ Our advertisement in *Pass*

☐ Our brochure with a letter through the post

☐ Our website www.bpp.com

Which (if any) aspects of our advertising do you find useful?
(Tick as many boxes as are relevant)

☐ Prices and publication dates of new editions

☐ Information on product content

☐ Facility to order books off-the-page

☐ None of the above

Which BPP products have you used?

Text	☐	**MCQ cards**	☐	**i-Learn**	☐
Kit	☐	**Tape**	☐	**i-Pass**	☐
Passcard	☐	**Video**	☐	**Virtual Campus**	☐

Your ratings, comments and suggestions would be appreciated on the following areas.

	Very useful	Useful	Not useful
Introductory section (Key study steps, personal study)	☐	☐	☐
Chapter introductions	☐	☐	☐
Key terms	☐	☐	☐
Quality of explanations	☐	☐	☐
Case examples and other examples	☐	☐	☐
Questions and answers in each chapter	☐	☐	☐
Chapter roundups	☐	☐	☐
Quick quizzes	☐	☐	☐
Exam focus points	☐	☐	☐
Question bank	☐	☐	☐
MCQ bank	☐	☐	☐
Answer bank	☐	☐	☐
Index	☐	☐	☐
Icons	☐	☐	☐
Mind maps	☐	☐	☐

Overall opinion of this Study Text	Excellent ☐	Good ☐	Adequate ☐	Poor ☐

Do you intend to continue using BPP products?   Yes ☐   No ☐

Please note any further comments and suggestions/errors on the reverse of this page. The BPP author of this edition can be e-mailed at: barrywalsh@bpp.com

Please return this form to: Nick Weller, CIMA Range Manager, BPP Publishing Ltd, FREEPOST, London, W12 8BR

Please note any comments and suggestions/errors below.

FREE PRIZE DRAW RULES

1   Closing date for 31 January 2003 draw is 31 December 2002. Closing date for 31 July 2003 draw is 30 June 2003.

2   Restricted to entries with UK and Eire addresses only. BPP employees, their families and business associates are excluded.

3   No purchase necessary. Entry forms are available upon request from BPP Publishing. No more than one entry per title, per person. Draw restricted to persons aged 16 and over.

4   Winners will be notified by post and receive their cheques not later than 6 weeks after the relevant draw date.

5   The decision of the promoter in all matters is final and binding. No correspondence will be entered into.

See overleaf for information on other
BPP products and how to order

CIMA Order

To BPP Publishing Ltd, Aldine Place, London W12 8AW
Tel: 020 8740 2211. Fax: 020 8740 1184
www.bpp.com Email publishing@bpp.com
Order online www.bpp.com

Mr/Mrs/Ms (Full name) _____

Daytime delivery address _____

Postcode _____

Daytime Tel _____   Email _____   Date of exam (month/year) _____

	7/02 Texts £20.95	1/02 Kits £10.95	1/02 Passcards £6.95	9/00 Tapes £12.95	7/00 Videos £25.95	Virtual Campus	7/02 i-Pass £24.95	7/02 i-Learn £34.95	7/02 MCQ cards £5.95
FOUNDATION									
1 Financial Accounting Fundamentals	£20.95	£10.95	£6.95	£12.95	£25.95	£50	£24.95		£5.95
2 Management Accounting Fundamentals	£20.95	£10.95	£6.95	£12.95	£25.95	£50	£24.95		£5.95
3A Economics for Business	£20.95	£10.95	£6.95	£12.95	£25.95	£50	£24.95		£5.95
3B Business Law	£20.95	£10.95	£6.95	£12.95	£25.95	£50	£24.95		£5.95
3C Business Mathematics	£20.95	£10.95	£6.95	£12.95	£25.95	£50	£24.95		£5.95
INTERMEDIATE									
4 Finance	£20.95	£10.95	£6.95	£12.95	£25.95	£80	£24.95	£34.95	£5.95
5 Business Tax (FA 2002)	£20.95 (10/02)	£10.95	£6.95	£12.95	£25.95	£80	£24.95	£34.95	£5.95
6 Financial Accounting	£20.95	£10.95	£6.95	£12.95	£25.95	£80	£24.95	£34.95	£5.95
6I Financial Accounting International	£20.95	£10.95				£80	£24.95	£34.95	
7 Financial Reporting	£20.95	£10.95	£6.95	£12.95	£25.95	£80	£24.95	£34.95	£5.95
7I Financial Reporting International	£20.95	£10.95				£80			
8 Management Accounting - Performance Management	£20.95	£10.95	£6.95	£12.95	£25.95	£80	£24.95	£34.95	£5.95
9 Management Accounting - Decision Making	£20.95	£10.95	£6.95	£12.95	£25.95	£80	£24.95	£34.95	£5.95
10 Systems and Project Management	£20.95	£10.95	£6.95	£12.95	£25.95	£80	£24.95	£34.95	£5.95
11 Organisational Management	£20.95	£10.95	£6.95	£12.95	£25.95	£80	£24.95	£34.95	£5.95
FINAL									
12 Management Accounting - Business Strategy	£20.95	£10.95	£6.95	£12.95	£25.95				
13 Management Accounting - Financial Strategy	£20.95	£10.95	£6.95	£12.95	£25.95				
14 Management Accounting - Information Strategy	£20.95	£10.95	£6.95	£12.95	£25.95				
15 Case Study									
(1) Workbook	£20.95			£12.95					
(3) Toolkit for 11/02 exam: available 9/02		£19.95							
Learning to Learn (7/02)	£9.95								

POSTAGE & PACKING

Study Texts

	First	Each extra
UK	£3.00	£2.00
Europe***	£5.00	£4.00
Rest of world	£20.00	£10.00

£ ____

Kits/Passcards/Success Tapes

	First	Each extra
UK	£2.00	£1.00
Europe*	£2.50	£1.00
Rest of world	£15.00	£8.00

£ ____

MCQ cards £1.00 / £1.00   £ ____

CDs each

UK	£2.00
Europe*	£2.00
Rest of world	£10.00

Breakthrough Videos

	First	Each extra
UK	£2.00	£2.00
Europe*	£2.00	£2.00
Rest of world	£20.00	£10.00

£ ____

Grand Total (Cheques to *BPP Publishing*) I enclose a cheque for (incl. Postage)   £ ____

Or charge to Access/Visa/Switch

Card Number _____

Expiry date ____   Start Date ____

Issue Number (Switch Only) ____

Signature _____

Total ____